PELICAN

Pelican Library of Busi...
Advisory Editor: ...

MANAGEMENT THINKERS

ANTHONY D. TILLETT was educated at Reading, Essex and Mexico Universities in history and sociology. He has carried out research at the University of Wisconsin. He has been mainly interested in the development of industrial sociology and its application to operational management problems, but has taught on a wide range of topics in schools, colleges and universities in Britain and in North and Central America.

THOMAS KEMPNER is Director of the Management Centre at the University of Bradford and Professor of Management Studies. He graduated from University College, London, in Economics. Subsequently he worked at the Administrative Staff College, Henley, and at the University of Sheffield. In 1963 he started the Management Centre in Bradford. Professor Kempner is the author of numerous articles, a consultant to several industrial companies and the editor of the Pelican Library of Business and Management. He says he is on too many committees!

GORDON WILLS is Professor of Marketing at the Management Centre in the University of Bradford, and editor of both *Management Decision* and the *British Journal of Marketing*. He graduated from Reading University in Politics and Economics and holds the D.E.S. Diploma in Management Studies with distinction. He is Chief Executive of Management Consultants (Bradford) Ltd, and an adviser to the B.B.C. and to the Office for Scientific and Technical Information on management topics. He is a frequent broadcaster, and author of numerous books and articles. He is a Director of Roles and Parker Limited.

MANAGEMENT THINKERS

Edited by Anthony Tillett, Thomas Kempner
and Gordon Wills

PENGUIN BOOKS

Penguin Books Ltd, Harmondsworth, Middlesex, England
Penguin Books Inc., 7170 Ambassador Road, Baltimore, Md 21207, U.S.A.
Penguin Books Australia Ltd, Ringwood, Victoria, Australia

—

First published 1970

—

This collection copyright © Penguin Books Ltd, 1970

—

Made and printed in Great Britain
by Hazell Watson & Viney Ltd
Aylesbury, Bucks
Set in Monotype Times

To Albert J. Thayre

Contents

Preface

THE grave temptation to study the panoply of modern management technology as though it were a panacea for corporate and industrial malaise must be resisted. As teachers, we have found that an analytic historical perspective on contemporary thought can be salutary. It was this which led to the collation of the ideas of the pioneers of management thought in book form. Our audience is the growing number of thoughtful practitioners in business and the students in business schools, universities, polytechnics and colleges who are now studying management.

From 1963 until 1966 the quarterly journal *Scientific Business* (now re-launched as *Management Decision*) carried a series of articles, under my general editorship, on the major contributions to management thought. Further contributions summarized the growth of new management subjects such as operational research, personnel management and marketing. At the conclusion of the series we felt that many of these articles showed a consistent pattern of development in management thinking from the early years of this century and that they could usefully be brought together in a single volume. Our experience as teachers has shown us that the demand from management students for a background to current ideas is growing even more strongly now than when the chapters which follow were initially drafted.

This, then, was the origin of the present book. All the original articles have, of course, been re-written so that the major themes are even more clearly recognizable. Our cordial thanks are due to the various authors, who so readily agreed to reconsider and recast their pieces, and to the Thomson Organization Ltd for their permission to reprint. The two junior editors, Gordon Wills and myself, also owe a special debt to Anthony Tillett, who synthesized into a coherent volume the discrete contributions, who then wrote the important introductory Part One as a conspectus of the book, and undertook the task of co-ordination throughout.

9

We have dedicated this book to Albert J. Thayre, Director and also General Manager of the Halifax Building Society. For many years he has made an outstanding contribution to the practice of management. More recently he has taken a prominent part in the growth of management education in the North of England, particularly through the development of the University of Bradford Management Centre as Chairman of its Council.

Finally, we should like to acknowledge the patience of our secretarial and literary advisers, Wendy Taylor, Elizabeth Tillett, Avril Wills, and Beth Wooding.

University of Bradford　　　　　　　　　　　　　Thomas Kempner
Management Centre

PART ONE

INDUSTRY AND MANAGEMENT

an historical perspective by Anthony Tillett

1. Industry and Management

ANTHONY TILLETT

IN recent years Management has become an established academic discipline. The earliest publications in which management situations were analysed appeared at the end of the nineteenth century but management problems, as distinct from management analysis, date back to the setting up of the first factories in the late eighteenth century.

The main task of the early factory owner was the co-ordination of resources. Although administration was not considered as a separate issue some code of practice became necessary if the factory was to deal efficiently with large numbers of workers, with several processes of production and with the exigencies of the market. At first the emergence of such a code was piecemeal. Problems were tackled as they arose and practices institutionalized at the discretion of the owner of the firm. Routine became established independently in different firms as ownership passed to the second generation and the process of production became more highly capitalized. It depended more on the men who ran the factory than on changing technology, markets or capital. The owner, who was also entrepreneur and manager, recruited his family and friends to help him run the factory, and with such small numbers of personnel little needed to be written down.

The actual experience of the men who ran the first factories and firms forms the foundation for the study of management. However, management was not recognized as being an important element in the success or failure of a firm until there were enough firms with common problems to enable administration to be picked out as a specific skill, independent of a particular firm or industry. It was found, for example, that size brought certain problems, and as firms grew in size they were confronted with the same type of difficulties. Management information, once it began to be communicated, was not confined to single industries,

13

or even to countries. There was a widespread exchange of books and journals between Britain and the United States, and as the United States began to take the lead in industrial innovation, so its management practices came increasingly to the attention of British industrialists. In fact, apart from Seebohm Rowntree and the examination of the beginnings of Operations Research, the writers and disciplines in this book originate largely in the United States.

An important influence leading to the growth of management was the specialization of personnel who held administrative and technical positions. Where occupations were held both to be specialist and to have a professional association there was a strong impetus to base management on their function and orientation. At the turn of the century the only professions based in industry were engineering and accountancy, and many of the early writings discussed in this book come from men trained in or influenced by these professions.

This introduction attempts to place British management in its historical perspective and explain why certain problems were dealt with before others in the literature of management. It is clear that much of British management is still traditional and has a limited view of its role and capacities. British management was backward by the end of the nineteenth century and, with notable exceptions, has never caught up. The reasons are to be traced to certain factors in the economy and to the organization of industry and of society. In Part One we discuss first the establishment of the factory and then the structure of British industry and the reasons for its backwardness. We then turn to the emergence of the social elements of management and finally we deal with the growth of literature on management.

Readers not interested in the early development of management may omit Part One of this book.

THE INDUSTRIAL REVOLUTION AND THE FACTORY

The administrative advantages of the factory can be shown by comparing it with the system it replaced, 'the putting-out system'. In the putting-out system the merchant co-ordinated the resources: he marketed the cloth, distributed it, gave instructions for its manufacture and, after an interval, collected it. However, compared with the owner of a factory, whose resources were concentrated in one place, he had little control.*

The factory evolved in the period known as the Industrial Revolution and for most of the nineteenth century the factory system and the cotton industry were synonymous. Concentrated industrial units were known before the eighteenth century in particular industries such as glass blowing, metallurgy and silk, but they were exceptions.[1] The first and most famous large factory was Lombe's silk mill in Derby, established in 1718, which was said to employ 300 men. Its influence extended to the whole textile trade. Dr Chapman, writing of the Midland textile owners, suggests that its impact as a social model was such that 'not only the design of the buildings, but also the details of administration and organization of the Derby mill had been absorbed by the local business community and accepted as procedures'.[2]

Factories were not costly to set up in the eighteenth century. Estimates based on insurance returns for this period and other documents calculate the price to have been between £1,000 and £4,000.[3] Fixed capital was rarely more than half the capital invested in the firm, and sometimes much less. The factory soon paid for itself. Cost became prohibitive either when the market was oversold or, more importantly, when the cost of fixed capital increased. The introduction of the Watt engine, patented in 1782, which led to larger buildings, doubled or even trebled the cost of fixed capital.[4] In the paper industry steam power increased the average cost of a factory from £4,000–5,000 to £10,000–12,000.[5]

*For a full description of this, see *Cambridge Economic History of Europe*, Cambridge University Press, 1965, vol. VI, part i, pp. 289–93.

Even so, capital was not a severe problem during the Industrial Revolution.

However, it must be emphasized that despite the growth of the factory system in the late eighteenth century, changes in technique were piecemeal, and the technological basis of the cotton industry has been described as 'exceedingly modest'.[6] Skills depended on experience and not on scientific knowledge, and the problems brought by simple mechanization were not difficult to solve. Indeed, taking a long-term view of industrial change, Boulding considers that the 'so-called Industrial Revolution of the eighteenth century was in fact the tag end of the long process of developing folk technology of the Middle Ages'.[7]

The changes of the Industrial Revolution in the late eighteenth century were as much social as industrial. Although the conditions of the work force were rapidly changing there were still, in the textile trade at the turn of the century, twice as many hand looms as power looms. The establishment of the factory did not at once disrupt the traditional forms of textile manufacture, and in the factory neighbourhood variants of the putting-out system developed under the control of the factory. Some of the early factories created factory 'villages' and ensured an adequate supply of labour for themselves by making work in the factory obligatory for all residents.

THE CHANGING ECONOMY AND THE FIRM

The nineteenth-century economy

During the nineteenth century the basis of the British economy changed from agriculture to manufacturing. This change is usually measured in terms of the national-income share of various sectors or by the distribution of the employed labour force. Neither method is entirely reliable, but they are adequate enough to demonstrate the major changes.* The clearest trend

*For these figures, and the discussion in the following paragraph, P. Deane and W. Cole, *British Economic Growth, 1688–1959*, Cambridge University Press, 1964.

is the decline in agriculture, whose share in the national income fell from one-third in 1800 to one-seventeenth in 1900. Manufacturing, mining and building increased their share, but unevenly. The transport and trade sector increased steadily at the beginning of the nineteenth century and continued to grow into the twentieth century. The national-income share of textiles, coal, iron and steel, and transport grew and prospered in that sequence. Changes in the economy were obviously interrelated, as for example the fortunes of the railway and shipbuilding industries with those of iron and steel. All industries grew in the nineteenth century, but not at the same rate. The 1870s saw a slowing up in industrial growth. This factor, together with the spur of international competition, led to greater mechanization and rationalization.[8] New attention began to be paid to the role of management.

The size of factories

As machines grew more powerful throughout the nineteenth century, so the number of men employed in factories increased; and for most industries increase in productivity depended on manpower. And, as factories grew in size, so did the need for administration increase. The average number of workers in a factory[9, 10] increased from 137 in 1838, 156 in 1861, 181 in 1870 to 191 in 1885. In 1871 the average number of workers in iron-making establishments was 219, in shipbuilding 570, and in machine manufacture 85.[11] These differences reflect both the different technologies and the varying number of separate skills involved in different industries, especially numerous in shipbuilding. These figures do not give a complete picture of the increase in scale. Factories had grown to a large size as early as 1833, when there were 7 mills employing over 1,000 people, 23 over 500, and 36 between 250 and 500.[12] In shipbuilding 30 firms in Scotland averaged over 800 employees; the typical primary iron works in South Wales numbered 350 men.[13] Already by 1849 the Dowlais works employed 700 men and had 18 blast furnaces.[14] These figures show that certain institutions had become large enough by the middle of the century to throw up substantial management problems. Yet there were few writings on management and little discussion of such problems.

The trend to greater size in factories reflected the widely held belief that increase in size would guarantee levels of output. In order to compete, a newcomer had to build larger factories, and this in fact occurred both domestically and internationally. Apart from limiting entry into a field the move towards greater size encouraged industrial concentration as smaller factories saw in integration the answer to increased competition. However, such movements towards increased concentration had to contend with tradition, which was particularly strong in areas where there were many small factories. Attempts were made from 1850 to 1870 to combine vertically the spinning and weaving operations in the cotton industry. The advantages would have included a lessening of administrative costs, but, because of the long lead in mechanization that the spinning process had, the separation from the weaving process was wide enough to be considered traditional, and the movement failed. In Europe and the United States, however, vertical integration was much more common than in Britain because of the different pattern of technical development and a clearer ability to see the advantages in terms of management efficiency.*

Factory and firm

The period saw the emergence of a distinction between the manufacturing unit or factory and the pattern of business aggregation within the legal entity of the firm. The growth of the factory and the development of large industrial units brought changes in the structure of the firm. Up to this point the average size of the factory has been used as an index for the growth of industrial organization, but in many ways this is misleading, since the firm was more important in gaining capital and markets, and

* For an examination of these moves see Checkland, *The Rise of Industrial Society*, p. 121, and A. J. Taylor, 'Concentration and Specialization in the Lancashire Cotton Industry', *Econ. Hist. Rev.*, 1, 1949, pp. 114–22.

in the nineteenth century these were the factors that guaranteed prosperity. The skills required for running a firm are different from those required for running a factory. The factory is concerned with labour, organization and productivity; the firm with finance, personnel and the market. In Britain in the nineteenth century the running of the firm took primacy over the running of the factory, and it was not until the development of larger firms in the late nineteenth century that it was recognized that the skills needed for each were distinctly different.

The success of a firm was not judged in terms of plant efficiency but by comparison with other firms; price was based on industrial consensus rather than on the cost of output. There was no accounting technique which could deal with individual component costs and so estimate plant contributions.

In the early nineteenth century the number of plants owned by firms was not large, as the textile industry illustrates. Robert Peel, who in 1819 owned 20 factories, was an exception. In 1830 the number of mills exceeded the number of firms by only 10 to 20 per cent.[15] The whole position changed with the growth of the large firm and the demise of the small firm of only 10 to 12 people.[16]

Throughout the nineteenth century the main type of firm was the family business. The great majority of firms remained private companies. In 1914 four fifths of the active joint stock companies were private companies.[17] Financial arrangements in Britain tended to be based on family reputation and personal recommendation rather than on large public subscription, and although there were exceptions, the main stream of business firms were private companies. The financial health of the firm was governed as much by the resources of the family as by its industrial position. Strong family ownership meant that any improvement in the efficiency of the plant depended on the initiative of the family.

With the growth of larger firms scale, in itself, became a criterion of efficiency and safety. The men running the larger firms were forced to pay more attention to the capital market and to domestic and foreign competition, and less to day-by-day production. These increases in scale were, at first, a hindrance to the growth of management. It was not until firms began to move towards rationalization that the role of management emerged.

CAPITAL AND INDUSTRIAL EFFICIENCY

Capital was plentiful in nineteenth-century Britain. The development of the capital market was largely a result of international trading. There were many who wished to invest their money, especially after the decline in the investment potential of the railways. The new combinations in the staple industries did not lack local or national support. The need for heavy capital investment did convert some firms into public companies, but in areas where little investment seemed to be needed, as in the textile industries, 'the slant of technical change after 1860 was largely towards capital saving'.[18] The ease of capital reinforced the established way of running companies and preserved the extant structure with its routine administration, family convenience, and productive short-term efficiency. These capital conditions did not exist in Germany or the United States, and their absence resulted in keener attention to administration and efficiency. In Germany the shortage of capital involved banks not only in lending, but in supervising the use of funds through positions on the board of directors. The fact that continued credit depended on satisfactory performance resulted in an attention to costs not found in British industry.

In the United States, where new industries like petroleum, meat, steel and packaged food competed with older industries, the pressure for capital was acute. The increasing size of American firms was the result of larger markets; costly and capital-intensive technology gave rise to a greater need for finance.[19] The need for capital encouraged a close attention to costs and the estimation of potential returns on the part of both lender and borrower. In this regard the career of Carnegie is instructive. Carnegie knew little about steel but much about company finance. Immediate or short-term returns were not enough, because capital-intensive industry depended on estimates of return over longer periods of growth. Long-term growth depended on innovation and up-to-date technology as much as on the present state of productive efficiency. Innovation and increasing returns could be most satisfactorily developed in monopolistic or oligopolistic markets. The elimination of competition had both domestic and international advantages.

The mergers which took place in the United States at the turn of the century were aggressive, the result of attempts to gain rewards in expanding markets. The consequence of these mergers was the separation of ownership from management, and the understanding that their respective successes depended on different skills. The division of these functions, which has been one of the main issues dealt with in management literature and comment, did not lead to the worst fears of some protagonists – irresponsible practice and weak control. Absence of the direct profit motive has not destroyed the private firm, nor have the technocrats become the new 'industrial elite' controlling a changed class system. More power has been put in the hands of managers, but this was necessary, given the larger firm and the tasks of reorganization. Reorganizing the small firm into larger units, and making and controlling policies for all units inside one firm, gave rise to an important literature about administration, typically found in 'house' and occupational journals.

Foreign competition from Germany and the United States in the late nineteenth and early twentieth century encouraged the belief that the industrial virility of Britain was being threatened, and that larger, less competitive industrial structures were the answer. Explanations for Britain's situation were many and various, and have a familiar ring – lack of tariffs, higher wages, laziness and industrial senility. Certain indicators support some of these views. For example, goods like machine tools and railway engines, which had previously been exported, were now being imported.[20] In comparison with American and German industrial structures the companies in Britain were overspecialized, over-competitive, and small. These factors produced severe problems of industrial organization, not only in markets, but also in the running of companies. For example, in the steel industry in 1907 100 blast furnaces were operated by 95 companies,[21] and there were 1,784 colliery businesses in 1911.[22] The reasons for an industrial structure characterized by small, inefficient and highly local industries can be found in the conditions of early industrial growth in Britain: early specialization, ease of entry, and a lack of interest in capital intensive innovations. The structure of the industry defined the kind of amalgamation that could take place. These conditions, particularly overspecialization and small size, encouraged the duplication of scarce resources, most noticeably administration.

Some of these conditions led to growth of *trusts* or *efficiency combinations* when pressure of international competition, falling prices, and tariff increases began to make reorganization of the industrial structure mandatory.[23] Dictated by business conditions, these moves can be described as defensive. Defensive combinations appeared in two major types – combinations of small firms into larger units and absorption of small firms by a dominant leader. The administrative problems differed for each category. In the first, individual firms and their traditions had to be accommodated into newly created larger bodies, and this called for sacrifices which were frequently opposed. The problems of relative power were less important for the second type of defensive combination, but strategies and choices were often limited by the fact that the major company did not wish to be seen as an industrial dictator. There was, however, a greater sense of market direction in the second type than the first. Examples can be found in most industries in the late nineteenth century. Coats of Paisley grew by buying up other firms and soon developed a selling agency which excluded the middle man. This became an established method of cost reduction and was practised by a large number of trades, notably in the larger homogeneous markets. Other instances can be found in food retailing where firms, such as Liptons and Home and Colonial, produced standardized foods and developed their own selling outlets. A notable example of the first type of amalgamation and its ensuing complications can be found in the cotton industry. Eleven firms came together to form the English Sewing Cotton Company. The companies had a central policy but no central control. Each firm retained its individual identity, the old directors remaining in charge. The subsequent losses led to a reorganization carried out, interestingly enough, by the chief executive of Coats – an American.[24] His reorganization resulted in the reduction of the number of constituent companies and, finally, in commercial recovery. Many other industries faced the problem of combinations containing too many firms with separate autonomy. For example, Calico Printers contained 28 limited companies and 21 other firms. Bradford Dyers consisted of 22 constituent firms, and the Yorkshire Woolcombers Association, 38 firms.

Although the creation of *efficiency combinations* led to greater attention being paid to management, this was often incidental. At the outset surprisingly little attention was paid to the quality of management. This was only partly due to the struggle for power between the directors of the constituent companies. A more fundamental reason was that the arrangements were based on financial criteria and not organizational ones. The causes and consequences of the use of financial, as against managerial, criteria are discussed below.

Efficiency and corporate policy

Finance is one sort of criterion which can be used to assess the health of a firm. Without finance there would be no firm. But the performance of a firm does not only depend on finance, and other tests of efficiency can be applied which are equally important. These include administration, production and technology.[25] The type of efficiency which has primacy in a firm will be a matter of choice but it will affect the character and structure of a firm, particularly its management. If finance is considered the most important criterion, then the orientation and policies of that firm will differ from those of a firm where the greatest stress is placed on technology. Firms use all criteria but with different stress. The order in which they place these efficiency values is due to a combination of environmental factors, such as the amount of available capital, and internal choices. In a modern company these values are departmentalized so that, for example, accounting, production or research and development will each have their advocates in the determination of company policy. The departments are subject to bargaining and negotiation and the end result should represent a balance of the various departments. Outright victory of one value at the expense of another may mean disaster for a firm. There are numerous instances where overproduction or 'featherbedding' of labour or the use of purely financial criteria have led to the demise of a company.

A certain key value may be emphasized when a company is established and its use reinforced by the administration. It has not been uncommon to find leading personnel in companies measuring performance by either productivity, stock market quotations, or labour achievement. Company traditions incorporate these values, so that without conscious change or failure the performance of the company is always judged with these values in mind. Other policy values may influence the manner in which the initial value is used, or lead to its replacement. A reduction of market share, or a high labour turnover, will bring more questioning of the key value than continued sales expansion and a growing market share.

Emphasis on one kind of performance criterion may lead to the failure to perceive alternative markets, or opportunities for diversification. Confidence in successful policies may be misplaced if the view of the leading personnel is based on one market or industry. Successful leadership depends on an understanding of the national, and latterly the international, economy particularly in selecting potential growth sectors. When potential sectors go unrecognized as at the turn of the last century, one reason is likely to be that firms have emphasized policies based on specific values rather than a mix of techniques and performance criteria. The institutionalization of values was one reason for the relative backwardness of British management. Companies provided their own education for administrative personnel, and there were few techniques which described the problems of policy making. Policy did not consider the means but the ends. In comparison to the United States, diversification does not seem to have been very common among large companies in Britain. The North American integration movement was a vitally important factor in shaking up management there, and bringing about changes in company policy.

Integration has more dramatic effects than the close trading or price agreements which were common in Britain. Horizontal integration is usually defensive, and has been so historically; it increases the size of the company, but the enlarged company maintains the same position in the economy. The market may be larger, but for the economy the function remains the same. Vertical integration has been more dynamic, introducing problems which frequently can only be solved by the total reorganization of the company on cross-industry lines. The problems of dealing with supplies, efficiency, and tailoring of processes, leads to a fundamental re-examination of values, particularly in administration. The range of choices widens and the potential avenues of growth for the company increase. The discussion assumes, as is usually the case, that vertical integration is based on one sound level.

There were fewer integration movements in Britain than the U.S.A., and the dynamic effect was less, mainly because Britain was an international economy, and could not control raw materials and markets in the same way. Close trading and price agreements were more common. Integration and close trading have different administrative effects, however, both in the degree of resultant efficiency and rationality. Price agreements maintain inefficiency by transferring responsibility to different institutions. Close trading also relied on separate institutions, and both were a positive hindrance to the rational allocation of resources. Market loyalty is confused in secure markets. An example of this latter problem is found in the British engineering industry of the nineteenth century where goods were custom-made, and the advantages of mass production with standardized parts went unrecognized for many years.

Apart from the environmental security of price agreements, and integration, the most important form of security for the internal working of the company is the stabilization of personnel.[26] The more stable the key personnel, the greater will be the commitment to present policies, and the nature of recruitment into the firm will reflect, if not mirror exactly, the nature of the leadership for the future. The stabilization of personnel will also have important effects on the kind of resources that the firm can command. Capital and returns on investment were partly assessed on these grounds in the nineteenth century, and capital was the measure by which to estimate the health or illness of the firm. Capital came to have an independent meaning away from its source, and provided the business continued to make profits the nature of the market was considered unimportant. Innovation was generally unimportant for the director of the British nineteenth-century firm for he could either rely on continuing profits or on switching markets. Markets like the British colonies did not inconvenience the structure of the firms.

The argument is not merely historical. Goals of efficiency always have some place in the formation of policy in a company; but the goals may be unhelpful to management development if certain efficiency values are emphasized at the expense of others.

The effects of efficiency values

The dominance of financial criteria in the British nineteenth-century firm was coupled with unwillingness to search for technologically possible and potentially advantageous types of production. Nothing illustrates this better than the then current views of machine running time and replacement. Output in the latter part of the nineteenth century was increasing, mainly as a result of additions to the efficiency of existing machinery. For example, in textiles output per operative increased from 2,800 lbs in 1844–6 to 5,500 lbs in 1880, and in weaving from 1,700 lbs to 4,000 lbs. The main cause for this increase was the greater number of machines that the individual could operate. Figures differ on this, but the most reliable estimate shows that power looms per man increased from 2·5 (1835) to 4 in 1887.[27] The average number of spindles per factory was also increased.

Clapham has correctly described this period in textiles as the era of *speeding up*.

The coal industry provides a fascinating case study of the criteria by which industries were judged. Although labour productivity increased phenomenally between 1879 and 1886, the coal owners regarded this as one of the least successful periods because of the low price of coal, and conversely the period after 1900, when productivity fell, as being the most successful. Innovation was not a necessity and even if it had been, the structure of the industry, typically family firms with one or two mines, would have hampered change. A. J. Taylor sums up the position of the industry: 'The weakness of the early twentieth-century coal industry was not that it was under-capitalized – the industry's profits if anything suggest the contrary – but that its assets were too thinly and too unevenly spread.'[28] Comfortable profits, combined with a lack of competition or any strong market leadership, led to an emphasis on financial efficiency. This was typical of much of industry at the time.

Productive efficiency, like financial efficiency, emphasized the current rather than potential returns to be gained from existing capital equipment and its use. The efficiency of the factory, particularly in middle-sized firms, was judged on the amount of time that machinery could be kept running. The writings of certain classical economists supported this view, which was followed by factory owners, and is shown by their utterances and practice.[29] Few managers considered other ways in which output could be improved, and so confirmed their belief that there was a fixed relation between labour and resources which could only be altered to the detriment of the manufacturer. The emphasis on short-term productive efficiency is also found in replacement policies. Replacement was based on the expected financial return from running the current machinery, rather than on the potential improvement from the installation of new machinery. Fixed capital was replaced when it ceased to be productive, rather than profitable or efficient. Numerous instances can be found in well-established industries like the railways, textiles and transport.[30] Decisions were taken with short-term perspective, and this kind of routine decision-making was a carry-over from the time when fixed capital had been profitable, and the machinery had an economic and technical, as well as productive, lead. This attitude to productive efficiency was helped by current accountancy practice which was employed to estimate costs on a very simple basis.

The emphasis on the short term, on steady returns and routine procedures, was also found in other directions. Harsh and competitive markets like the United States were replaced by primary producing countries, where goods met little competition. Productive and financial efficiency supported the social requirements of managers and owners who relied on fixed income estimates, and consistent, if not increasing, profits. Financial returns dominated the assessment of the firm.

The importance of technology for the growth of the economy has been illustrated by several startling calculations for the United States. Abramovitz has shown that between 1869 and 1944–53 the *per capita* output of the U.S.A. increased fourfold, but that capital and labour could only account for 14 per cent* of the increase. Even if these figures are inaccurate, they call into question the contributions of entrepreneurship, craftsmanship, labour hours and the organization of the economy as explanations of this growth. Clearly the limits are difficult to assess, but company and industrial histories show that administration, business skill, and hard working personnel were important, but only when combined with an understanding of the technology of the industry. The stabilization of the company, through markets, policy and administration, depended on the success of the product, and this, in turn, depended on the capacity of the technology.

By the end of the nineteenth century Britain was looking to U.S. and German technology for its industrial growth. British

* This is a simplifying paper which has already made heroic simplifying assumptions; it shows clearly, however, the limits of our knowledge, especially about the kinds of change that have created economic growth. M. Abramovitz, 'Resource and Output Trends in the U.S. Since 1870', *Am. Econ. Rev. Papers and Proc.*, 46, May 1956, pp. 1–23.

technology had become defensive and was no longer copied and imitated. As Landes graphically puts it, 'even the best of her enterprises were usually being dragged in the wake of foreign precursors, like children being dragged along by impatient adults'.[31] Landes points also to two important pieces of evidence further demonstrating the defensive nature of British technology. British inventions were being exploited more effectively abroad, and foreign personnel were beginning to make important contributions to the development of British technology and industry. The lag in technique, and lack of concern with innovation, even discounting new industries like motor cars and electricity, was noticeable in most sectors. Experience in the coal industry is typical. 'Some years ago I asked a user of a coal-cutting machine to allow me to add such appliances (for the improvement of the machine). His reply was that he had trouble enough with his machine already ...'[32] This lack of interest in technology has severely hampered the development of modern management in Britain, and in large measure our attitude to technology has remained defensive.

Standardization and technical efficiency

The great increase in technical efficiency was the result of mechanization. Its rate of growth depended on extending the range of actions that could be mechanized or simplified by the use of the machine. It would seem worth while to show the stages into which this process can be analysed and its effect on management in Britain and the United States.

The first phase of mechanization consisted in linking as many processes as possible to steam energy. Throughout the nineteenth century the steam engine was improved, and the power generated by the engine doubled and trebled. The range of industries using steam power was extended by the invention of such machines as the steam hammer and the power loom. The application and use of steam power put great pressure on those processes which could not deploy this form of energy.

The second phase of mechanization is characterized by the

improvement of powered machines, particularly where speeds and standards were related to them. At first this was accomplished by craftsmen in the factory, but over a period of time, as machines became more complex, improvements originating from the factories diminished and machine-building firms became one of the most important centres for the improvement and diffusion of techniques.

The third phase is the standardization of machines through the use of interchangeable parts, and the development of mass production. By working out a select number of parts, machines could be assembled and used with little skill, and a standard knowledge transferable between industry and the firm. Precision of manufacture was particularly important, and this depended on the development and use of accurate lathes, milling machines and cutting devices. There was a shift in the focus of skill from production to preparation. Interchangeable parts became the principle of production for the sewing machine, bicycle, typewriter and the motor car industries, all producing goods which could reach a mass market. The development of standard systems of production was the basis of planned management, and had an enormous impact on the organization of the factory. Standard equipment used in a standard way led to standard problems, and the pooling of information to solve them.

The situation in the United States has been described by Rosenburg as technological convergence, where 'industrialization was characterized by the introduction of a relatively small number of broadly similar productive processes to a large number of industries'.[33] The production history of the United States shows how firms discovered that the fine precision tools developed for one industry could be applied to another. Thus the Baldwin Locomotive Company of Philadelphia had previously manufactured textile printing machinery; Browne and Clark developed from clocks and watches to sewing machines and then progressed rapidly to tools for the bicycle and car industry. The evolution was particularly marked for those firms that produced fine precision tools for the arms and textile industries, the first industries to require such tools. In the United States the trend soon led to the end of the general workshop, and the specialization of the workforce.

However, the same convergence of problems did not occur in Britain because of the different development and structure of industry. Machine tools were custom built for individual factories and firms, and specifications for each differed considerably. They were serviced by men at the factory, rather than by independent agencies or itinerant craftsmen. The arrangement had great initial advantages. Many improvements were carried out on the existing stock of machinery, and workmen gained a great deal of technical knowledge from this experience. But this knowledge was limited to the individual factory and firm and did not give rise to a common stock of knowledge in the sense described above by Rosenburg. Although machines became more complex the style and servicing of the machine did not change. By the end of the century there had been little standardization or specialization. Rule of thumb and imprecise workmanship were coupled with designs which were conceived independently of actual production. In the locomotive industry, for example, design and production were independent functions, and this is one reason why, in contrast to the United States, the railway industry in Britain had little influence on the cycle and car industry. The early development of railways had created a structure of work in which there was a clear distinction between craft and professional tasks; design in Britain was a profession, and as such limited itself to the task of designing. The only contribution of the craftsmen was in following instructions when making the product.

The importance of machine tools was not marked in Britain until the influx of American machinery and patents at the end of the nineteenth century, when the consequent fierce competition demonstrated the importance of technological efficiency based on standardization. Although both engineers and the government had known of American machine tools and the American system of manufacture from the mid-century, most craftsmen and manufacturers saw standardization as synonymous with poor quality and shoddy craftsmanship – views consistent with their general attitude to replacement. But the advantages of standardization were there for all to see. The influx of bicycles, sewing machines, locomotives and machine tools imported from the U.S.A. demonstrated their superiority in terms that were difficult to deny. A Westinghouse subsidiary and Thomson Houston dominated the electric tram industry, and machinery for the Central Underground Railway was supplied by American firms.[34]

The reaction of British firms took two forms: buying patents and the use of American personnel. Some of the conditions for technological convergence and standardization did exist in Britain however. Herbert began an engineering works, producing machine tools, including the first automatic lathes. His brother formed a company with William Hillman which made roller skates, then sewing machines, bicycles and finally the Hillman car. Much of this industry was localized in Birmingham. However, few of the older industries took much account of this development.

The most significant move to standardization in Britain was in the field of consumer goods, the retail food industry being perhaps the best example. Unlike the U.S.A. there was no immediate mass market. Lack of demand was a problem of market education amongst potential consumers in large cities. However, the rising standard of living brought mass production techniques to the chocolate, boots and shoes, tea and meat industries at the start of the twentieth century. They were produced in standard qualities and sold at cheap prices with great efficiency. The retail grocery trade relied on cash payments, high turnover, bulk-buying and the development of particular lines with which to pull in the customer.[35]

Uniformity was not demanded in the producer goods industries, largely because the structure of the market was over-specialized, diverse, and in the main highly profitable. The main emphasis in the British firm on financial and productive efficiency was the concomitant of rising markets, easy profits, and an early international lead. The failure to develop standardized goods was not only a blow to the basis of management, but to the future development of British industry.

Why was British technological performance so unsatisfactory? Was it the result of industrial laziness or social inertia? Was it a reflection of the character of the whole society? Some writers have offered explanations which discount social conditions as secondary, and explain the variation between countries in terms of the different demand and factor abundance of nations. Compared to the United States, with its expanding markets and relatively unskilled labour force, there was little need for the British industrialist to introduce labour-saving devices. There was no encouragement because of the relative factor abundance and labour supply. This argument is most forcibly advanced by Habakkuk to explain the differential change in the two countries. He writes of Britain as having 'relative abundance of labour, [which] means the absence of restraint on the rate of profit, and in so far as capital accumulation depends on the rate of profit on capital; the relative scarcity of labour means the converse'.* This argument is supported by Aldcroft, who shows that the very abundance of factors such as capital and profits was taken, with good cause, to prove that the economy was not in need of any radical change. Such complacency led to industrial inefficiency, particularly in regard to fuel.[36] Cheap labour, market shares and capital abundance all led to an overestimation of the health of the economy.

These conditions were the result of the cumulative effect of company policy and factory management. Where an industry was highly interrelated individual firms could do little to change the operating conditions of their factory. Kindleberger cites the example of the railway industry, where the introduction of longer and more economical wagons depended on the agreement of the railway proprietors to introduce them unanimously.[37]

*

The family firm in the nineteenth century was less concerned with

* Habakkuk, *American and British Technology in the Nineteenth Century*, Cambridge University Press, 1962, p. 162. In the words of the cabinet minister James Graham: 'Low profits stimulate ingenuity whereby the machinery makes fresh inroads on the demand for manual labour', p. 186.

the individual plant, and more with the goals of the company. Implicit in its policy was a concern with financial criteria, which resulted in a systematic lack of interest in management as such. Only with the combinations of the 1890s and with the introduction of new personnel did administration and organizational planning become important for the health of the company. Recognition of these qualities was more likely to occur in larger units, particularly where mass production and its control made good organization a necessary function for the firm. The control of finance and the management of the plant were finally differentiated. With the institutionalization of planning many anomalies were recognized and corrected. Trained personnel replaced family authority and company habits gave way to attention to factory co-ordination. Technology, unlike finance, could not be left to fend for itself, but needed a commitment from the firm in terms of personnel, policies, research and administrative structure.

MANAGEMENT AND THE FACTORY

The changing scope of management

One of the main concerns of factory management is to gain a high commitment from labour to the goals of management. Labour is a common and continuous property of all factories; techniques change but the day-to-day running of the factory is essentially concerned with labour and organizational problems. As the various labour groups within the factory changed, so the task of management changed from the co-ordination of labour to the co-ordination of knowledge. This was the result of changes both in industry and society. Relations with labour became institutionalized and organized and the ambitions of labour, both as a movement and among individuals, became conditioned and framed by industrialism. Increasing population, growing literacy and differing skills had an important bearing on the change in the labour movement and relations with management.

Part of this shift is due to the changed role of the state in relation to business and society. In the nineteenth century the influence of the state was growing in a patchy way to regulate the conditions of work and the payment of wages. Its growing interest as an arbiter in the labour market is first seen in the various Factory Acts, the regulations for safety, public welfare and provisions for health, housing and education. The Factory Acts were enforced by the state through a central inspectorate. State influence over the factories was mainly confined to the establishment of minimum standards and humanitarian prohibitions concerning the treatment of women and children. However, the bargain to work made between master and man was still considered to be an individual contract, negotiated in a free market and enforceable in the courts. This position only changed in the late nineteenth and early twentieth century with the growth of the trade unions.

The increasing education and skill needed by the company from its employees has altered the relations between labour and management. The changed relationship, true now for most of labour, is most clearly marked where a firm is dealing with professional and scientific employees who have more bargaining power than skilled or semi-skilled workers. The problem for the manager is to integrate the specialist into the power structure of the firm and allow him more autonomy than the workman, in an attempt to identify him with the company. To resolve the conflict that the professional will find himself in – on the one hand required to innovate, on the other subject to the control of the company – certain high technology firms in computers and electronics, for example, have replaced hierarchical with communal decision-making. Management has changed from overseer to organizer and management specialisms like accountancy and works management have emerged.

The Industrial Revolution and labour commitment

The commitment to factory work by labour always depends on a variety of circumstances of which alternative work is the most important. The social patterns and expectations found in the domestic industry were particularly difficult to change to an acceptance of factory work. Factory work demanded discipline, in time and practice, which resulted in far less autonomy for the individual worker. Descriptions of factories in the early part of the Industrial Revolution show that many were based on *unfree* labour, paupers and Poor Law apprentices. Much of the dislike of factory work resulted from associations of these *houses of industry* with the Workhouse. The situation was such that employers accepted it. Robert Owen, who was a sympathetic observer, wrote: 'Such was the general dislike of the occupation at that time, that with few exceptions only persons destitute of friends, employment and character were found willing to try the experiment.'[38] The discipline demanded by the factories was viewed, in the minds of owners and men of property, as a moral corrective for godless men. Conditions without work were worse than conditions within the factory, and the decline in traditional industries increased the dependence of the unskilled on the factory.

The reliance on child labour was the feature that most distinguished the cotton industry, but it is important to remember that the core group of operatives were women, and that women throughout the nineteenth century continued to make up one half of the working population of the industry. They provided a cheap and ready supply of labour, and were considered more reliable than male adults.[39]

The clearest form of the creation of commitment in the early Industrial Revolution is found in the establishment of factory villages, often built by the owner around the factory. They were particularly important and effective where there had been no previous industry. The earliest examples are found in the coal industry, where the standards of layout and building were poor. Better examples of this neo-feudalism could be found in Scotland, where the villages were provided with schools and chapels. For example, in the Lea Mill of Peter Nightingale, coal and provisions could be bought cheaply and in some firms medical and sick clubs were organized. The growth of towns providing a natural source of labour supply led to a decline in the necessity for factory villages.

Attempts to improve the lot of the whole labour force, rather than white-collar groups alone, were found particularly in the chocolate trade, as at Bournville, or in soap, as at Port Sunlight. A good workforce was not the only reason. Moral conscience and welfare played their part; the result was paternalism, at best benevolent, at worst authoritarian.

Division of labour and the factory floor

The advantages of the division of labour were, in the classic argument of Adam Smith, an

increase in the dexterity of every particular workman; secondly the saving of time which is commonly lost in passing from one species of work to another; and lastly the invention of a great number of machines which facilitate and abridge labour and enable one man to do the work of many.[40]

Increases in production in the factory supported all the claims for the division of labour in the nineteenth century. Three types of division of labour will be considered: through job, technology, and organization. The first two relate to the factory floor, the latter to the rationalization of the elements of production and their control.

An examination of trade books which appeared in the early nineteenth century* shows that many of the new trades listed were the result of a subdivision of previous employment categories. Several men might be completing the job that previously one man was able to do, with the intention of increasing productive efficiency. This can be seen in the Birmingham and London works of Wedgwood, where each room was organized so that there was a flow from process to process, and the subdivision of skills was such, in the words of Wedgwood, as to 'make machines of men as cannot err'.[41] Diligence and care

*E. P. Thompson, *The Making of the English Working Class*, Gollancz, London, 1963, pp. 244–5. In 1818 the *Book of English Trades* did not mention the engineer, boilermaker, etc. By 1828 the influx of new skills had increased the *Operative Mechanic and British Machinist* to 900 pages.

rather than technical knowledge were the main requirements of the labour force.

The higher the technical base of an industry, the greater the propensity to do away with subcontracting and include all the processes in the factory. However, this was frequently hampered because the labour force was unskilled. One way to counter this was to develop machines to perform the jobs of men, a division not by job, but by technology. In engineering, reliance on hand labour was replaced by the invention of the slide rest, planing machine, and machine tools. The popularity and great advantage of the 'self-acting machine tools' led Nasmyth, in his important Bridgewater Foundry, to produce 'planing machines and lathes ... all ready to supply the parties asking for them every day'. These were the seeds of mass production and automation. The convenience of this kind of technical division of labour was apparent especially with the use of heavy materials. Such a technical division had an important effect on the running of the factory, and Nasymth developed what he called the 'straight line system' because

the various workshops are all in line, and so placed that the greater part of the work, as it passed from one end of the foundry to the other, receives in succession each operation which ought to follow the preceding one, so that little carrying backward and forward or lifting up or down is required.[42]

In each successive department there was a foreman to see to the quality of the work. But little was made of this as an organizational principle or a management technique. It was treated rather as common sense.

Machine tools made their most important mark in the sewing machine, bicycle and car industries. These industries all developed techniques of mass production as a result of a speed-up of production found to be possible with the new machine tools. Pools of craftsmanship in factories were slowly eroded. A witness told the Royal Commission on the Poor, in 1906: 'In all highly organized shops most of the boys are taught to do one part of an engine and little else.'[43] Improvements in machine tools required an improvement in labour and work layout. The craftsman who owned his tools, and the long queue for the grinding machine, were replaced by the tool room; work became subject to closer control through the increasing importance and practice of checking and measuring. Such changes had two effects: a decline in subcontracting to the individual craftsman, and a greater concern with layout and systems of control. The decline in subcontracting has been estimated to be one of the main reasons for the increase in factory size by one half in the period 1895–1919.[44]

The increasing size of the labour force, and of the number of tasks in the factory, led to a concern with control and coordination on the factory floor. At the same time the increasing size of the firms led to an increase in the administrative staff. Both are different aspects of the organizational division of labour, which has its roots in the standardization of the tasks of the factory and the firm.

Standardization and the organization of the workshop

Standardization spelt the demise of many of the conventions by which the workforce conceived of their job. One major consequence of standardization on the factory floor was in methods of payment.

The high cost of machine tools, as against craft tools, led management to account for costs at this level, for the first time, and to pinpoint waste and utilization. When machine tools were first introduced into the factory it was considered they should be used sparingly, and saved for as long as possible; an example of productive efficiency in the short term. This view was gradually superseded by the assumption that tools should be used as much as possible, and replaced, a gain in both efficiency and up-to-date models. Output per day had to be more efficiently organized; increasing output was also helped by process improvements such as the use of high speed steel, which allowed metal to be cut at rates as much as 100 per cent above previous speeds. Such changes in timescale led to problems of inflow and outflow to and from such a process. As a result there was greater pressure for rational organization. Aitken commented:

The innovation in high speed steel spread much more quickly through American industry than did the innovation of scientific management. Its advantages were more obvious, its nature more familiar, and its adoption more easy. Employers and wage earning machinists alike might well be suspicious of Taylor's managerial reforms, but they would find it much more difficult to resist the introduction of a superior piece of technology. But if the high speed tool was to be effectively used, scientific management or something very close to it had to be adopted too.[45]

High speed steel led to the re-organization of work, and labour-saving mechanisms brought a different attitude to the conduct of the workshop.

The changing conditions of work, both in pace and skill, led to a closer attention to the norms under which tools should operate. The most useful instrument for this was found in the manipulation of wages. The reduction of craft skills and the use of semi-skilled labour released management from the problems of accepting the wage norm, on which craftsmanship and the idea of the labour aristocrat depended. Some labourers had remained on 'payment by results' by sustaining their old pre-factory structure, but this was not prevalent in industries where craft predominated.[46] Payment by results was based on the premise that money was the real reason for hard work. Early schemes could not test the success or failure of this assumption, for payment was not calculated in terms of portions of work, but as a proportion of a day's output. There was no accurate way to calculate costs for individual work. Often payment was hierarchically distributed so the overseer or the manager would get a share of the profits. Payment by results was slowly accepted because management in general held that the more work hours a person gave the greater would be the profits; so shifts of twelve hours were considered profitable, while those of eight hours were not. There were no norms for independent pieces of work, and any use of piece rates to influence the workforce would need to depend on this kind of information.

The search for information about individuals and the establishment of standards through wage payment schemes was one of the major contributions associated with F. W. Taylor. Behind his work there is a tradition of concern and speculation about wages and waste which he organized into coherent practice, and institutionalized into a distinctive approach to the study of the worker. The literature on wages begins in the 1880s. Work-study based on observation, cost and norms can be found, for example, in the work of Lammond du Pont. Britain was behind the practice of the American workshops, although there were some examples of elementary concern with organization.

Administration and the organization of the factory

The introduction of payment by results was an administrative mechanism to increase labour output, and decrease waste. To obtain the required information, detailed studies had to be made on each shop floor, and this was carried out by professional engineers. The main impetus for such studies was the introduction of new machinery, with a new emphasis on costs. At the same time the administrative apparatus of the firm was increasing, and cost became for bureaucracy an important test of efficiency in the firm. Unlike the works engineer, the clerk had few skills, and bureaucracies developed in firms by accepting and acting on standards set by the owners of firms. The values of most owners were built into the development of bureaucracy and these values tended to be pecuniary, not technical. These values found their best expression in the norms of nineteenth-century book-keeping and accountancy. It was therefore unlikely that those most closely concerned with administration would initiate any kind of changes that would lead to the development of management. Indeed, the structure of administration became one of the most serious stumbling blocks in the early writings on management.

As a simple index of the growth of administration for the whole population of Britain one estimate could be given by the total number of clerks in the population, although the majority were in finance and commerce. In 1851 they were 0·8 per cent of the population, in 1891, 3·3 per cent, and in 1901, 4·8 per cent. Since that time the proportion of clerks and professionals in the working population has continued to rise, while the proportion of managers and employees has remained stationary. From the date of the first Industrial Census, 1907, one can use a better index of bureaucracy in the firm: the proportion of administrators or white-collar workers to operatives or blue-collar workers.

Clerks were needed in greater numbers because of the changing structure of industry. The increasing scale and precision of the new industries and the growth of suppliers dealing with the firm, led to a greater volume of paper work in and outside the factory. The sales of typewriters and copying machines are indicative of this change. The changing legal structure of firms also called for information for shareholders and partners. Inside the factory the use of double ledgers and the new emphasis on cost accounting required more staff. In certain industries, particularly those directed at new consumer markets, like multiple grocers, an unending flow of information and advertising was disseminated, necessitating a large administrative staff.

The growth of bureaucracy can best be understood by looking at an example from the soap trade. At Crossfields in the period 1907–8, the administration of the factory was divided into secretarial (commercial) and the works (manufacturing). The secretarial side consisted of the following departments: 'cashiers, ledgers, forwarding home sales, export sales, buying, traffic, lighterage, Erasmic, and advertising'.[47] New offices to house this section were built in the 1880s and again in the early twentieth century. With the addition of the auditing department in 1911, the company was provided with monthly, quarterly, half-yearly, and annual figures. The size of the firm grew from 800 (1896) to 2,500 (1913) and the above list illustrates the ranges of administrative activities that went with such an increase in size. The increasing number of functions could no longer be carried out by small numbers of men, especially where the industry was competitive and technical.

Between 1907 and 1962 it is possible to index the changing

relation of administrative to productive personnel, by finding the average number of administrative to manual personnel. In 1907, for every 100 operatives there were 8·6 administrative personnel, while by 1948 the number of administrative personnel for every 100 operatives had risen to 20.[48] The figures in other studies are not as high as this, but according to Galambos it can be shown that the employment of non-operatives has increased by 82 per cent and that of operatives by 22 per cent since 1948. Much of this increase can be accounted for by the subdivision of functions found in the modern management structures, and associated with increasing size, but it is important to note that where employment concentration is high 'a large percentage of the labour force is concentrated in a few enterprises, and the proportion of non-operatives tends to be smaller'.[49] In the present decade (1962), the largest percentage of all non-operatives continues to be office staff, between 51·5 per cent for engineering and 71 per cent for printing and publishing. The increase in administrative labour has been used to illustrate the problems of production costs in the modern factory. It is ironic that the level of productivity per operative continues to rise, but overhead costs are increasing largely because of the number of administrative workers.[50] The large number of administrative personnel is partly a result of technological lag. The low cost of clerks did not at first encourage any search for office innovation; even now firms have to be a critical size before computers are viable.

Bureaucracy by the end of the nineteenth century was an essential characteristic of the firm in industry. The increase of separate functions in the firm, the extension of departments, the greater emphasis on paper and costing, all contributed to the growth in importance of administrative personnel. This was institutionalized by a division of most factories between the office and the works, and the establishment of administrative controls in both divisions.

The growth of the commercial side of industry was not based on an increasing technical knowledge but on a growing need to control the functions of the expanding firm. Decisions taken by the innovator or partners were soon established as routine. Central to this routine was the *counting house*, the simple ledgers of profit and loss preserved for the partners by the chief cashier and his department. The task of the office was to provide the firm with suitable information upon which the state of the company could be assessed and policy formulated. When companies grew, the simple response was to add clerks where necessary, and to develop separate departments within the commercial administration. The functions of the departments would differ, but the main body of personnel would continue to be clerks or secretaries. Many of these departments would not be autonomous, for the work would be assessed by the accounting and book-keeping department. There was a subtle difference in assessing the efficiency of labour in the technical and commercial parts of the factory. Labour would be assessed by the wages bill; clerks would be assessed by the amount of work that needed to be done. The increase in the number of clerks in administration was regarded as an indicator of efficiency itself.

The core department in administration was book-keeping or accounting. Other departments were its offspring aiding in the estimation of costs and the control of production. In the late nineteenth and the early twentieth century, the values of book-keeping were the values of the administration. The strength of this value was reinforced by the circumstances of employment. The clerk was expected to be loyal and obedient. His education was little more than preparation in the tidiness and care needed by the counting house. Indeed, accounts of work in elementary schools suggest the values and habits of the counting house were synonymous with those of the school, with emphasis on appearance and neat handwriting. There seemed to be no difficulty in finding clerks for employment. The advantages of security, and the work circumstances of the gentleman, were enough to encourage many artisans' sons to seek employment in this capacity.

The value of a clerk to the business increased with experience, and as he continued in the same firm so his choice of alternatives lessened. Loyalty was rewarded with security and personal esteem. The main aim of the clerk was to be indispensable.[51] The conditions of his employment and his general predisposition did not allow him to promote change. Bureaucracy was hierarchic and inflexible. When men gained influence by the secretarial or accountancy route they were unlikely to change the system that had served them so well. Pressure for administrative change came from external forces, not only from mergers, combinations, greater competition and new technologies, but also from new ideas about administration, and the techniques of workshop management. These new ideas became most powerful when advocated by men who were not dependent on bureaucracy, but had an independent source of knowledge, linked to professional status.

THE FORMATION OF MANAGEMENT INQUIRY

Education and professions

The major social division of the nineteenth century lay between the man who worked with his hands and the man who did not, the latter being clearly the occupation with more status. The ideal of the gentleman was firmly upheld at the end of the nineteenth century, to the detriment of technical education. Managers, owners and clerks received little or no education to prepare them for industry. Technical and scientific subjects were not generally taught at school; the stress in public schools lay on classics. This lag in applied science has even yet to be overcome.

In the last few decades universities and higher educational institutions have become centres of industrial research and development. However, in the nineteenth century, the role that universities played in industry was extremely slight. There had been some alliance in the late eighteenth century between industrialists and science but this soon gave way to the belief that practice and experience were what made for success in the factory.* This was paralleled in science by the stress laid on the

---

*For the early connexion of science and industry in the eighteenth century, see the article by A. E. Musson and E. Robinson (*Econ. Hist. Rev.*, 13, 1960, pp. 222–44). It is interesting to note that the decline of the Manchester Philosophical Society was in part due to '. . . superstitious dread of the tendency of science to unfit young men for the ordinary details of business', p. 225.

brilliant amateur. The division between science and industry widened, and there was a strong belief that success in one field precluded success in the other.* Although universities were founded by commercial interests and with commercial backing, it was not until the First World War that industry began to appreciate science, and the importance of technical education.

There were exceptions like the technological work of Sheffield University but, in general, the value of science was not accepted by those industries which depended on it most. For example, the chemical industry had few graduates and some firms relied on very few to do a large amount of work, treating them as little more than clerks. At Saint Rollax there were nineteen chemists of whom only seven were full-time students; the rest attended evening school.[52] Compared with his counterpart in Germany, the chemist in Britain had far less prestige and was far less well paid. Because of the lack of suitable chemists many British firms recruited from the continent. Much of the new knowledge that made other nations so technically formidable had to be bought in the form of licences, rather than developed.

Apart from apprenticeship and education, the other method of gaining knowledge was through a profession. The traditional professions have usually been able to control entrance into practice by statute. The church, law and medicine did have educational qualifications and demanded some kind of attendance at a university or its equivalent, but their role in the social structure came from their ability to practise their skills in their own way. The advantages were large enough to encourage engineers and accountants to professionalize their skills during the nineteenth century, but the division of older and newer professions remained.

The main educational reforms came at the end of the nine-

---

*Playfair pointed out that 'In this country we have the eminent "practical men" and the eminent scientific men, but they are not united and generally walk on paths wholly distinct ... From this absence of connexion there is often a want of mutual esteem and misapprehension of their relative importance to each other.' D. Cardwell, *The Organization of Science in England*, Heinemann, London, 1957, p. 68.

teenth and the beginning of the twentieth century. One of these was the introduction of examinations. Many were thoroughly opposed to the whole style of education that this implied, and argued that this could only end with the 'smart cocksure style of the trained examinee'.[53] Whatever the merits for science, about which this controversy mainly raged, the introduction of examinations can be seen as part of the standardization of knowledge. Knowledge was now to be written down and independently assessed. Examinations also altered the method of judging a person's success in education; the stress was laid on qualifications rather than skill.

Educational institutions began to play an important part in the creation of new professions like accountancy and engineering, encouraging specialization and imposing a standard that could only be reconciled with a period of study. Such standards were independent of the business world. They did not rely on apprenticeship, and the move to professionalization can be seen as the attempt to create an autonomy not possessed by the clerk or the employee. The creation of engineering groups within industry, and the growing demand for engineers and accountants, allowed men to practice their skills and claim exemption from the demands of company bureaucracy. However, there remained some ambiguity about their professional status and their role as either an industrial occupation or a professional service.

These professions were the foundation for modern management in industry at the turn of the century, depending not only on their position, but also on their skill. As yet there was little education that was concerned with management. Pure science was taught at the university, and practical training for apprentices and clerks was supplied by technical schools and colleges. Commerce was studied in evening classes in London, but it was little more than book-keeping and law, with a smattering of office practice. The discussion of management depended on the newer professions and the creation of pressure groups within them. Education and industry were more solidly joined with the foundation of the National Certificate Movement, beginning with the creation of a national examination for mechanical engineers in 1921. Together with engineering and accountancy the technical colleges were the seedbed of management education.

The growth of a business press

The growth of the business press in the nineteenth century was directly related to the growth of stockholding in the community. The growing number of companies depending on public issues called for greater information on financial security than in the past. Much of this demand for information came from fear; the probity of certain companies could not be trusted. The railways, for example, after the speculative boom of the mid-nineteenth century, were under the near permanent scrutiny of Parliament; the financial press called for more information, and gave unceasing streams of advice. The *Economist* gained a particular reputation for its care of the small investor, and its belief that this was best served by the promotion of *laissez faire*. On these grounds it attacked the efficiency combinations, for monopolies of this nature would give the investor little control over the policies. Other sources of information included government investigations, and independent institutes, such as the various statistical and economic societies. Little of this was concerned directly with management, but it did bring to the public mind the importance of sound business administration.

Before the end of the nineteenth century there had been little systematic and consistent discussion of organization and management. Various books were published in the cotton industry describing the technical problems of setting up and running a factory, but little was said about the organization of the works.* Some went beyond the establishment of a factory code and tried to allocate responsibility and authority between the works and commerce departments, management and technicians. One particular example is worthy of note: William Brown of Dundee

---

*See E. J. Hobsbawm, *Labouring Men*, Weidenfeld & Nicolson, London, 1964, p. 354, where it is pointed out that the *Carding and Spinning Master's Assistant* (1832) felt that reorganization would be less important than wage saving.

tried to establish the relationships between eleven departments and created a special department of 'Improvement or Alteration'.[54] Other examples of this concern with organization would include Boulton, Owen and Nasmyth from published accounts of their work, but none would add up to a discussion of management technique.

The main discussion of management problems was allied to the development of occupational journalism. Before 1850 there were journals of mining and banking which contained technical articles and occupational comment. With the continued move to professionalization in the latter half of the century most of the engineering groups published transactions, the most influential journals being *The Engineer* and *Engineering*. In the United States the *American Machinist* had been published before the American Society of Mechanical Engineering was formed to safeguard its sale. The other important journal to concern itself with problems of organization was the *Engineering Magazine*. The growing circulation of magazines of this kind depended as much on the advertising for durable and industrial goods as on the wisdom of the articles. But both were part of the increasing need of the specialist to have technical information across a wide range of industries.

Problems of the large organization; the contribution of the railways

Engineers and accountants appear to have contributed most to management thinking, particularly when viewed from the perspective of the twentieth century. But both engineers and accountants were only a small part of the total organization and used their knowledge only in specific areas. The development of railways in the United States in the third quarter of the nineteenth century faced the problem of the creation of a whole organization. (Partly because of size and the piecemeal development of the railways in Britain these questions of co-ordination and control of a large organization were not faced until the 1920s.) The only precedent for such large-scale organization was the Army, and much of the vocabulary of management comes from analogies with the Army.

Railways had to cope with a large number of uncertainties not faced by the ordinary firm: passengers, freight, sales, maintenance, and flow. The problems were new enough to encourage speculation about general management questions. Company officials met and corresponded with each other, and under the editorship of Henry Varnum Poor, the *American Railroad Gazette* became a leading journal disseminating management information. The whole literature on the development of railway management was an important contribution to the growing concern over administration.

The most difficult problem for the organization of the railways was the basis of authority on which they were to be run. The technology of railways was extremely complex, dependent on many sources of information, and this conflicted with the initial authority structure, usually built around the owner. Locally this could be seen as a conflict between the engineer and the agent. One of the solutions was to make clear the line of authority, and organizational charts were designed to give personnel a clear view of their responsibilities. McCallum of the Erie Railroad was singled out by the *American Railroad Gazette* for his distinction of responsibilities which the railway put in hierarchical terms.

All the subordinates shall be accountable to and be directed by their own immediate superior only; and the interference cannot be enforced where the foreman in immediate charge is interfered with by a superior officer giving orders directly to his subordinates.[55]

Even if an organization chart could be successfully designed, a decision would have to be made on what basis of authority this should be, for the administration of railways was complicated by the obvious factor of territory. Two different forms of territorial organization existed to cope with this problem. *Divisional*, in which each area was considered separately, gave each territory a complete structure which was duplicated in all other territories. The total was co-ordinated by representation at the highest level. *Departmental* organization, in which the network was considered as a whole, meant each member owed allegiance to departments, not divisions. In each system there were problems of co-ordination and responsibility, and the literature on responsibility, and on technical and service departments, was to have an important influence on later management writings, particularly in the United States.

The maintenance of organizational control depended on information and personnel who understood the purpose of the organization. McCallum was followed by others in building on the daily reports of engineers and guards. These detailed accounts were issued weekly, and were the basis of control in the company, showing immediately the position of rolling stock, men, and the operating conditions of the company. This information was also used for detailed auditing, based on actual operation, which resulted in detailed budgeting and forward planning. Other elements in the railway literature included the importance of work discipline, which followed organizational charts and reports, and methods of inspection of performance. Behind these developments stood a vigorous and critical press which strongly advocated the use of professional engineers in the running of the railway.[56] The growth of the railways in the United States made these techniques more important, and resulted in greater discussion of essentially managerial problems, particularly those of administration and control in large-scale organizations. The techniques of accountancy worked out in the railways were to spread rapidly to other industries.

Engineers and the management of the factory

The main concerns of engineers were not organizational, but limited to the cost, standardization, and work incentives of the workshop.

Like the railway officials, the engineering profession differed from the rest of business in trying to find information which would increase the control of management. In the professional press, articles appeared, usually in the form of case studies and individual investigations, presenting reports of particular problems. Gradually management writing shifted from case studies to systematization and finally the establishment of management principles.

Much of the concern with management in the U.S.A. was linked to a debate, current through the last part of the nineteenth century, over high wages and low costs.[57] Wage rates in the United States and Britain were compared, and the U.S.A. felt that Europe had the advantage in terms of costs. It was assumed that the workforce of the United States was characterized by high wages and little skill. This led to investigations of the best conditions for the introduction of machinery, so that the United States could remain competitive. The criterion was to be cost, but to determine the costs, the work of the factory had to be standardized, observed and accounted, and a routine developed so that judgements could be made of expected performance. Particularly important was the establishment of predetermined costs as one of the major tools by which to control organizational and individual performance. The more complex the techniques within the organization, the more difficult it became to ascribe costs to different parts of the firm. With the introduction of new machinery and the breakdown of the social distinction of craft and labour, greater attention was paid to the constituent tasks in the job to maximize the performance of the man running the equipment.

The importance of accounting for determining the performance of new machines was not solely related to labour costs. Labour under these conditions was one of the most controllable of factors, but standards for labour also involved standards for the performance of the whole factory. If costs could be predetermined then calculations could be made of the various factors of production in the plant for the assessment of potential and actual performance. It would also be possible to pinpoint waste in the factory. The elimination of waste, one of the major motives in early management writing, had the advantage of being morally acceptable to both labour and management.

The move to standardization involved the move to standard performance, and a discussion by writers of the best way to measure and cost such performance. One of the earliest writers was J. Slater Lewis, who emphasized the need for the investigation of past performance for the control of the future. Apart from this British contribution most of the work came from the United States. An important early paper on this question is that of Henry Metcalfe illustrating the close connexion between problems of labour control, costs and shop management. Working in the U.S. Government ordinance shops, Metcalfe established costing estimates for work which depended on permanent records, not on individual knowledge. The standards established were based on 'accumulated observations' and were to help with any assessment of efficiency and costs. Cards, on which details of work were classified, were passed to foremen, assessed at the completion of work, and then stored. The cards were divided into Time and Material cards, and to Metcalfe they had the advantage of giving 'the foreman an assurance that good work done cheaply would be known as such and that a method was provided by certain and automatic action of which their work would be surely gauged,'[58] as well as reducing book-keeping and waste. The cards were both an order and a record. Few took up the ideas in the form proposed, even though the basic method of recording both orders and performance was followed by Taylor. In the period before 1900 most attention was paid to the question of productivity, particularly labour productivity, rather than to administration as such.

The engineer or the shop manager did not have the right to order new machines but had to arrange the present resources at his command; the easiest way to do this was to alter the wage rates, to get labour to do more by establishing standards of productivity. The methods developed to establish standards measured individuals and their performance. The layout of work allowed the engineer to know the face of the person doing each job. Measurement layout and ideology established the individual as the producer of work, rather than the group. Behind this view lay the commonsense assumption about human nature, for wage schemes in the words of Taylor would stimulate '. . . each workman's ambitions by paying him according to his individual worth, and without limiting him to the rate of work or pay of the average of his class'.[59]

Taylor put forward an influential wage scheme but his was not the first. Wages, effort, and their relationship, were discussed on both sides of the Atlantic, but the most important discussions took place before the American Society of Mechanical Engineers. In 1889 H. R. Towne unveiled his 'gain sharing' scheme, by which savings on the product were split among the labourers; in 1891 F. A. Halsey introduced his 'premium plan' by which savings on a given time would be paid to the operative. The switch from output to time was crucial, and this was paralleled in Taylor's own work by his change in estimating performance from physical quantities in foot pounds to minutes. The result of this change was to create for observers a 'standard individual', a model for appropriate performance.[60]

The success of such schemes would not depend on management alone but on the willingness of labour to accept them. Even with unions Taylor felt that workers would accept the advantages of time and motion, for

The workmen see clearly that without the constant help and guidance of those on the management side, they could not possibly earn their high wages and the management see that without the true friendship of the workmen their efforts would be futile, and they are glad to have their workmen earn higher wages than they could elsewhere.*

The friendly help, the picture of hands across the industrial divide, was premature and misunderstood both the nature of unions and their role in the industrial world. In 1911 J. R. Commons in his essay *Unions and Efficiency* pointed to the inherent conflict between the aims of management and the aims of unions, a conflict between restriction and efficiency, which could only be settled as the result of bargaining. 'The place where the minimum wage, or the piece rate, or bonus rate, shall be placed is partly a matter of evidence and partly a matter of strength,'[61] and was not so much the result of science, but of a series of approximations, or 'adjustment to circumstances'.

Settlement by bargaining limited the scope of the new science.

*Comment on the 1912 report by Taylor. This is a toning down of previous remarks.

The establishment of performance criteria was not a matter of discussion to Taylor and his disciples, but one of industrial acceptance in the way the world had accepted gravity. The elaborate techniques of measurement by chart, slide rule and camera (the respective contributions of Gantt, Barth and Gilbreth) were not open to question. Nor did Taylor allow that they were open to question by management once arrived at. In this way the whole Taylor movement, whatever his views on unions, implied criticism of the existing practices of management. Interestingly enough, the major critics of his famous paper, *Shop Management*, came from the proponents of the 'open shop' movement. The distinguishing mark of the Taylor proposals was the insistence on the systematization of the whole factory and the work process, and these proposals were often not acceptable to management. Both Halsey's 'premium plan' and Emerson's 'bonus plan'[62] were more popular, calling for less change whilst concentrating on what seemed to management the main issue of wages and labour. Even some of the firms which claimed to follow Taylor seemed to have selected those parts that would give them a comparative wage advantage over other firms, rather than the full implementation of the scientific system. The whole scheme was not well received in Britain, and industrialists considered that it lacked humanity, or was little more than common sense. Levine has argued that the caution shown to organizational improvement and scientific management was typical of a reluctance to innovate in British industry at the end of the nineteenth century, and a cause of the decline from international industrial leadership.[63] However, it should be noted that the caution concerning scientific management was shared in the United States and echoed in the A.S.M.E. report on industrial management in 1912.[64]

Taylor's work was centred on the shop; for him the principles of the workshop were the principles for the management of all industrial organizations. Moreover

the same principles can be applied with equal force to all social activities; to the management of our homes, the management of our farms: the management of business of our tradesmen large and small; of our churches, of our philanthropic institutions, our universities and our government departments.[65]

Taylor's system, however, was not employed by large firms, because of the special problems relating to their size, but by small and medium-sized firms. Taylor discounted problems of bureaucracy; he considered that the institutionalization of his planning department would solve any administrative difficulties. Many managers understood that the organization was important, but saw it in terms of 'a process of procedures rather than as a matter of structure'[66] and this was particularly the case with those who saw the organization through workshop eyes.

It was gradually realized that Taylor had dealt systematically with only one part of the factory, and that administering an organization depended on a view of the whole organization. The literature had no clear focus and dealt with records, communications, the use of organizational charts, and line of authority. Writers recognized the problem of confused authority, the difficulties of co-ordination, and the problems of size, for the plant

becomes every day more and more an assemblage of independent powers operated still, it may be, in thorough harmony to a common end, but on wholly independent lines of management in different departments, and always approaching a point where these independent subordinate managers of either real or recognized authority are secretly or openly jealous of each other, and where each sees that the less anyone knows about the actual facts of his department, the better the chances are for the continuance of his position.[67]

The solution to the problems of the organization (rather than workshop) was felt to be the systematization of management so as to bring managers into harmony with the organization. Men like Alford Hamilton Church and Robb saw their task as broader than the shop engineer, as 'readjusting the balance of responsibilities disturbed by the expansion of industrial operations, and to enable control to be restored to its essential features'.[68] Sets of maxims were produced to guide the manager, as the ten commandments advise the worthy.

The discussions about wages, systems, and labour-saving

management took place against a great growth in the number of engineers in the United States. Between 1880 and 1920 the numbers grew from 7,000 to 136,000. The most important engineering association was the American Society of Mechanical Engineers. From 1907 management was one of the bases for membership, but not until 1920 was a separate division for management set up. The lack of clear acceptance by the senior engineering association of any particular management scheme led to the establishment of various societies claiming professional status, and supporting various branches of the new management. The most famous, or notorious, was the 'Society for the Promotion of the Science of Management', commonly called the Taylor Society, founded by his disciples to promote and perpetuate his principles. Proceedings were published and the orthodoxy, at least during Taylor's lifetime, sternly defended. Other societies included the Efficiency Society, supporting the work of Emerson and the Society of Industrial Engineers. Each society promoted both the gospel and the status of the industrial and consulting engineer.

The urge to professionalism in business was made in a famous lecture by Brandeis in 1912. The conditions he laid down for a profession were independent knowledge, the idea of service, and success in other than monetary terms, such as 'excellence of performance'. Many claimed these conditions to be unfulfilled. Several themes ran through the literature which emphasized the non-pecuniary advantages of the new professions, the belief that scientific management promoted peace and harmony in the factory and the industrial world, and that it eliminated waste and increased production. These were counted as advantages for human welfare and reinforced a distinction that professional engineers were anxious to make, that service to industry was beneficial in comparison with service to commerce. Symbolic of this distinction was the Code of Ethics drawn up in 1919 by M. L. Cooke for the A.S.M.E. which emphasized the obligation of the engineer, not to the firm, but to his profession. It was not that profits should not be made but that the calling of science was higher and more demanding. The engineer could contribute to the welfare of society and guide its welfare in the most efficient way. An example of this exaggerated opinion was held by Veblen; in *The Engineers of the Price System* (1919) he claimed that engineers could provide the basis for a 'practicable Soviet of Technicians'. Much of the writing which promoted the importance of the engineer was euphoric and boastful. But in these schemes there was the attempt to come to terms with the needs of social efficiency, if not organization, and an understanding that society in the future would need special skills, and the applied expert had much to offer.

The ideological bias of American management

The ideological elements that management held in common with other groups in American society in the nineteenth century included Social Darwinism and populism and, in particular, individualism and pragmatism. One of the most important elements of the individualistic ideology was the emphasis on character. Character was prized above intelligence and education, for it carried with it the promise of hard work and diligence. For Taylor it was 'the real monotonous grind that extolled character', with the implication that those among the workmen who did not accept his scheme deserved to be sacked for they would not in any case get on. The rags to riches story was part of the folk ideology of the United States; the successful were formed in the 'College of Hard Knocks'. Allied with character was an emphasis on personal experience, and a denigration of education and learning that did not have any immediate use. Carnegie was stating the obvious for the business world when he observed that such education gave 'false ideas and . . . a distaste for the practical life'.[69]

Underneath these assumptions lay a set of views about the individual and particularly about the motivation of the employee. Like many of the views held by engineers they were made up of a combination of folklore and commonsense. No analysis of the human personality existed in scientific terms and even if it had, it is doubtful if it would have changed their minds. The history of the application of psychology to industry shows how it has been used to justify and support pre-determined interests.[70]

Most early management schemes concentrated on the individual worker and on his self-interest. Some schemes, like profit sharing, attempted to identify the common interests of the worker with the union, but these were unsuccessful either because the schemes were ultimately inequitable, or because they resulted in the unions becoming the agent of business. Too often they consisted of a set of 'engineering details', and it was doubtful if scientific management as embodied in the work of Taylor was capable of dealing with organizational problems.

The individualist presumption took for granted that a man would work if he was paid enough, and that if he were paid more, then he would work harder. But a balance had to be kept between being under- and overpaid, for if overpaid he would become, in the words of Taylor, 'more or less shiftless, extravagant, and dissipated'. For Taylor the task was not to innovate but to work, which is reminiscent of Andrew Ure's demand for 'docility' from the good workman. The organization of the work would be dealt with by the foreman in conjunction with the planning department. Union leaders like Gompers were not inaccurate in their description of the process.

Here is the idea that all labour consists simply in moving things. See? Just as all the work done by the machine is one motion after another, all manipulation of matter by human beings is made up of motions and series of motions. So there you are, wage earners in general, mere machines – considered industrially of course.[71]

This complaint was common, both inside and outside the unions. Coupled with the idea of motivation and the machine role of the worker, was the view that men were best fitted for what they did firstly as workers, and secondly in the industrial organization. The division of mental and physical labour was a division best suited for efficiency and work in the plant. The division was common in the writing of the period; Taylor institutionalized the division and created 'a radical separation of thinking from doing' as one of the principles of the well-run factory.[72]

It is important not to overestimate the originality of Taylor and his fellow writers of this period. The division of mental and physical labour, the survival of the fittest and the pecuniary motives of workmen, were part of the fund of ideas current in the nineteenth century, and in some cases before. Shovelling, heavy labouring, and an emphasis on time had all been discussed before, the most important single contribution being Charles Babbage's *On the Economy of Machinery and Manufactures*, published in 1832. Taylor wrote at a propitious time, and fulfilled a need; he combined this with his flair for publicity and a bold claim that all that needed to be known could be found in his own work.[73]

Another source of knowledge for the new science was the Army. Analogies drawn between industrial and military organizations were common, and this was not surprising as the Army was the only large-scale organization before the railways with which to compare industrial organizations. The U.S. Army was an innovator in the use of scientific management. Military terms were also transferred, the most famous being the distinction between 'line' and 'staff' used by Emerson in 1913.

Social inquiry and management science

Management writing has never shown a complete unity, and one of the main distinctions that can be drawn in the literature is that between books coming out of universities and books written by managers. In Britain in particular, a distrust exists between the two, partly based on the complications of academic writing and partly on the demand for simplicity by the busy manager. Nevertheless, today all writing on management incorporates academic findings in some form or another. Perhaps it is surprising that even by the beginning of the twentieth century other disciplines did not take management seriously. The contributions of economics and sociology were at first peripheral, but as they became more relevant the engineering concept of man had to be modified.

The modification came from several sources: studies of the labourer and his environment and studies of the psychology of the workman, his home conditions and his life. The former studies were an added help to the control of labour, while the latter were concerned with 'betterment' or 'welfare'. Studies of factory labour had been carried out in Germany in the last half of the nineteenth century and by officials in various countries, but this had rarely influenced management policy. Industry did not encourage investigations by psychologists until World War I, when the success of the selection programme for the army became known. These tests followed those of Binet in France, examining men for their skills in both literary and non-literary form. Companies 'besieged the unit for information'.[74] Most of the selection procedures were worth very little, and psychologists were worried at their failure to show the limitations of such tests to business users. The boom slowed and, although some firms continued to use them, they did not become important again, in an improved form, until World War II.

The consideration of labour turnover as a separate problem after 1910 was particularly important in those industries, with a large proportion of semi-skilled workers, which needed some degree of labour stability. The Ford Motor Company in 1913 had 13,000–14,000 positions with a turnover of 50,000 men in that year. This resulted in increased attention to factory welfare and an attempt to build up loyalty to the firm by payment and fringe benefits. This had an important effect on the development of management.

But there were longer term changes which were to have a more profound effect on the study, and ultimately the practice, of management. These changes were part of an attempt to test assumptions about industrial society in a more scientific manner. Many assumptions about poverty, family income and health were changed by these investigations and a different picture of society emerged, altering views about the relationship of work to the rest of living.[75] In Britain the most important survey was that of Charles Booth who found that the main cause of widespread poverty was not fecklessness but unemployment. A further development was the use of the case study in charity work, and this was later adopted by welfare workers to investigate conditions of the workforce. These inquiries gave a great fillip to the development of welfare in enterprises, for, even if conditions of work could not be altered, personal conditions could be improved by facilities and services, however rudimentary, at the factory.

The increasing number of perspectives involved in the sociological examination of society can be illustrated by one concept, the division of labour. The view cited from Adam Smith earlier illustrates the popular view of the division of labour in the nineteenth century. Writers like Ure considered it to be inevitable and necessary for the progress of the economy and society. Most writers accepted this and concentrated on the effects of the division of labour on the ordinary workman. Smith examined the question again in Book V of *The Wealth of Nations* when he wrote that the effects of extreme specialism resulted in the worker becoming 'as stupid and ignorant as it is possible for a human creature to become ... His dexterity at his own particular trade seems to be aquired at the expense of his intellectual, social and marital virtues,' [76] but the social effects of the division of labour meant an increase in the collective knowledge of the whole society. There are, then, two traditions arising from the division of labour: that concerned with the effect on the individual worker, and that concerned with the benefits for the whole society. Both sprang from Smith's work. The first may be called the humanistic tradition: it deplores the effects of the division of labour, and takes the problem of the individual's freedom as being the main criterion of assessment. The second is the tradition of social development.

The humanist tradition is found in the writings of many social observers, but none put their position more succinctly than de Tocqueville in his observations on the United States. 'In proportion as the principle of the division of labour is more extensively applied the workman becomes more weak, more narrow-minded and more dependent. The art advances, the artisan recedes.' [77] Marx also considered the division of labour to be the prime reason for the alienation of the labourer from his product, although he was arguing this in the context of property and capital which the division of labour served. Together with the concentration of the means of production and the creation of a world market, Marx made the division of labour one of the three characteristics of Capital. Marx saw the advantages of the division of labour in terms of wealth, but felt that it divided the common interests of the workers. The extension of the principles of the division of labour can be found in the work of Durkheim, and particularly in his *Division of Labour in Society*. This aimed to show the 'function of the division of labour, that is to say what social need it satisfied', particularly the way it contributed to the legitimacy and moral basis of society, that is, to its social solidarity. The view that the individual's moral well-being depended on the collective well-being of society gave meaning and stability to the individual. Durkheim opened up a new dimension for the study both in substance and method. In methodology he believed in 'social facts', data that did not depend on individual assumptions, and he considered this to be the proper basis for a study of society.[78] In substance the study emphasized the importance of social relations *per se* over economic relations: 'The division of labour presumes that the worker far from being hemmed in by this task does not lose sight of his collaborators, that he reacts upon them and reacts to them.'[79] The appropriateness of Durkheim's discussion for industry has been questioned by Georges Friedmann. He criticizes the assumption that the worker can find meaning in his work, and therefore moral stability (i.e. lack of alienation) through an understanding of the purpose of his work. He also finds that workers are not interdependent, given the character of job specialization and repetitive nature of the semi-skilled work. Even so, Durkheim's work is important because he looked at society rather than industry alone, and because his emphasis on the morale of workers served as an important premise for later industrial sociology, including the Hawthorne investigations (see Part 4.4). The growth of interest of sociologists in industry extended the intellectual scope of the study of management and, ultimately, its improvement in practice.

Psychology was also influential, in other ways than the mechanics of personality testing. It emphasized the importance of social relations in the study of individuals. Münsterberger, who produced some of the first psychological work in the U.S.A. dealing with industry, considered to be misguided Taylor's view of man as a helpless, psychological dilettante and felt that the task of the professional psychologist was to correct this error by experiment and study. Within social thought there was also the tradition that collective behaviour and individual behaviour had to be studied together. The tradition of Cooley in the United States, that 'man's psychological outfit is not divisible into the social and the non-social; but that he is all social in a larger sense, is all part of common human life',[80] was supported by the writings of Freud on group psychology and played an important part in the thinking of Elton Mayo. These contributions of the emerging social sciences to the study of management could be multiplied, but it is enough to indicate that a fund of ideas was available to be studied in universities and research institutions.

The aim of most of the writers discussed in Parts 2, 3 and 4 of this book is to contribute to or proclaim the science of management. Many of the early writers felt that they had found the secret of scientific management, but later writers grew more cautious as the complications of the methods, approach and results became more apparent. The overconfidence of the early writers was misplaced but the approach was not, for Taylor and his colleagues were the first to take the workings of the factory as being worthy of detailed and systematic study. In the context of this book, it is worth pondering the kind of science they saw management to be.

The early studies of management were both positivist and pragmatic. Metcalfe had argued that the art of management must be founded on 'accumulated observations which could be built up to check performance and would be more trustworthy than individual impressions'. Some writers felt that these impressions, by themselves, would make a science, while others considered that they needed to be presented systematically. The debates after the 1912 report to the A.S.M.E., *The Present State of the Art of Industrial Management*, illustrate both these approaches. Three groups emerged with different attitudes to the future development of management. First there were those who were openly sceptical of scientific claims, and who felt that management itself would remain 'an art for selecting and applying the most appropriate methods', and those like A. Hamilton Church who felt that what was new about labour-saving management was its scepticism.

> Take nothing for granted
> See that every effort is adapted to its purpose
> Cultivate Habit.

Secondly there were those who followed Taylor in thinking that both the results and the applications, properly conducted, were scientific. To quote H. P. Gillette in the debate: 'The science of management is a comprehensive code of demonstrable and formally enunciated laws for so directing energies of men as to secure the most economic production and marketing of utilities.' Thirdly came the group who felt that if basic principles could be enunciated and followed, then management would become scientific and more successful. These systematizers differed from Taylor in that they did not conduct studies but relied more on their own experience. All shared the view that such studies must be pragmatic, and those not working in industry followed this assumption.[81]

Each of the scientific management proponents felt that they had the one best way, and that they had achieved it. Taylor and Gilbreth emphasized studies and measurement, and from the results inferred the proper and most efficient way to run the factory. Too often the studies became absolutes and were transferred into standards of performance and proper practice. Those who argued for first principles were more openly normative, but their proposals were generally less useful as principles and more interesting in their detail. All wished their approach to be useful, but few distinguished between discovery and application, which depended on specific conditions of leadership and policy. Policy depends on values and criteria of performance: efficiency, welfare and cooperation. Although these are not mutually exclusive, they highlighted different management problems, as essays later in the book will consider.

The development of management concepts depended on a

variety of factors: the growing size of the firm, the importance of technological efficiency, the need for greater standardization of labour and costs, the growth of administrative control, and the increasing interest in management. Writings on management have continued to emphasize three kinds of performance criteria. The concern with the optimization of production, with betterment, and with the total organization express the different conceptions of success contained in the roles of the production, personnel and general management functions.

NOTES

1. See J. U. Nef, 'The Progress of Technology and the Growth of Large-Scale Industry', in E. Carus-Wilson, ed., *Essays in Economic History*, Arnold, London, 1954, vol. I, pp. 88–107.

2. See S. D. Chapman, *The Early Factory Masters*, David & Charles, London, 1967, p. 41.

3. S. Pollard, 'Fixed Capital in the Industrial Revolution in Britain', *Journal of Economic History*, 24 September 1964, pp. 302, 304.

4. Chapman, op. cit., p. 133.

5. D. C. Coleman, *The British Paper Industry, 1495–1860*, Clarendon Press, Oxford, 1958, p. 232.

6. E. J. Hobsbawm, *The Age of Revolution*, Weidenfeld & Nicolson, London, 1962, p. 48.

7. K. Boulding, in his essay in B. M. Gross, *Great Society?*, Basic Books, New York, 1968, p. 212.

8. See C. Wilson, 'Economy and Society in Late Victorian Britain', *Economic History Review*, 18, 1965, pp. 183–98.

9. H. D. Fong, quoted in J. Clapham, *Economic History of Modern Britain*, Cambridge, 1932, vol. II, p. 117.

10. M. Blaug, 'Productivity of Capital in the Lancashire Cotton Industry during the Nineteenth Century', *Econ. Hist. Rev.*, 13, 1961, p. 379.

11. Clapham, op. cit., vol. II, p. 117.

12. S. Checkland, *The Rise of Industrial Society, 1815–1885*, Longmans, London, 1964, p. 120.

13. Clapham, op. cit., vol. II, p. 116.

14. D. Landes, 'Technological Change and Development in Western

Europe', in *Cambridge Economic History of Europe*, vol. VI, part i, pp. 350–1.

15. Blaug, op. cit., p. 32. Also for the 1851 census, Clapham, op. cit., vol. II, p. 35.

16. H. D. Fong, *Triumph of the Factory System in England*, Nankai Univ., Tientsin, 1930, p. 28.

17. D. Landes, 'The Structure of Enterprise in the Nineteenth Century' in D. Landes, ed. *The Rise of Capitalism*, Macmillan, New York, 1966, p. 105.

18. Blaug, op. cit., *Econ. Hist. Rev.*, 13, 1961, p. 360.

19. L. Davis, 'Capital Markets and Industrial Concentration', *Econ. Hist. Rev.*, 19, 1966, pp. 255–72.

20. S. B. Saul, 'The Motor Industry in Britain to 1914', *Business History*, 5, 1962, pp. 22–44.

21. David, op. cit., p. 266.

22. C. P. Kindleberger, *Economic Growth in France and Britain, 1851–1950*, Harvard Univ. Press, Cambridge, Mass., 1964, p. 177.

23. Clapham, op. cit., vol. III, p. 225.

24. Clapham, op. cit., vol. III, pp. 225–6, 228.

25. See E. Penrose, *The Theory of the Growth of the Firm*, Blackwell, Oxford, 1960, p. 88 ff., for a fuller treatment of this theme.

26. For these themes see P. Selznik, *Leadership in Administration*, Harper, New York, 1957.

27. Blaug, op. cit., pp. 365–6.

28. A. J. Taylor, 'Labour Productivity and Technical Innovation in the British Coal Industry, 1870–1914', *Econ. Hist. Rev.*, 14, 1961, pp. 48–70.

29. H. J. Habakkuk, *American and British Technology in the Nineteenth Century*, Cambridge Univ. Press, 1962, pp. 161–2.

30. See Kindleberger, op. cit., pp. 141–56, for a good discussion of this.

31. D. Landes, 'Factory Costs and Demand Determinants of Economic Growth', *Bus. Hist.*, 7, 1965, pp. 15–33.

32. Taylor, op. cit., *Econ. Hist. Rev.*, 14, 1961, p. 59.

33. N. Rosenburg, 'Technological Change in the Machine Tool Industry, 1840–1910', *J. Econ. Hist.*, 23, 1963, pp. 414–46.

34. Saul, op. cit., p. 31.

35. P. Mathias, *The Retailing Revolution*, Longmans, London, 1967, pp. 44–5.

36. D. H. Aldcroft, 'Technological Progress and British Enterprises, 1875–1914', *Bus. Hist.*, 8, 1966, pp. 122–39.

37. Kindleberger, op. cit., p. 141 ff.

38. S. Pollard, *The Genesis of Modern Management*, Arnold, London, 1965, p. 173.

39. Blaug, op. cit., p. 368, and for the handloom weavers, D. Bythell, 'The Handloom Weaver in the English Cotton Industry during the Industrial Revolution', *Econ. Hist. Rev.*, 17, 1964, pp. 339–53.

40. A. Smith, *The Wealth of Nations*, Everyman edition, vol. 1, p. 7.

41. N. McKendrick, 'Joseph Wedgwood and Factory Discipline' in D. Landes, *The Rise of Capitalism*, p. 67, and Pollard, op. cit., p. 179.

42. A. E. Musson, 'Nasmyth and the Early Growth of Mechanical Engineering', *Econ. Hist. Rev.*, 10, 1957, pp. 121–7.

43. E. H. Phelps Brown, *The Growth of British Industrial Relations*, Macmillan, London, 1959, p. 91.

44. ibid., p. 90.

45. H. J. Aitken, *Taylorism at the Watertown Arsenal*, Harvard Univ. Press, Cambridge, Mass., 1960, p. 32.

46. Pollard, op. cit., p. 190. In 1833, 47·1 per cent of the cotton industry were on piece-work.

47. A. E. Musson, *Enterprise in Soap and Chemicals: Crossfields of Warrington*, Manchester, Univ. Press, 1965, ch. XI.

48. S. Melman, *Dynamic Factors in Industrial Productivity*, Blackwell, Oxford, 1956, p. 73.

49. P. Galambos, 'On the growth of employment of Non-Manual Workers', *Oxford Univ. Inst. Econ. and Stats. Bul.*, 26, 1964, pp. 369–87.

50. ibid., table XIV, p. 379.

51. D. Lockwood, *The Blackcoated Worker*, Allen & Unwin, London, 1958, p. 22.

52. L. Haber, *The Chemical Industry during the Nineteenth Century*, Oxford Univ. Press, 1958, p. 190.

53. Q. in Cardwell, op. cit., p. 133.

54. D. Chapman, 'William Brown of Dundee', in H. Aitken, *Explorations in Enterprise*, Harvard Univ. Press, Cambridge, Mass., 1965.

55. Q. cited in A. Chandler, 'Henry Varnum Poor', in W. Miller, ed., *Men in Business*, Harvard Univ. Press, Cambridge, Mass., 1952.

56. For the problems of the Pennsylvania Railroad, and the attempts to deal with them, L. H. Jenks, 'Early History of Railroad Organization', *Bus. Hist. Rev.*, 35, 1961, pp. 153–79.

57. See the important article by J. Litterer, 'Systematic Management: the Search for Order and Integration', on which the passage is based. *Bus. Hist. Rev.*, 35, 1961, pp. 461–76.

58. Q. from the introduction to his book, *The Cost of Manufactures and Administration of Workshops Public and Private* (1885) conveniently reprinted in H. F. Merril, ed., *Classics in Management*, A.M.A., New York, 1960, pp. 47–56.

59. Q. in M. Nadworny, *Scientific Management and the Unions*, Oxford Univ. Press, 1955, p. 5.

60. For the question of science see L. Haber, *Efficiency and Uplift*, Chicago, Univ. Press, 1964, p. 21, and the phrase 'standard individual' comes from the A.S.M.E. 1912 report on management, reprinted in *Fifty Years of Progress in Management*, A.M.A.

61. Reprinted as Chapter X, *Labour and Administration*, Macmillan, New York, 1913, see pp. 145–6.

62. Nadworny, op. cit., p. 19.

63. A. L. Levine, *Industrial Retardation in Britain, 1880–1914*, Weidenfeld and Nicolson, London, 1967.

64. Paragraph 48 of the 1912 report.

65. F. W. Taylor, *The Principles of Scientific Management*, Harper, New York, 1911, p. 8.

66. L. H. Jenks, 'Early Phases of the Management Movement', *Admin. Sci. Q.*, 5, 1960, pp. 421–47. This is the best account of early management, and I have relied on it often.

67. ibid., p. 472, from Henry Roland, *Engineering Magazine*, 1898.

68. A. Hamilton Church, *Engineering Magazine*, 1900, q. in Haber, *Efficiency and Uplift*, p. 19.

69. Q. in E. Kirkland, *Dream and Thought in the Business Community, 1860–1900*, Cornell Univ. Press, Ithaca, N.Y., 1956, p. 86.

70. L. Baritz, *The Servants of Power*, Wesleyan Univ. Press, Middletown, Conn., 1960.

71. Q. from D. Weiner, 'The Man with the Hoe and the Good Machine', in J. J. Kwiat and M. C. Turpie, eds., *Studies in American Culture*, Minnesota Univ. Press, 1959, p. 71.

72. The point is made in Haber, op. cit., p. 21.

73. J. Hoagland, 'Historical Antecedents of Organizational Research', in W. Cooper, ed., *New Perspectives in Organization Research*, Wiley, New York, 1964, pp. 27–38.

74. Baritz, op. cit., p. 37, 43.

75. See G. Stigler, 'Empirical studies of consumer behavior' in his *Essays in the History of Economics*, Chicago, Univ. Press, 1965.

76. A. Smith, *The Wealth of Nations*, Book V.

77. A. de Tocqueville, *Democracy in America*, Vintage edit., ed. Phillips Bradley, vol. 2, p. 169.

78. See G. Friedmann, *The Anatomy of Work*, Heinemann, London, 1961, pp. 68–81.

79. Friedmann, op. cit., p. 69.

80. R. Hofstadter, *Social Darwinism in American Thought*, Beacon Press, Boston, 1944.

81. For examples, the deans of business schools, Kirkland, op. cit., p. 111, psychologists, Baritz, op. cit., p. 52–3. Münsterberger felt that social scientists should keep out of industrial conflict and not make value judgements on the use of work.

PART TWO

THE CRITERION OF EFFICIENCY

2.1 Introduction: the Criterion of Efficiency

THE criterion of efficiency, as applied to the firm or organization, is cost. Changes in organization or work procedure which diminish cost are considered to be more efficient; those which increase cost, less efficient. Stated in this way efficiency seems to be a simple concept involving only the manipulation of factors within the organization. But as soon as one begins to examine the reasons for efficiency or lack of efficiency in any given firm one realizes that it is, in fact, far more complex. This is illustrated by the writers and disciplines discussed in Part Two.

Taylor saw labour as the main source of efficiency, the workshop as the main unit of application for his system, and activity measurement as the major tool for improvement. He aimed to limit the actions used in performing a task to the most essential, and to improve the *flow* of work between individual workers in the workshop. Gilbreth took Taylor's ideas in one direction to their logical conclusion, but both Taylor's and Gilbreth's ideas on efficiency were based on over-simplified views of human motivation and factory administration. Taylor considered that men would maximize their effort and consequently the efficiency of the factory if they felt that they were doing the job in the best way and were thus able to earn more. Administration was regarded as little more than the means for introducing and controlling the new methods. But labour had to work within the framework of administration, and improvement of the worker depended, in part at least, on improvement of the administration.

Fayol dealt with institutional costs such as those associated with administration and changes in organization. He was not concerned with immediate output but rather assumed that good administration was bound to bring better results. For Fayol the source of efficiency was proper management procedure, the unit of application was administration and the method for its attainment was the establishment of correct principles. To cut through the vast amount of data and to distinguish the important from the unimportant for the manager, Fayol used a common strategy of analysis – the establishment of principles for managers which, if followed, would result in organizational control. He wrote in the early twentieth century at a time when such reflections on management were uncommon, and he helped to shift the perspective of management studies away from the workshop and the labourer towards problems of administration. Organizational problems were not merely the result of uncooperative workmen but also of failures in communication and co-ordination inside the whole organization.

Efficiency, as a criterion for the organization, has now become subject to more rigorous and scientific techniques, particularly in econometrics and operational research. Both disciplines specify their assumptions, quantify data and set up models. Taylor, Gilbreth and Fayol based their assumptions on industrial values as they saw them, and their methods were not scientific in the sense of the two previously mentioned disciplines. This, of course, is not to belittle their work which had an immediate utility.

Operational research is based on a number of disciplines of which statistics is the most important. Its task is to convert observations to numerical values which can then be manipulated to improve performance.

2.2 Frederick Taylor and Scientific Management

THOMAS KEMPNER

ASSESSMENTS of important figures from the past suffer from the difficulty that few characters fall into tidy categories. Taylor is no exception. Many of his views are strange to us today; others were the forerunners of important techniques still in use. For the purpose of this chapter, I wish to identify only the main elements in these ideas. First, the improvements in production management from which sprang the application of scientific methods, and hence 'Scientific Management'. Second, the systems of pay designed to produce 'a fair day's work for a fair day's pay'. Third, a 'grand design' for an industrial society which would produce improved standards of living. Fourth, and linked with the first three, Taylor's importance as the founder of the 'Scientific Management' movement, whose ideas were influential long after his death.

Taylor was born in 1856 into a well-established middle-class family in Philadelphia.[1] His family intended him to become a lawyer like his father, and he passed the Harvard entrance examinations; but, before he could take up his place, he developed eye trouble and headaches (probably of a nervous origin) and, on medical advice, abandoned thoughts of university study.

Shortly after this, in 1874, he began an apprenticeship as a pattern maker and machinist; his eyesight improved even though work of this kind could hardly be described as undemanding for his eyes. Indeed, it has never been adequately explained how he chose a career which, in the social milieu of the time, would hardly have been thought appropriate. The puzzle increased in 1878. By this time, he had completed his apprenticeship and had obtained a post with the Midvale Steel Company, but he started as a labourer even though there seem to have been family connexions with Midvale. Within a few years he had worked his way through the ranks to chief engineer. It was during these years that he obtained a degree in engineering by evening study from Stevens Institute. At Midvale too he had his first clash with labour. As he rose in the Midvale hierarchy, he sought to impose his gradually acquired ideas, which were to develop into 'Scientific Management'. In this firm Taylor won, but only after the most bitter struggle.

There followed a period with the Bethlehem Steel Company, where Taylor had been brought in to reorganize the plant. This appointment ended in disaster. Once again he tried to impose his methods, but met the concerted opposition of other managers. He did little to conciliate his opponents and, without warning, he was sacked* and his system abandoned.

After Taylor left Bethlehem he immediately wrote *Shop Management*. It proved an effective way of advertising his system, and from then on until his death in 1915 his advice was regularly sought.

We are not concerned with the non-management side of his activities, but he was an extremely competent engineer. He was responsible for a number of inventions or improvements in production technology, including the improvement of 'high speed' steel.

Taylor left some of his contemporaries and later writers with a feeling of unease about his personality. He was determined to the point of obsessiveness in all he did – determined to succeed and unwilling to compromise. In his childhood he had had to adapt himself to an easy-going and weak father and a mother of strong personality. By inclination he probably took after his father, but by training, followed the precepts of his mother. He lived in a generation which worried about the 'softening' effects of easy living and believed that toil was 'character building'. Taylor himself repeatedly described toil as a virtue and perhaps this explains his early career choice. For him, grace could be achieved by hard and monotonous toil; he advocated shop-floor experience as part of graduate training for moral as much as for practical reasons.

*He was given a fortnight's notice which read, 'I beg to advise you that your services will not be required by this company after 1st May 1901'.

TAYLOR AND SCIENTIFIC METHOD

Taylor's first interest had been to increase output on the shop floor, but he soon realized that this was only one aspect of the management problem. He therefore made the heroic attempt to apply scientific methods to industry. Of course, he was in advance of his time and he was often wrong or blind to ideas other than his own, yet there can be little doubt that he led a major change.

The basis of the method was detailed and careful analysis of all tasks and functions, together with time studies of the component parts. It was assumed that new machines and tools would often be needed. Next, the analysis would shift to the other associated routines: production planning (which Taylor really helped to invent), stock control and office procedures. This would be followed by standardization of equipment, methods and procedures.

The next stage would consist of the selection and training of a staff of 'first-class men', producing 'a fair day's work'. All work would be planned and carefully co-ordinated at every phase; finally, the results would be checked and adjustments made where necessary. In the years after his death, these ideas were absorbed into the growing body of knowledge of management as a subject for serious study. Systematic analysis was shown to be applicable to all aspects of business, from the planning of new products to the control of a machine shop.

'Scientific Management', as the name of the movement associated with Taylor, was coined in 1910 by Louis D. Brandeis, a well-known American lawyer. He had been retained by those opposing certain railways that had applied to the Interstate Commerce Commission for an increase in freight rates (the Eastern Rates Case). In the course of a conference with Gantt, Gilbreth and others in October 1910 in New York, the movement was named; and his contention that the railways would need no increase in rates if they used scientific management helped Brandeis to win the case.

Taylor's shop-floor experience is important because it influenced his later thinking. He was impressed by the amount of deliberate output restriction. This, as we shall see later, he considered a criminal waste. He knew that threats and dismissals could do little to change this situation. The problem was, of course, the difficulty of setting a standard acceptable to both employers and employees as a fair day's work. Taylor's attempt to find a way of measuring such an output is the key to all his later work. It led him on to an investigation of the physical abilities and aptitudes required in a variety of jobs. Simultaneously, he and his associates used elementary time and motion study techniques.

Taylor's solution was that the standard should be the work done by a 'first-class man' in favourable conditions. The last phrase contains two interrelated ideas which were fundamental to Taylor's system. First, the men had to have an aptitude for their particular work. Secondly, it was the duty of management to determine correct methods of work by careful analysis, to provide suitable machinery and good working conditions, and to select and train those men who would be first-class at their jobs. The standards required from first-class men would be high and those who did not qualify would have to find work elsewhere. The next step was to persuade men capable of first-class work to produce the 'fair day's work'. This was to be done by an incentive piece-work plan. It gave higher wages to those who accomplished the set task, plus a substantial bonus for extra work done. Work which fell below the standard was, however, penalized and an alternative method of payment was developed by one of Taylor's associates, H. L. Gantt, which was not so harsh.

Taylor had immense faith in the possibility of accurately measuring the requirements for first-class performance.[2] Because he thought that he had discovered what constitutes a 'fair day's work', he believed he could solve the problem of output restriction. One can sympathize with the attempt even if it did not come off. It ignored all the difficulties of creating an absolute standard in situations where men's judgements can differ and still be reasonable. It was not enough for Taylor to say that a fair day's work is done by a first-class man under the best possible conditions which management can create. Admittedly, to say that much was a big step forward at the time. But even if we leave aside the problem of measuring performance, we still have to decide the 'fair day's pay' which goes with the 'fair day's work'. These are shifting standards and so too are all the non-monetary conditions which surround the job. A great deal of this Taylor seems to have recognized implicitly. We know that he looked forward to rising standards of living, but all his views were essentially long-term with little allowance for those human weaknesses which spring from short-term needs.

TAYLOR AND UNIONS

Taylor accepted the basic organization of the American capitalist society of his time. In this context Taylor was writing as a man within his period, and it would be unfair to be critical. This applies also to Taylor's negative view of trade unions.

The growth of Taylor's ideas on 'Scientific Management' at the turn of the century coincided with the growing strength of American unionism and militant anti-union campaigns by many employers, individually or through their associations. It was the era of the Open Shop Campaign which had the purpose of maintaining the authority of employers by denying unions the right to speak or act on behalf of workmen.

Taylor's position was predictable. His attitude to lazy or 'soldiering' workmen was often stated; this, together with his ideal of a 'fair day's work', gave him a pre-disposition against trade unions. But his objections went much deeper and followed logically from other parts of his theories. He believed that his methods were capable of assessing 'scientifically' – and therefore beyond argument – a 'fair day's work' and appropriate pay. As all aspects of work, pay and conditions could be, according to him, objectively assessed, there could be no place for collective bargaining. Of course, if one holds such views, then unions are, at best, a nuisance and at worst, a sign of decadence and unreasonableness. Not that employees were solely to blame. Management, said Taylor, did not know what constitutes a proper day's work and seemed reluctant to find out.

A sophisticated argument would probably go as follows: Taylor claimed that unions practised output restrictions. This is an unmitigated evil but, given the laxity of management in setting and maintaining proper standards, union behaviour was inevitable. With his 'system' men would leave their unions and become part of a cooperative enterprise. Working together with management, instead of in opposition to it, output, pay, profits and the standard of human welfare would rise, and a higher individual output would produce a better moral tone.

It is important to stress the nature of the cooperative system between management and men which Taylor advocated. Once an extremely detailed production plan had been made by management, workers would be trained to do exactly what they were told and would then be expected to obey in a docile way. But if Scientific Management removed the need for collective bargaining and trade unions, then it also removed the need for authoritarian managements. Scientific Management would determine the activities of both. Many employers resented it for that reason.

For their part, the unions retaliated against a system which both denied the usefulness of collective bargaining and threatened loss of control over the working environment. To some extent the Taylorites and the unions were agreed: both opposed rate cutting; the former because it undermined the 'scientific' basis of their work and the latter because they feared speeding up and 'sweated' conditions. Employers and hack consultants, under the halo of Scientific Management, were cutting wage rates with little attempt to implement the rest of the system. Inevitably, when things went wrong, Taylor and his disciples were blamed. There was a further reason for disagreement. The powerful unions were those of the craftsmen, but Taylor's system threatened to erode the importance of skilled men for it proposed a system of training outside union control to produce 'first-class men'.

A change of attitude began in 1914 when the U.S. Commission on Industrial Relations discussed, among other topics, the impact of Scientific Management. For the first time it seemed that, if the Taylorites were prepared to concede the importance of collective bargaining, then the unions might swallow at least part of the 'system'. To the end of his life Taylor himself refused: he insisted, with increasing irritation, that the system was 'scientific' and that there could be no argument about it.

However, even before his death, some of the younger disciples were making concessions. As the years went by these men began to accept the role of unions. They agreed that no system, however scientific, could be imposed without discussion and consent. It was a major advance. Attempts to build a bridge between the two sides had also been helped by the investigations of the committee presided over by Professor R. F. Hoxie.[3] His committee had been given this task by the Commission on Industrial Relations. Hoxie's detailed survey pointed to both the strength and weaknesses of the system – it was highly efficient on the production side, but tended to aggravate, rather than solve, the social problems of industry. This was because it refused to accept that the individual worker could not bargain with an employer. (Of course, Taylor would have argued that he had no need to do so.)

In the years after Taylor's death, the anti-union attitude of the disciples lessened. Partly this was because the movement itself was subject to new ideas and new men for whom the old orthodoxy was not sufficient. Partly also, it was due to the widening interest in management as a subject for research and discussion so that 'Taylorism' was seen as one aspect of a much larger whole. There were related reasons. The 'scientific basis' continued to be challenged with increasing effect. Gilbreth himself showed how unreliable time studies were; others did the same. When doubts of this kind could not be answered, then the payments system could no longer be considered objective and bargaining with unions had to be accepted. Finally, the increasing influence of behavioural scientists, as distinct from engineers, had an impact on the theoretical assumptions made about industrial society – a subject further discussed in later chapters of this book. Non-financial incentives became accepted as an increasingly important area of discussion.

As the Taylorites abandoned their anti-union stance, so the

unions by the 1920s were ready to accept the new version of scientific management. This no longer had the precision of a dogma, but now both sides approved of the aim of higher production which would lead to higher standards of living.

IMPROVEMENTS IN MANAGEMENT TECHNOLOGY

It is easy to be critical. Taylor's ideas were formed fifty to seventy years ago. So much has happened to change society that it would be unfair to blame him for sharing many of the ideas of his contemporaries. None of this should be allowed to detract from Taylor's major contribution, which has stood the test of time: namely, the idea of applying scientific methods, of inquiry and experiment, first to production problems and then to management as a whole.

In this area Taylor was an innovator of outstanding fruitfulness. Many of his ideas brought system, order and logic to areas where previously rule of thumb had prevailed – production planning, analysis of costs, systems of payment and many more. If he did not always invent such systems, he did carry them several stages further. The increasing complexity and size of managerial tasks have made such systems essential.

Many of Taylor's ideas were, of course, far more fundamental. It is well known that he was one of the founders of time and motion study. His interest developed through his need to determine a 'fair day's work'. To know this, he had to try and discover what would be the reasonable output for a first-class man. His studies to determine the causes of fatigue and the influence of rest pauses, and the attempt to determine the physical abilities required for particular jobs, all hold within them the seeds of things which have become of major importance since then. An interesting and often misunderstood proposal was Taylor's plan to introduce what he described as 'functional foremen'. He criticized the concentration of numerous functions in the hands of a single subordinate manager. This he described as the military type of organization where orders are transmitted in a straight line down a chain of command. Taylor wanted to change this by adding specialists, responsible for planning, inspection, maintenance and so on. A great deal of this has happened in recent years as new roles have needed the creation of specialists to fill them. Unfortunately, in practice the division of responsibility between line managers and specialists is not as simple as Taylor supposed and continues to trouble us.

Many of Taylor's views read strangely now. He had a puritanical zeal about work and regarded the practice of 'soldiering', as he described it, as a very great crime. For example, in *The Principles of Scientific Management* there occurs the following phrase: 'There is hardly any worse crime to my mind than that of deliberately restricting output; of failing to bring the only things into the world which are of real use to the world, the products of men and the soil.' He goes on to say that the history of mankind has shown that whenever production increases, so does consumption and that in the long run fears of overproduction were unjustified. This is true, but Taylor was not the first, or indeed the last, to discover that the long-term process of economic adjustment is not an argument acceptable to those who will lose their jobs.

It must be appreciated that Taylor's ideas on restriction of output were part of a comprehensive pattern of industrial, if not of social improvement. In Taylor's world only first-class men were allowed to do any particular job. The justification was partly moral and partly economic. First-class work and a full day's work (very full indeed if one accepts his standards) were an ethical requirement. But Taylor was also driven on by the logic of economic events as he saw them. Since harder work by first-class men, aided by production improvements, increased the volume of goods and services available to all, it would also be bound to increase earnings per head in real terms.* The creation of greater wealth for such a purpose could not be challenged; hence, said Taylor, output restriction meant the continuance of poverty and was a crime against humanity. From increases in productivity could come other improvements: greater pride in

*Taylor did not use this terminology but the meaning is clear enough.

work, an identification of interests between employer and employee, the former obtaining greater use of overhead equipment and the latter higher standards of living. The division of the spoils would become less important than the increase of total output.

Unfortunately, men who did not fit into the category of 'first-class' would have to find work elsewhere. Taylor assumed that there must be, somewhere, a job where a particular individual could be first-class by his definition.

To achieve his utopia, Taylor required first, a technically enlightened but autocratic management willing to use all the latest devices to increase output. Such managements would deal justly with their employees and in return for an end to output restrictions, there would be no attempt to cut piece rates. Secondly, he needed a docile labour force prepared to have their working conditions constantly changed,[4] for in the nature of things, this would be a dynamic system. As improvements occurred in methods, so working groups would be altered, methods would change, and skills which had made a man first-class under the previous system, would now put him into a lesser category. One doubts whether Taylor really understood the full implication of all this.

Even as Taylor was writing, the social and economic backgrounds which are so important a part of his theories were undergoing change. Higher standards of living were beginning to create quite different demand conditions. Taylor's arguments were based solely on the efficiency of economic incentives. He assumed that men could be persuaded to work for an individual incentive and that this would spur on the 'first-class man' to do the 'fair day's work'. Implicitly he understood many of the group pressures to which the individual workman is subject, but at the crucial points in this theory he believed these to be less important than the possibility of pecuniary gain. What he did not, and perhaps could not have realized, was the paradoxical effect of that very increase of output per head which he hoped to achieve by scientific management. Far from increasing the desire for money it lessened its importance in relation to the other social needs and the needs for individual development. As far as we can tell, the further men move away from the subsistence level, the more important do non-monetary incentives become. Money is still very important – there is no question of that – but it now ceases to have the dominating influence which it must have at a much lower standard of living.

TAYLOR'S DISCIPLES

In his lifetime, Taylor had many disciples. Two of these who developed his ideas into new fields were Gantt and Gilbreth. At this point, it is necessary to describe only briefly their immediate links with Taylor.

Gantt worked for Taylor for a number of years, but his experience of the latter's system of pay caused him to amend and improve it. Gantt also had a much clearer understanding of the place of trade unions in an industrial society and tried to co-operate with them rather than oppose them. His contribution was particularly useful in one area of Taylor's work: the improvement of production control techniques and the information required for decision making. All these are described in another chapter. In his later years, labour problems increasingly took Gantt's attention. He dreamt of applying scientific management to the industrial problems of society as a whole and sponsored a short-lived movement for this purpose—'The New Machine'. Its objectives were sincere if idealistic. It appealed for a new spirit of harmony between workers and employers, for justice in industry and restraint from arbitrary power. Human behaviour as an independent constraint was beginning to be accepted; Gantt realized this; it is doubtful if Taylor saw people as anything other than inefficient and unpredictable machines.

Gilbreth developed another line of Taylor's thought and both time and motion study and ergonomics owe much to him. He continued that part of Taylor's work which dealt with the scientific investigation of work. In the narrow but important areas in which Gilbreth specialized, his work was original and useful. On management—worker relations and the factory system he held much the same views as Taylor.

Taylor lived long enough to see his 'system' become the subject of endless discussions and copied by countless imitators, many of whom gave the original an undeservedly bad reputation. Employers used Taylor's system 'exactly as Taylor had insisted that they should not; as an arsenal of devices designed to simplify and improve the management of labour'.[5] He had had the (for him) prized honour of becoming president of the American Society of Mechanical Engineers, and in 1911 his friends had founded a society in his honour to propagate his ideas.

Many of Taylor's ideas were to become fruitful in work study, production planning and control, and ergonomics; the failures were where too much was claimed. It was not a comprehensive system of work because its advocates were slow in seeing the weaknesses of the payments system. It was very rare for firms to apply Taylor's ideas in full. Yet this does not detract from the impact which the movement had on management thinking. It became absorbed into a larger framework, but there are few areas of management studies which do not owe a debt to the ideas, the debates and controversies of 'Scientific Management'.

By the time Taylor died, there were probably 140 establishments which used the system, of which 120 implemented it more or less in full.[6] But Hoxie's report showed great differences between the writings and statements of the Taylorites and the practical application. Employers, it seems, wanted quick results and some of the consultants were prepared to compromise. The biggest flaw was in the variation in time study methods and results. Hoxie believed it could be used properly even though the situations he had seen had dismayed him.

The movement had aroused a large amount of public controversy, and in 1915 Congress forbade the use of some of the Taylor pay and time study methods in military establishments. While the effects were not, in the long run, important, it did give an indication of the strength of union feeling.

Taylor was a great production manager. He believed that every job, no matter how simple, could be improved by study and the application of scientific techniques. It is this part of his thinking which provides the best possible example today.

READINGS FROM FREDERICK TAYLOR

Taylor on the new 'Science'[7]

In addition to developing a *science* in this way, the management take on three other types of duties which involve new and heavy burdens for themselves.

These new duties are grouped under four heads:

First. They develop a science for each element of a man's work, which replaces the old rule-of-thumb method.

Second. They scientifically select and then train, teach and develop the workman, whereas in the past he chose his own work and trained himself as best he could.

Third. They heartily cooperate with the men so as to insure all of the work being done in accordance with the principles of the science which has been developed.

Fourth. There is an almost equal division of the work and the responsibility between the management and the workmen. The management take over all work for which they are better fitted than the workmen, while in the past almost all of the work and the greater part of the responsibility were thrown upon the men.

It is this combination of the initiative of the workmen, coupled with the new types of work done by the management, that makes scientific management so much more efficient than the old plan.

Taylor defending the 'System'[8]

Scientific management is not an efficiency device, not a device of any kind for securing efficiency; nor is it any bunch or group of efficiency devices. It is not a new system of figuring costs; it is not a new scheme of paying men; it is not a piece-work system; it is not a bonus system; it is not a premium system; it is no scheme for paying men; it is not holding a stop watch on a man and writing things down about him; it is not time study; it is not motion study nor an analysis of the movements of men; it is not the printing and ruling and unloading of a ton or two of blanks on a set of men and saying, 'Here's your system; go use it.' It is not divided foremanship or functional foremanship; it is not any of the devices which the average man calls to mind when scientific management is spoken of. The average man thinks of one or more of these things when he hears the words 'scientific management' mentioned, but scientific management is not any of these devices. I am not sneering at cost-keeping systems, at time study, at functional foremanship, nor at any new and improved scheme of paying men, nor at any efficiency devices, if they are really devices that make for efficiency. I believe in them; but what I am emphasizing is that these devices in whole or in part are not scientific management; they are useful adjuncts to scientific management, so are they also useful adjuncts of other systems of management.

Taylor on his Utopia[9]

The great revolution that takes place in the mental attitude of the two parties under scientific management is that both sides take their eyes off the division of the surplus as the all-important matter, and together turn their attention toward increasing the size of the surplus until this surplus becomes so large that it is unnecessary to quarrel over how it shall be divided. They come to see that when they stop pulling against one another, and instead both turn and push shoulder to shoulder in the same direction, the size of the surplus created by their joint efforts is truly astounding. They both realize that when they substitute friendly cooperation and mutual helpfulness for antagonism and strife they are together able to make this surplus so enormously greater than it was in the past that there is ample room for a large increase in wages for the workmen and an equally great increase in profits for the manufacturer. This, gentlemen, is the beginning of the great mental revolution which constitutes the first step toward scientific management. It is along this line of complete change in the mental attitude of both sides; of the substitution of peace for war; the substitution of hearty brotherly cooperation for contention and strife; of both pulling hard in the same direction instead of pulling apart; of replacing suspicious watchfulness with mutual confidence; of becoming friends instead of enemies: it is along this line, I say, that scientific management must be developed.

Taylor on Utopia[10]

The general adoption of scientific management would readily in the future double the productivity of the average man engaged in industrial work. Think of what this means to the whole country. Think of the increase, both in the necessities and luxuries of life, which becomes available for the whole country, of the possibility of shortening the hours of labour when this is desirable, and of the increased opportunities for education, culture, and recreation which this implies. But while the whole world would profit by this increase in production, the manufacturer and the workman will be far more interested in the especial local gain that comes to them and to the people immediately around them. Scientific management will mean, for the employers and the workmen who adopt it – and particularly for those who adopt it first – the elimination of almost all causes for dispute and disagreement between them. What constitutes a fair day's work will be a question for scientific investigation, instead of a subject to be bargained and haggled over. Soldiering will cease because the object for soldiering will no longer exist. The great increase in wages which accompanies this type of management will largely eliminate the wage question as a source of dispute. But more than all other causes, the close, intimate cooperation, the constant personal contact between the two sides, will tend to diminish friction and discontent. It is difficult for two people whose interests are the same, and who work side by side in accomplishing the same object, all day long, to keep up a quarrel.

The low cost of production which accompanies a doubling of the output will enable the companies who adopt this management, particularly those who adopt it first, to compete far better than they were able to before, and this will so enlarge their markets that their men will have almost constant work even in dull times, and that they will earn larger profits at all times.

This means increase in prosperity and diminution in poverty, not only for their men but for the whole community immediately around them.

As one of the elements incident to this great gain in output, each workman has been systematically trained to his highest state of efficiency, and has been taught to do a higher class of work than he was able to do under the old types of management; and at the same time he has acquired a friendly mental attitude toward his employers and his whole working conditions, whereas before a considerable part of his time was spent in criticism, suspicious watchfulness, and sometimes in open warfare. This direct gain to all of those working under the system is without doubt the most important single element in the whole problem.

Taylor on 'First-Class Men'[11]

In preparation for this system the writer realized that the greatest obstacle to harmonious cooperation between the workmen and the management lay in the ignorance of the management as to what really constitutes a proper day's work for a workman.

Among several investigations which were undertaken at this time, one was an attempt to find some rule, or law, which would enable a foreman to know in advance how much of any kind of heavy labouring work a man who was well suited to his job ought to do in a day; that is, to study the tiring effect of heavy labour upon a first-class man. Our first step was to employ a young college graduate to look up all that had been written on the subject in English, German and French. Two classes of experiments had been made: one by physiologists who were studying the endurance of the human animal, and the other by engineers who wished to determine what fraction of a horse-power a manpower was. These experiments had been made largely upon men who were lifting loads by means of turning the crank of a winch from which weights were suspended, and others who were engaged in walking, running, and lifting weights in various ways. However, the records of these investigations were so meagre that no law of any value could be deduced from them. We therefore started a series of experiments of our own.

Two first-class labourers were selected, men who had proved themselves to be physically powerful and who were also good steady workers. These men were paid double wages during the experiments, and were told that they must work to the best of their ability at all times, and that we should make certain tests with them from time to time to find whether they were 'soldiering' or not, and that the moment either one of them started to try to deceive us he would be discharged. They worked to the best of their ability throughout the time that they were being observed.

Now it must be clearly understood that in these experiments we were not trying to find the maximum work that a man could do on a short spurt or for a few days, but that our endeavour was to learn what really constituted a full day's work for a first-class man; the best day's work that a man could properly do, year in and year out, and still thrive under. These men were given all kinds of tasks, which were carried out each day under the close observation of the young college man who was conducting the experiments, and who at the same time noted with a stop-watch the proper time for all of the motions that were made by the men. Every element in any way connected with the work which we believed could have a bearing on the result was carefully studied and recorded. What we hoped ultimately to determine was what fraction of a horse-power a man was able to exert, that is, how many foot-pounds of work a man could do in a day.

After completing this series of experiments, therefore, each man's work for each day was translated into foot-pounds of energy, and to our surprise we found that there was no constant or uniform relation between the foot-pounds of energy which the man exerted during a day and the tiring effect of his work. On some kinds of work the man would be tired out when doing perhaps not more than one-eighth of a horse-power, while in others he would be tired to no greater extent by doing half a horse-power of work. We failed, therefore, to find any law which was an accurate guide to the maximum day's work for a first-class workman.

A large amount of very valuable data had been obtained, which enabled us to know, for many kinds of labour, what was a proper day's work. It did not seem wise, however, at this time to spend any more money in trying to find the exact law which we were after. Some years later, when more money was available for this purpose, a second series of experiments was made, similar to the first, but somewhat more thorough. This, however, resulted as the first experiments, in obtaining valuable information but not in the development of a law. Again, some years later, a third series of experiments was made, and this time no trouble was spared in our endeavour to make the work thorough. Every minute element which could in any way affect the problem was carefully noted and studied, and two college men devoted about three months to the experiments. After this data was again translated into foot-pounds of energy exerted for each man each day, it became perfectly clear that there is no direct relation between the horse-power which a man exerts (that is, his foot-pounds of energy per day) and the tiring effect of the work on the man. The writer, however, was quite as firmly convinced as ever that some definite, clear-cut law existed as to what constitutes a full day's work for a first-class labourer, and our data had been so carefully collected and recorded that he felt sure that the necessary information was included somewhere in the records. The problem of developing this law from the accumulated facts was therefore handed over to Mr Carl G. Barth, who is a better mathematician than any of the rest of us, and we decided to investigate the problem in a new way, by graphically representing each element of the work through plotting curves, which should give us, as it were, a bird's-eye view of every element. In a comparatively short time Mr Barth had discovered the law governing the tiring effect of heavy labour on a first-class man. And it is so simple in its nature that it is truly remarkable that it should not have been discovered and clearly understood years before. The law which was developed is as follows:

The law is confined to that class of work in which the limit of a man's capacity is reached because he is tired out. It is the law of heavy labouring, corresponding to the work of the cart horse, rather than that of the trotter. Practically all such work consists of a heavy pull or a push on the man's arms, that is, the man's strength is exerted by either lifting or pushing something which he grasps in his hands. And the law is that for each given pull or push on the man's arms it is possible for the workman to be under load for only a definite percentage of the day. For example, when pig iron is being handled (each pig weighing 92 pounds), a first-class workman can only be under load 43 per cent of the day. He must be entirely free from load during 57 per cent of the day. And as the load becomes lighter, the percentage of the day under which the man can remain under load increases. So that, if the workman is handling a half-pig, weighing 46 pounds, he can then be under load 58 per cent of the day, and only has to rest during 42 per cent. As the weight grows lighter the man can remain under load during a larger and larger percentage of the day, until finally a load is reached which he can carry in his hands all day long without being tired out. When that point has been arrived at this law ceases to be useful as a guide to a labourer's endurance, and some other law must be found which indicates the man's capacity for work.

When a labourer is carrying a piece of pig iron weighing 92 pounds in his hands, it tires him about as much to stand still under the load as it does to walk with it, since his arm muscles are under the same severe tension whether he is moving or not. A man, however, who stands still under a load is exerting no horse-power whatever, and this accounts for the fact that no constant relation could be traced in various kinds of heavy labouring work between the foot-pounds of energy exerted and the tiring effect of the work on the man. It will also be clear that in all work of this kind it is necessary for the arms of the workman to be completely free from load (that is, for the workman to rest) at frequent intervals. Throughout the time that the man is under a heavy load the tissues of his arm muscles are in process of degeneration, and frequent periods of rest are required in order that the blood may have a chance to restore these tissues to their normal condition.

To return now to our pig-iron handlers at the Bethlehem Steel Company. If Schmidt had been allowed to attack the pile of 47 tons of pig iron without the guidance or direction of a man who understood the art, or science, of handling pig iron, in his desire to earn his high wages he would probably have tired himself out by 11 or 12 o'clock in the day. He would have kept so steadily at work that his muscles would not have had the proper periods of rest absolutely needed for recuperation, and he would have been completely exhausted early in the day. By having a man, however, who understood this law, stand over him and direct his work, day after day, until he acquired the habit of resting at proper intervals, he was able to work at an even gait all day long without unduly tiring himself.

Now one of the very first requirements for a man who is fit to handle pig iron as a regular occupation is that he shall be so stupid and so phlegmatic that he more nearly resembles in his mental make-up the ox than any other type. The man who is mentally alert and intelligent is for this very reason entirely unsuited to what would, for him, be the grinding monotony of work of this character. Therefore the workman who is best suited to handling pig iron is unable to understand the real science of doing this class of work. He is so stupid that the word 'percentage' has no meaning to him, and he must consequently be trained by a man more intelligent than himself into the habit of working in accordance with the laws of this science before he can be successful.

The writer trusts that it is now clear that even in the case of the most elementary form of labour that is known, there is a science, and that when the man best suited to this class of work has been carefully selected, when the science of doing the work has been developed, and when the carefully selected man has been trained to work in accordance with this science, the results obtained must of necessity be overwhelmingly greater than those which are possible under the plan of 'initiative and incentive'.

NOTES

1. For detailed biography see F. B. Copley, *Frederick Winslow Taylor: Father of Scientific Management*, Harper and Row, New York, 1928.

2. As an example, see his description of the discovery of the 'law of heavy labouring' in *The Principles of Scientific Management*, Harper and Row, 1947, p. 57.

3. *Scientific Management and Labor*, New York, 1915.

4. See the description of the selection of pig-iron handlers in *Principles of Scientific Management*, Harper, 1947, p. 64.

5. R. Bendix, *Work and Authority in Industry,* Wiley, 1956, p. 286.

6. Estimated by C. B. Thompson, 'Scientific Management in Practice', *Quarterly Journal of Economics*, February, 1915. (Quoted by Nadworny, *Scientific Management and the Unions 1900–1932*, Harvard University Press, 1955, p. 85.)

7. F. W. Taylor, *The Principles of Scientific Management*, Harper and Row, 1947, pp. 36–7.

8. F. W. Taylor, 'Testimony before the Special House Committee', in *The Principles of Scientific Management*, Harper and Row, 1947, pp. 26–7.

9. ibid., pp. 29–30.

10. ibid., pp. 142–4.

11. ibid., pp. 53–60.

FURTHER READING

F. W. TAYLOR, *Scientific Management*, comprising: 'Shop Management', 'The Principles of Scientific Management', 'Testimony before the Special House Committee', Harper, 1947.

J. J. NADWORNY, *Scientific Management and the Unions 1900–1932*, Harvard University Press, 1955.

F. B. COPLEY, *F. W. Taylor* (2 vols.), Harper, 1923.

R. BENDIX, *Work and Authority in Industry*, Wiley, 1956.

H. AITKEN, *Taylorism in the Watertown Arsenal*, Harvard University Press, 1960.

S. HABER, *Efficiency and Uplift*, University of Chicago Press, 1964.

H. S. PERSON, Article in Seligman and Johnson, *Encyclopedia of the Social Sciences*, vols. 13–14, p. 603 ff.

R. F. HOXIE, *Scientific Management and Labor*, Appleton, New York, 1915.

H. B. DRURY, *Scientific Management: A History and Criticism*, Columbia University Studies in History, Economics and Public Law, vol. 65, No. 2, New York, 1915.

2.3 Gilbreth and the Measurement of Work

MICHAEL THICKETT

ANYONE who has been a student of work study is familiar with two names, Frederick Winslow Taylor and Frank Bunker Gilbreth. For most of his working life Gilbreth was a contemporary of Taylor and one of the small band of pioneers of 'Scientific Management'. This was a system of management, the basic purpose of which was to quantify work and so be able to allocate it sensibly and check on its performance. The first measure that was used on work by scientific management was that of time, and Taylor was the initiator. Gilbreth was a great admirer of Taylor. He regarded him as being the 'father of scientific management' – in fact he campaigned for the movement to be called the 'Taylor System of Management' – but he had a wider view than Taylor as to its principal objective. Taylor regarded scientific management as being a system for discovering a worker's true capacity and thus providing a means for paying him his true worth. His motto is quoted as being 'a fair day's work for a fair day's wage'. Gilbreth agreed with this philosophy, but he had an additional and more important objective. This was to use the worker's 'fair day's work' in the most efficient way, by discovering and showing to him the best way for him to do his job.

Gilbreth was born in 1868 in Fairfield, Maine. His early life bears a remarkable resemblance to that of Taylor. He was of middle-class origin and when seemingly destined to continue his studies at university, he entered the building trade at the age of seventeen, as an apprentice bricklayer. Within ten years he became superintendent of his company and then set up his own contracting business, undertaking work all over the United States and Great Britain. While working in the construction industry he was struck by the amount of wasted effort and some of the illogical practices that were carried out, and took positive steps to try to eliminate them. He became fascinated by this side of his work, which can best be described as motion study, and this interest eventually became so strong that he gave up his construction business and devoted the rest of his life to this work, achieving an international reputation as a consultant and writer on the subject. In all this he worked in close collaboration with his wife, Lillian, a trained psychologist, and after his early death in 1924 she carried on their work with great distinction.

One of the first things that Gilbreth noticed, when he was an apprentice, was that bricklayers had three different ways, or, as he later described it, three different sets of motions for doing their work. They had one set for use when working quickly, another for working slowly, and a third for teaching their trade to an apprentice. Gilbreth could not accept that this was a correct state of affairs. One of these ways, or a combination of different parts of all three, must be the best way, and this should always be used.

To find the best way of doing a job became Gilbreth's life work. He first applied himself to the building industry, where he discovered a method for laying bricks which reduced the motions required to lay a brick from eighteen to less than five, and at the same time he increased individual output from 120 to 350 bricks laid per hour. When he became a consultant he aimed to find the best method of doing work in many different industries and claimed many successes. His method was as follows:

– He defined the current situation, noting everything that could have any possible effect on the job and its performance.

– He analysed the job using the special equipment that he had either invented or adapted for use for this purpose, and he used one of several systems of analysis that he had devised.

– He examined the results of these analyses, cutting out any parts of the job he found unnecessary, combining different parts where possible, and, if practical, designing equipment that would reduce still further the motions required to do the job.

– Taking what was left of the job he would synthesize this into a new job method, which, to him, was the best way the job could be done in the given circumstances.

Gilbreth was not the first to use this system. Taylor used it in his studies, but Gilbreth was the first to prove and advocate its universal application. He laid down detailed instructions on how to find out the best way of doing any job. These instructions, and the apparatus he devised for use in carrying them out, were possibly Gilbreth's greatest contribution to the science of work study. They are very numerous and diverse, but for the sake of convenience they are best considered under the following headings.

ANALYTICAL APPARATUS

Gilbreth realized that to make an accurate analysis of a job one had to have some sort of record of it being carried out. The motion picture camera was an obvious answer to this, and he was the first to use it for this purpose. This did not give him all the information he required, a big deficiency being that it only gave a series of pictures taken at timed intervals. For his analyses Gilbreth wanted a record of paths of hand movements made while doing a job. He solved this problem by fixing lights on to the worker's hands and getting him to do his job in front of a photographic plate, thus getting a permanent record of his hand movements. He further improved on this system by having the lights flash at fixed intervals, thus putting a time scale on the record. This method of job recording was called 'The Chrono-cyclographic Method' and it provided a cheap and easy way of recording performance. It has been greatly used in all sections of industry, especially in mass production.

ANALYSIS OF WORK

Gilbreth devised several systems of analysing work into different distinct elements. He used flow process charts which break work down into five basic elements – Operations, Transportation, Inspection, Storage and Delay. He then took work analysis further and eventually arrived at a micro-analytic system by which he could break down all hand work into seventeen basic elements, called 'THERBLIGS' (Gilbreth spelt almost in reverse). Examples of these are:

Grasp Begins when hand or body member touches an object.

Consists of gaining control of an object.

Ends when control is gained.

Assemble Begins when the hand or body member causes parts to begin to go together.

Consists of actual assembly of parts.

Ends when hand or body member has caused parts to go together.

Release load Begins when hand or body member begins to relax control of object.

Consists of letting go of object.

Ends when hand or body member has lost contact with object.

Transport loaded Begins when hand or body member begins to move with an object.

Consists of hand or body member changing location of an object.

Ends when hand or body member carrying object arrives at general destination or movement ceases.

Plan Begins when hand or body members are idle or making random movements while worker decides on course of action.

Consists of determining a course of action.

Ends when course of action is determined.

PRINCIPLES OF MOTION ECONOMY

Once a job has been recorded the analysis must be used to discover whether there is a better way for the task to be performed. Gilbreth did much original work in this field. He laid down rules for finding out which of the motions a person was using were necessary to the job's completion and which were not. The latter, which he described as 'wasted motions' were to be immediately discarded. The former were to be examined again in close detail to see if different separate motions could be combined, or if special equipment could be designed to eliminate some of them completely. For example, in bricklaying he noticed that many bricklayers had to bend down to pick up bricks. He easily eliminated these bending motions by providing a table, on which the bricks were placed, that was of such a height that all bending was eliminated. When as many motions as possible had been either combined or eliminated, what was left had to be put together to form the new method of doing the job, and Gilbreth formulated a set of basic rules to aid in synthesizing these remaining elements. These rules were called Rules for Motion Economy and Efficiency. They consisted of guidance in setting out a job in such a way that it could be performed with a minimum of effort, and hence fatigue, and a maximum of achievement. These principles were tested by Gilbreth both in the laboratory and in the field; they harnessed the natural co-ordination of the body and utilized its easiest paths of motion. Like his work on analytical equipment and analysis procedure they have stood the test of time, requiring few modifications or additions.

INTERACTION OF THE TASK, THE WORKER, AND THE SURROUNDINGS

In addition to all the tangible steps that could be taken to ensure that a job was done in the best way, Gilbreth identified two relatively undefinable factors that could affect its actual execution. One of these was the worker and the other was the working environment. He listed fifteen different characteristics of a worker that could have a bearing on his performance on a specific job. These were anatomy, brawn, contentment, creed, earning power, experience, fatigue, habits, health, mode of living, nutrition, size, skill, temperament and training. However, these factors and their possible effects were not studied by him scientifically in controlled conditions. He mainly used his own experiences and possibly those of others to describe their likely effect. He quoted several examples to strengthen his case. A simple one, illustrating the effects of a worker's religion (creed), was 'The motions of a bricklayer working upon the wall of a church differing from his own religion are often vastly different from those that he is careful to make when the congregation to occupy it coincides with his belief'.[1]

In his analysis of environment he identified fourteen possible factors that could affect performance. These were appliances, clothes, colours, entertainment (reading, music, etc.), heating (cooling, ventilation), lighting, quality of materials, reward and punishment, size of unit moved, special fatigue-eliminating devices, surroundings, tools, union rules, and weight of unit moved. Like his worker analysis they were mainly of an empirical nature, based on his own experience and that of others. He quoted the possible effect of entertainment on workers by giving the experience of a German working in a tobacco factory in Mexico, who stated: 'The four packers under me knew no greater joy than to listen to a fairy tale, with the regulation princess and dragon, and if I could but tell them one, or one of their number did so, the work went twice as fast, and they were happy.'[2] Unlike his other work, these analyses may seem somewhat old-fashioned today, but the basic ideas behind them are still relevant – perhaps more so. Work on the interaction of environment, worker characteristics and job performance has been pursued vigorously since Gilbreth, but much of the work has been of an academic nature and there have been relatively few industrial applications.

All Gilbreth's work had one objective – to discover the best method of doing a job. Once at an exhibition in London he gave a devastating display of his ability to do this. The example is quoted by Henry L. Gantt in his introduction to Gilbreth's book on *Motion Study*.[3]

... While in London with the American Society of Mechanical Engineers, Mr Gilbreth cornered an old friend of his and explained to him the wonderful results that could be accomplished by motion study. He declared that he did not care what the work was, he would be able to shorten the time usually required, provided that nobody had previously applied the principles of motion study to the work.

A few days before, this friend had been at the Japanese-British Exposition and had seen there a girl putting papers on boxes of shoe polish at a wonderful speed. Without saying what he had in mind, Mr

Gilbreth's friend invited him to visit the exposition, and in a most casual way led him to the stand where the girl was doing this remarkable work, with the feeling that here at least was an operation which could not be improved upon.

No sooner had Mr Gilbreth spied this phenomenal work than out came his stop-watch and he timed accurately how long it took the girl to do twenty-four boxes. The time was forty seconds. When he had obtained this information he told the girl that she was not working right. She, of course, was greatly incensed that a man from the audience should presume to criticize what she was doing, when she was acknowledged to be the most skilled girl that had ever done that work. He had observed that while all her motions were made with great rapidity, about half of them would be unnecessary if she arranged her work a little differently. He had a very persuasive way, and although the girl was quite irritated by his remark, she consented to listen to his suggestion that he could show her how to do the work more rapidly. Inasmuch as she was on piece work the prospect of larger earnings induced her to try his suggestion. The first time she tried to do as he directed she did twenty-four boxes in twenty-six seconds; the second time she tried it she did it in twenty seconds. She was not working any harder, only making fewer motions.

This account the writer heard in Manchester, England, from the man himself who had put up the job on Mr Gilbreth, and it is safe to say that this man is now about as firm a believer in motion study as Mr Gilbreth.

Gilbreth appears to have been a 'larger than life character', and his boast that he was prepared to improve any kind of work was not an idle one. He had twelve children and when it became necessary for the majority of them to have their tonsils removed he decided that this was an excellent opportunity to study this operation with a view to finding the best way of doing it. He arranged for the operations to be carried out and persuaded the surgeon to allow him to film them. He himself, probably to placate his children, also underwent the operation – though this was not medically necessary. Unfortunately the results of this experiment were never made available to the medical profession, as the cameraman forgot to put any film in the camera and a similar opportunity to repeat the process never occurred!

Gilbreth's basis for scientific management was the concept of the one best way. A worker entering an organization where this system was in operation would be examined and classified, mainly from a physical and mental point of view, to see what work he was most suitable for. He would then be trained to do his allocated job in the best way, and he would be paid high wages, even when training, for doing this. These wages would be much higher than he could expect under a traditional management system, the reason for this being that he was doing his job in the best way, and was therefore working more efficiently. Scientific management insisted that the worker should share the benefits of his increased efficiency. The exact amount of his wages would, where possible, be decided by a piece-rate system. If he could not achieve his expected level of earnings, the reasons would be scientifically investigated. If he was not using the best way that he had been taught, he would be re-educated, or, if his failure were due to a personal deficiency he would be reclassified and placed in more suitable work. Careful records of performance of all workers would be kept and those with outstanding achievements would be promoted to positions such as foremen, or instructors. Personal initiative was encouraged from the workers, especially in the form of suggestions for improvements, even for the best ways being used, and rewards were paid for any used suggestions. Gilbreth considered that this sort of cooperation between workers and management was very important, and in this he differed from Taylor. He particularly disapproved of Taylor's practice of carrying out secret time studies on men, and ruled out any clandestine activity where matters appertaining to workers and management were concerned. Gilbreth was a disciplinarian, but he did have a respect for workers and as far as is known was never subjected to their animosity as Taylor was.

Gilbreth was convinced of the absolute ethical rightness of what he did. He visualized a society in which every job was performed in the best way. He claimed that the advantages of such a society would be enormous, stating that at least 50 per cent of all work being carried out consisted of wasted and unnecessary motions. By doing all work in the best way output would be doubled and he called on the United States Congress to look into this possibility. He was positive that the total application of the principles of scientific management could bring about this society. Realizing that he could not do this himself, he set out to persuade his fellow beings to help him perform this task. He became the great publicist for scientific management both by the written and spoken word and by demonstration, an example of which has already been given. This was Gilbreth's second great contribution to the cause of work study, possibly of equal importance to that of devising methods and equipment.

So far we have considered the mechanics of scientific management; we must now consider its social implications. It invariably tended to make work simpler and of shorter duration or cycle time. This tendency was accentuated by Gilbreth's insistence on job specialization. Thus we find that scientific management tended to create monotony in work. Gilbreth did not avoid this issue and dealt at length with the question of whether scientific management would make 'machines out of men'[4] and eventually 'cause the men to become insane'. He stated that this would not be the case as workers would be happy knowing that they were doing the work for which they were best suited, and of which they were complete masters. He further argued that even if the workers did experience boredom, the extra wages that they were paid when working for a scientific management organization would amply compensate them for this inconvenience.

Though Gilbreth stated that specialization and shorter job cycles should not cause the worker any unhappiness, it is noticeable in reading certain sections of his work that he was perhaps not sure that the question could be dismissed quite so easily. He described systems of moving people on short-cycle work between different jobs with appropriate rest periods, and he also devoted much space to what he termed 'athletic contests'. These were simply competitions between different groups of workers to see who could do the most work in a given time. The groups were often based on the worker's original nationality, in which case the winning group's prize could be the privilege of flying the flag of their country of origin on the site flagpole on the following day.

Other methods of forming teams were by matching the tall men against the short, or the married against the single, in which cases the prizes would be of money or time in lieu. By using these 'athletic contests' Gilbreth claimed up to 20 per cent increases in productivity, but he never attempted to give any specific reason for these improvements in performance, and so far as it is known he never subjected their effects to scientific investigation, being content to say that it appealed to the men's sense of competition, the material reward being of secondary consideration for them.

Gilbreth's own work and achievements were outstanding, but criticism can be directed at his successors. The main theme of his work was that there is a best way to do any job, and this should be searched for, and, when discovered, implemented. This philosophy is sound and widely accepted by management, but it has tended to be interpreted as meaning that there is a best physical way of doing a job, to which the worker must adapt himself. It is readily recognized that this best way has altered as science has advanced, and new tools and techniques have become available, but while this aspect of work has been recognized as being dynamic, the human side has been looked on as being static, by which it is meant that though the job changes, the worker who performs it does not. In his writing Gilbreth treated the worker as a fairly static factor, but this has since been interpreted by many to mean that the worker would always be a static factor, although Gilbreth in fact never said this. The advances that have come from the uses of his techniques have invariably been concerned with the improvement of the physical side of the job, which have led to more repetitive work and boredom, and the possible adverse effects of this policy on the worker have been ignored.

Gilbreth's work pointed to increasing specialization and short job cycle work because in his working life it appeared to him, and to many of his contemporaries, that this was the best way. It is unfortunate that his hypothesis, that a man could be satisfied by becoming the complete master of a well-paid mundane job, has been regarded by some to be an eternal law. It may have been true when Gilbreth enunciated it, but it is very open to question today when a far more sophisticated and questioning labour force is being shaped by the education system.

Gilbreth's great service to work study was twofold. Primarily he was a method study engineer and first rate equipment inventor, who took the techniques and methodology of his subject to a stage at which they are still being used today. Secondly and almost of equal importance he was a tireless messiah for the cause of scientific management at a time when suspicion and prejudice were widespread.

NOTES

1. Frank B. Gilbreth, *Motion Study*, Van Nostrand, New York, 1911.
2. ibid.
3. ibid.
4. Frank B. Gilbreth, *Primer of Scientific Management*, Van Nostrand, New York, 1912.

SHORT BIBLIOGRAPHY

Frank B. Gilbreth, *Field System*, Clark, New York, 1909.

Frank B. Gilbreth, *Concrete System*, Engineering News, New York, 1908.

Frank B. Gilbreth, *Bricklaying System*, Clark, New York, 1908.

Frank B. Gilbreth, *Primer of Scientific Management*, Van Nostrand, New York, 1912.

Frank B. Gilbreth, *Motion Study*, Van Nostrand, New York, 1911.

Frank B. and Lillian M. Gilbreth, *Applied Motion Study*, Sturgis and Walton, New York, 1914.

Motion Study for the Handicapped. Presented at the Tenth Sagamore Sociological Conference, 27–9 June 1917, Routledge, 1920.

Frank B. and Lillian M. Gilbreth, *Fatigue Study*, Sturgis and Walton, New York, 1916.

F. B. Gilbreth Jr and E. G. Carey, *Cheaper by the Dozen*, Heinemann, 1949.

F. B. Gilbreth Jr and E. G. Carey, *Belles on their Toes*, Heinemann, 1950.

2.4 Fayol and the Principles of Organization

NORMAN CUTHBERT

HENRI FAYOL was concerned with efficiency at the level of the organization rather than at the level of the task; with general management rather than with departmental management or supervision; with overall control rather than the detail of operations. His emphasis reflects his experience as a chief executive.

From this experience Fayol developed a framework for a unifying doctrine of administration that he hoped would hold good wherever the art of government had to be exercised. He was one of the first to stress the key position of that symbol of formal organization, the organization chart, which, with his organizational manual of job descriptions, remains the chief instrument of business management.[1] He produced ideas on human relationships which preceded those of Mary Parker Follett. Not least, he was a firm advocate of the view that management can and should be taught. This was a revolutionary idea when he first propounded it in 1908.

Fayol's first paper on management theory was read to the *Congrès des Mines et de la Métallurgie* in 1900. He followed this with his 'Discourse on the General Principles of Administration' at the Jubilee Congress of the *Société de l'Industrie Minérale* in 1908, a paper which appeared in the third number of the *Bulletin de la Société de l'Industrie Minérale* for 1916 and was published as a book by Dunod of Paris. This was translated into English by Conbrough in 1929, and again by Constance Storrs in 1949. It is the latter translation which is in widespread use under the title *General and Industrial Management*,[2] and by which Fayol is primarily known to the British and American reader.[3]

Fayol was born in 1841 of the French *petite bourgeoisie*. He was educated at the *lycée* in Lyons and thereafter at the National School of Mines in Saint Etienne. On graduation in 1860 he was

108

appointed engineer to the Commentry pits of the Commentry-Fourchambault Company.

His working life fell into four periods. For twelve years from 1860 he was a junior executive interesting himself in the problems of mining engineering, especially fire hazards. Promoted to manager of a group of pits in 1872, he became concerned chiefly with the factors determining the economic life of the pits in his charge. This not only stimulated him to write a geological monograph but aroused his interest in thinking and planning ahead. In 1888 he was appointed managing director of the combine, taking over when the group was on the verge of bankruptcy. He closed uneconomic metallurgical works, replaced exhausted mines with rich acquisitions and expanded the whole organization. When he retired in 1918 the financial position of the combine was impregnable. It had made a contribution of the greatest value to the Allied cause in World War I, and it had an administrative, technical and scientific staff famous throughout France.

In his retirement Fayol devoted his time to the popularization of his own views on management and to the development of theoretical studies. He immediately founded the Centre for Administrative Studies, which had a profound influence on business, the Army, and the Navy in France, and attempted to persuade the French government to pay attention to principles of administration. By invitation of the Under-Secretary of State for the Postal and Telegraph Service he undertook an investigation of that department.[4] At the time of his death in 1925 he was engaged in investigating the organization of the French tobacco industry.

UNITY OF ADMINISTRATIVE THEORY

In the study of business and other concerns terminology is no longer the battleground it was, but confusion and controversy persist. These are exemplified in the use of the term 'management' by most businessmen for the concept known as 'administration' in the state and elsewhere. Fayol employed the word *administration* in his native French. It has been claimed, *inter alia*, by

Urwick[5] and Brodie[6] that this would have been better translated into English as 'administration'. Brodie has gone further, alleging that if contact with Fayol's writings is limited to the Storrs translation, the impression cannot be avoided that Fayol was a writer and thinker dominantly concerned with industrial management, and that such a view would be mistaken.

Brodie suggests alternative translations of key terms and in particular that the title, *Administration industrielle et générale*, should never have become in English, 'Industrial and General Management'. Certainly the term 'general management' has a technical meaning which is not 'management in general'. 'Business and General Administration' would therefore have been a more correct translation and a more faithful reflection of Fayol's purpose.[7]

Fayol himself continually reiterated his belief in the unity of administrative theory. Nowhere does he distinguish business management from public administration. Indeed, for Fayol administration was an activity pertaining to government in all its diverse forms, ranging from the running of a home to matters of state. Whether one was considering 'commerce, industry, politics, religion, war or philanthropy' an administrative function had to be performed, and it was this common activity which made possible the development of a common code of administrative knowledge and principles.

Even in the Storrs translation this emerges clearly: 'Management plays a very important part in the government of undertakings: of all undertakings, large or small, industrial, commercial, political, religious or any other.'[8]

In his address to the Second International Congress of Administrative Science he declared:

The meaning which I have given to the word 'administration' and which has been generally adopted, broadens considerably the field of administrative science. It embraces not only the public service but enterprises of every size and description, of every form and every purpose. All undertakings require planning, organization, command, co-ordination and control, and in order to function properly, all must observe the same general principles. We are no longer confronted with several administrative sciences, but with one which can be applied equally well to public and to private affairs.[9]

Elsewhere he wrote: 'There is no one doctrine of administration for business and another for affairs of state; administrative doctrine is universal. Principles and general rules which hold good for business hold good for the state too, and the reverse applies.'[10]

Fayol's far-ranging interests and activities bear out these words. He delivered papers on higher education,[11] the reform of the public services,[12] military administration,[13] and the theory of administration in the state.[14] The scope of the Centre for Administrative Studies which he had established covered all forms of administration.

THE FAYOL MODEL

The concept of the model was not commonly used in the social sciences in any sophisticated form until well into the twentieth century. Possibly as a consequence of his engineering training, Fayol was thinking in terms of theoretical and practical models in the field of management from the beginning of the century.

In his discussions of planning he recommended that models 'be sought in business practice, after the fashion of the architect with a building to construct'.[15]

In Waldo's terminology, administrative models fall into four categories: 'machine models', conceived in terms of efficient business procedures; 'organic models', which present the relationships of the concern and its members with the total environment; 'business models', with activities expressed in terms of profitability; and 'pure systems models', emphasizing the nature of such organizations as systems with special systematic needs.[16] Using this classification Burns and Stalker see Fayol's system as a 'machine model'.[17]

Certainly Fayol attempted to set up efficient business procedures and produced ideas which appear mechanistic. He asserted, for example, that all organizations at the same stage of expansion are alike, with the qualification that this did not imply the same detailed structure nor the same organic quality. His by no means inflexible view of the ideal model and his writing on human relations, however, render superficial any assessment of his model as purely mechanical. He noted that the personal qualities of individuals could have 'enormous importance outweighing the system', and seems to have been aware of an informal organization existing alongside the formal one.

Fayol himself would have approved recent attempts to fuse the many approaches to model construction into one synthetic appreciation of the concern which will accept the fact that it is both a bureaucratic institution with a specific social purpose and a community of people with distinct purposes and institutional forms.[18]

In referring to contemporary comparisons of the organization with the machine, with the plant and with the animal, Fayol expressed his preference for the last and expounded the analogy in terms of the nervous system, reflexes, organs, etc.

His term *corps social*, meaning all those engaged in any given corporate activity, was translated by Storrs as 'body corporate', and it is significant that she retained this unusual term partly because of the implied biological metaphor.[19] Fayol had behind him here the whole tradition of French political and social thinking.[20] This mode of thinking in biological terms continues and forms one of the sources of the modern study of cybernetics.[21]

THE ROLE AND ELEMENTS OF MANAGEMENT

The process of conducting an undertaking towards an objective by seeking to derive optimum advantage from all available resources Fayol entitled 'government'. Within this process he divided the activities of industrial undertakings into six groups: technical, commercial, financial (capitalization), accounting, security (property and persons) and managerial.

In Fayol's view of these terms, none of the first five groups was concerned with drawing up the broad plan of operations of a business, or with assembling personnel and co-ordinating effort. That is, all these fields were techniques, the term 'technical activities' being reserved for 'production', 'manufacture' and 'adaptation'.

But these technical activities needed to be supplemented by managerial activity, and 'to manage is to forecast and plan, to organize, to command, to co-ordinate and to control'.[22] These were the essential elements of management, which was thus a process spread throughout the organization structure.

In Britain Fayol clearly influenced Lyndall F. Urwick, who likewise started from the viewpoint of the chief executive and attempted a macro model.* He became similarly impressed by the unifying nature of management.† Urwick adopted Fayol's elements of management as basic functions in his 'general principles', dividing them into 'process' (forecasting, organization, direction – Fayol's 'command') and 'effect' (planning, co-ordination, control), adding corresponding 'principles' (investigation, appropriateness, order).[23] Perhaps by virtue of his military background, Urwick readily adopted Fayol's hierarchical structure and its consequent 'chain of command'.

Urwick himself recognizes his indebtedness to Fayol, and there seems little doubt that this influence on Urwick was stronger than that of other early writers.[24] In admitting his own deficiencies in his later work, Urwick points to the inadequacies of

---

*E. F. L. Brech is in the same school. Brech reduced Fayol's six elements to four: planning, control, co-ordination, and motivation (Fayol's 'command'). He included organization structure, together with policy-making, in the planning category, declaring that Fayol's emphasis on organizing may have been due to his participation in a large-scale enterprise where problems of hierarchy and of channels of delegation and communication loomed large. E. F. L. Brech, ed., *The Principles and Practice of Management*, Longmans, 1963, 2nd edition, pp. 20, 21.

† 'It is no longer possible, even for the most extreme individualist, to fail to recognize that the business of Government and the government of business are, in fact, a single problem.' L. Urwick, 'A Short Survey of Industrial Management', British Institute of Management, Occasional Papers, No. 1, revised edition 1962.

Fayol.[25] A detailed discussion of motivation was missing. He had stated the necessity for it, but had said little about the means of attaining it.[26]

PRÉVOYANCE

Gouverner c'est prévoir; 'to govern is to foresee'.[27]

In giving prominence to foresight as the first characteristic of sound administration, Fayol laid stress on that judgement and intelligent anticipation which is prerequisite to the success of the whole management process. Fundamental, however, was the necessity to prepare an appropriate plan of action.

Fayol emphasized that any plan produced must be dynamic rather than static. Not only must unity and precision be secured, but also flexibility and continuity. The plan must 'have as much accuracy as is compatible with the unknown factors bearing on the fate of the concern'. In this he was groping towards the concept, long before it made its appearance in management literature, of corporate strategy.

The forecasting and planning which were part of Fayol's lot as a colliery manager so impressed themselves upon him that he suggested for large concerns a whole array of forecasts, daily, weekly, monthly, yearly, ten-yearly, and special, where, for example, an activity-cycle exceeded one or more ten-year periods. None of these should be introduced for forecasting's sake; necessity in relation to purpose should be the criterion.

Apart from their main purpose, Fayol saw forecasts as increasing the involvement, and therefore the interest, of staff. A further side-effect of forecasting was its action as a training device.

ORGANIZING

Here Fayol concerned himself both with structure and process, listing sixteen managerial duties and emphasizing the necessity for clear objectives, authority, decisions, and tasks.

It is in his discussion of organization structure that one can see Fayol at his best. He regarded specialization and the division of labour as the classical economists had done in Britain and fitted the concepts into his biological analogue:

Specialization belongs to the natural order; it is observable in the animal world, where the more highly developed the creature the more highly differentiated its organs; it is observable in human societies where the more important the body corporate the closer is the relationship between structure and function. As society grows, so new organs develop destined to replace the single one performing all functions in the primitive state.[28]

Fayol saw responsibility as the corollary of authority, at once its consequence and its counterpart. Long before the appearance of industrial sociology he noted the distinction which can often be made between a manager's authority deriving from his office and that deriving from his personality and experience. He wryly observed that responsibility was feared as much as authority was sought.

Fayol listed disastrous cases of dual command, for example imperfect demarcation of departments and badly defined duties, in order to stress the necessity for unity of command. He similarly insisted on unity of direction, that is, one head and one plan for any group of activities having the same objective.

Like the division of labour, he believed centralization to belong to the natural order of things, and conceived the notion of an optimum degree of centralization for each concern. Any equilibrium between centralization and decentralization had, however, to be conjured in dynamic terms, partly because 'Each employee, intentionally or unintentionally, puts something of himself into the transmission and execution of orders and of information received too. He does not operate merely as a cog in a machine.'[29]

Fayol's central theme in his discussion of organization is the *hiérarchie*. This was translated into English as 'scalar chain',[30] an expression which has taken root in management writings. It has been asserted that since organizations are often hierarchal in

115

character and structure, the notion of hierarchy may be necessary and appropriate to define an ordered system of authority, so that the English translation should read 'hierarchy'.[31] Others defend the 'scalar chain'.[32] The chain constitutes the process of co-ordination through which the supreme co-ordinating authority becomes effective throughout the entire structure. It implies a grading of duties according to degrees of authority and corresponding responsibility.

Fayol not only introduced the notion of the 'line of authority', but described some simple communications nets. So concerned was he with good order that he emphasized his concept of the organization chart to indicate that a formal plan of the organization could and should be constructed. His concept of clarity and order led him to suggest that each role on the organization chart be accompanied by a job description, defining duties clearly, and that lists be prepared to accompany the charts showing the 'value' of each employee. Here lay the foundation for his scheme of management development.

In his examination of the composition of the organization, Fayol laid down that each superior should normally have a 'span of control' comprising no more than four or five immediate subordinates, a concept which has been attributed to his compatriot, Graicunas.[33] Most management thinkers and practitioners would not agree with this view today.

Being impressed with the fact that managers, absorbed by current work, have not normally the time, nor perhaps the specialized knowledge, to devote themselves to research, Fayol conceived the idea of the staff of specialized assistants. He observed that two classes of work were often deplorably neglected, future planning and studies of development. For the staff to acquit itself of these portions of its role, however, he insisted that it must be free of all responsibility for running the business. Fayol extolled Taylor's functional foremanship in its principle of a staff provided to assist supervisors, while expressing his concern that functionalism implied the negation of unity of command.

CO-ORDINATION, CONTROL AND COMMAND

Fayol's conception of co-ordination he elaborated from the organization structure of the 'scalar chain'. Co-ordination across the organization should be effected by weekly conferences of departmental heads; further, in order to keep objectives in the forefront of the mind, targets should be set up.

Clearly this action was of little use without control, which should be all-embracing. Inherent pitfalls to avoid in the control mechanism were information arriving too late for usefulness, the neglect to act on the evidence thrown up by the system, and the danger of the infiltration of control into operational management. At all costs one must 'fight against excess of regulations, red tape and paper control'.

In his notion of command Fayol insisted on the necessity for the manager himself to set a good example and to aim at making unity, energy, initiative and loyalty prevail. He should not become engrossed in detail, but should develop initiative by allowing subordinates 'the maximum share of activity consistent with their position and capability, even at the cost of some mistakes. . . .'[34] The freedom to use initiative was a source of job satisfaction. Here again, control was vital, and for this purpose Fayol suggested a periodic 'management audit' using summarized charts to aid the process.

HUMAN RELATIONS

Comments on the human relationships within a concern occur throughout the whole of Fayol's general principles and elements of management. 'Not very much time is required', he asserted, 'for changing, either for good or for ill, the attitude of the personnel, through able or misguided management.'[35] Further, 'discipline is what leaders make it', defects in discipline and poor relationships between superiors and subordinates mostly resulting from the ineptitude of the leaders.

Treating employees with equity, a 'combination of kindliness and justice', did not imply kid-glove management. Incompetent employees must be 'eliminated', but in the imposition of sanctions 'individual people and attendant circumstances' must be taken into account.

Fayol continually affirmed the necessity for fairness in industrial relations. Agreements must be clear and as fair as possible. The miners', railwaymen's and civil servants' strikes which plagued France around the turn of the century he felt to have arisen partly as a result of disputed agreements. He deprecated national bargaining and frequent state intervention in industrial relations, favouring plant agreements. In an analysis of payments systems of all types he emphasized the need for remuneration as far as possible to afford satisfaction to employee and employer alike, encouraging keenness by rewarding well-directed effort.

One of his main preoccupations in the human aspect of management concerned the impact of the stability of the labour force on morale. Such were the undesirable consequences of insecurity of tenure, especially in large concerns, where the settling of managers was generally a lengthy matter, that a mediocre manager who stayed was infinitely preferable to outstanding managers who came and went. Here Fayol was in conflict with many practising managers today.

In his discourse on *esprit de corps*, Fayol decried the splitting up of personnel. 'There is no merit in sowing dissension among subordinates; any beginner can do it.' But real talent was needed to co-ordinate effort, encourage keenness, use each man's abilities, and reward each one's merit without arousing jealousies and disturbing harmonious relations. Face-to-face contacts were part of the process, and should not be abandoned for written communication unless absolutely necessary.

Before the advent of industrial psychology Fayol observed that the attitudes and activities of employees in the workshop were affected by their life outside the factory. This led him to suggest a modicum of 'benevolent collaboration' in their welfare. Lest it be thought that his view of senior management was too paternalistic, it must be emphasized that he saw management and labour as fundamentally in conflict.

SENIOR MANAGERS

In his requirements of senior managers Fayol listed health and intelligence; the 'moral qualities' of determination, energy, courage, sense of duty and care for the common good; a sound general education; managerial ability, comprising a competence in his five 'elements' of management; a general knowledge of all the essential functions; and the widest possible experience in the specialized activity characterizing the concern. He made the point that only this last varies with each kind of concern. Moreover, it was most frequently by this specialized ability that men who became senior managers first attracted attention. But the most brilliant specialized ability was not enough for good senior management, where a general ability was required.

The proportion of specialized ability, whether 'technical', commercial, financial, accounting or security, to managerial ability was considered by Fayol to be fundamental. He attempted in tabular form to set a numerical value to the relative importance of each ability in the evaluation of employees and heads of businesses. Such coefficients he then incorporated in organization charts. He concluded that with the exception of the head of the small concern, where the main quality required was technical ability, the essential ability of the higher ranks was managerial. This may sound trite and obvious today, but ignorance of this fundamental fact still bedevils many a small business in the throes of expansion.

EDUCATION AND TRAINING FOR MANAGEMENT

Clearly if management ability was so important, preparation was necessary for those posts requiring it. Specialized expertise in engineering or accounting was inadequate, and might even be a hindrance.

Fayol rejected the view that managerial ability could be acquired only in business practice. It could, and should, be acquired in the same way as technical ability, first in educational institutions, later in the workshop or some other appropriate place. The real reason for the absence of management teaching in engineering and other higher educational institutions was the absence of management theory; without theory, no teaching was possible.

He went further, asserting that there should be some management teaching at an elementary level in schools, with particular emphasis on planning and organization structure. Indeed, higher technical colleges should require more clarity of expression and some management knowledge of their entrants. He did not see this as a panacea, alleging that such teaching would no more make good managers from its pupils than technical teaching necessarily made excellent technicians out of its trainees.

Fayol had another criticism of the French universities and higher educational institutions of his time which is relevant to some British equivalents today. He felt that these institutions did not give a general education. The manager, however, should not only be well-educated, but should be a man of culture, demonstrating a breadth of education, discrimination and quality of judgement befitting an 'intellectual *élite*'.

Fayol was impressed by the difficulties of selecting managers and the dangers inherent in engaging men from outside the company. It was logical, therefore, for him to advocate the steady, methodical training of all employees at all levels within the company. A manager should 'preach by example' and introduce to his subordinates the general problems of management at his level. He thus saw training as a continuous process and was without doubt one of the first to write on management development.

A difficulty which he envisaged in this field was that posed by the increasing scale of business units. This at once eliminated many smaller concerns which might have been used as training establishments for managers, while at the same time calling for more capable men. Additionally, specialization became so significant in large organizations that exceptionally gifted men were often excluded from training for general management. Here he failed to foresee the devices which would be developed to combat this problem: the buying up of smaller businesses specifically for use as training grounds; the development of job rotation, which he would have abhorred; and the like.

FAYOL'S CONTRIBUTION

Henri Fayol was an able man whose talents had a fertile field for development in the social and economic environment of France between 1860 and 1925. His abilities placed him in the *élite* comprised of those who had attended the *grandes écoles*, the most senior administrators in business, government, the armed forces and in other fields. At the time he commenced his business career the French economy had 'taken off' and was passing through the stimulating 'drive to maturity'.[36] In this period of rapid growth there was a sense in which French business needed a theory of management, however rudimentary, as did American business in a similar stage of development. Fayol's work in France, a country with a long tradition of administration, was complementary to that of Taylor in the U.S.A., a nation which revered the principle of 'coming up the hard way'. That Taylor worked primarily on the operative level, from the bottom of the hierarchy upwards, while Fayol concentrated on the senior manager and worked downwards, was not merely a reflection of their different careers; it was also a reflection of the political and social history of the two nations.*

Fayol's views on management theory contain weaknesses of analysis and assessment. His principles, elements and duties over-

* A somewhat different view of the complementarity of these two contributors to management thinking is expressed by N. Pearson, 'Fayolism is the Necessary Complement to Taylorism', *American Political Science Review*, 1945, 39, pp. 68–80.

lap; he confuses structure and process; and there is a vagueness and superficiality about some of his terms and definitions. He hinted at, but did not elaborate, the limitations of his view that management can and should be taught. Senior managers and administrators he imagined as an intellectual *élite*, a view which could not be supported universally although true of his own circle and still largely obtaining in France today. He placed a higher value on management theory than it could be expected to support, addressing in 1924 a conference on the importance of administrative doctrine as a contribution to peace.

Nevertheless Fayol's contribution to management theory is unique and valuable. He was a generation ahead of his time in proclaiming its significance and he propounded many views which have been attributed to others who followed. While acclaimed for emphasizing the organization chart, the job specification and the concept of management education and training, he has been underestimated. His views on human relationships at work anticipated some of the basic findings of industrial psychology. His idea of flexible planning at all levels lies behind the development of the *Commissariat du Plan*[37] which has played such a significant part in the recent expansion of the French economy.

Although it is clear that he was exceptionally gifted, Fayol maintained that his phenomenal business success was due primarily not to his personal qualities but to the application of simple principles which could be taught and learned. These constituted his theory of management. It exercised, and continues to exercise, a profound influence on efforts to clarify thinking on organization, and is one of the foundations of organization theory. His emphasis on unremitting effort has the flavour of Samuel Smiles of latter nineteenth-century Britain, but it is probable that his biological model could have only been produced by a Frenchman.

It is regrettable that the third and fourth parts of his book on business and general management, in effect comprising case material from his experience, were never published, although an indication of the practical applications of his principles appeared elsewhere.[38]

While Fayol was less clear, his principles of management are akin to the characteristics of the formal organization, or 'bureaucracy', laid down by Max Weber, although it is extremely unlikely that Weber's work was known to him. Fayol was, however, less rigid and mechanistic than he has sometimes been judged, even though he did not have the benefit of the considerable developments in sociological and psychological theory which have taken place since his death. Even so, more mechanistic systems of management, with unified command and complete authority, seem appropriate to stable conditions; organic forms, where communication between people of different rank resembles consultation rather than command and the location of authority is settled by consensus, being more suitable for changing environments.[39]

Fayol was a technocrat-scholar, and as such a forerunner of businessmen-theorists like Chester I. Barnard in the U.S.A. and Wilfred Brown in Britain. He practised 'positive' management, at the same time pursuing the research approach to management problems.[40] Contemporary debate still centres on questions which occupied him half a century ago.

READINGS FROM HENRI FAYOL,
General and Industrial Management

Planning[41]

The maxim, 'managing means looking ahead', gives some idea of the importance attached to planning in the business world, and it is true that if foresight is not the whole of management at least it is an essential part of it. To foresee, in this context, means both to assess the future and make provision for it; that is, foreseeing is itself action already. Planning is manifested on a variety of occasions and in a variety of ways, its chief manifestation, apparent sign and most effective instrument being the plan of action. The plan of action is, at one and the same time, the result envisaged, the line of action to be followed, the stages to go through, and methods to use. It is a kind of future picture wherein proximate events are outlined with some distinctness, whilst remote events appear progressively less distinct, and it entails the running of the business as foreseen and provided against over a definite period.

The plan of action rests: (1) on the firm's resources (buildings, tools, raw materials, personnel, productive capacity, sales outlets, public relations, etc.) (2) on the nature and importance of work in progress (3) on future trends, which depend partly on technical, commercial, financial and other conditions, all subject to change, whose importance and occurrence cannot be predetermined. The preparation of the plan of action is one of the most difficult and most important matters of every business and brings into play all departments and all functions, especially the management function. It is, in effect, in order to carry out his managerial function that the manager takes the initiative for the plan of action, that he indicates its objectives and scope, fixes the share of each department in the communal task, co-ordinates the parts and harmonizes the whole; that he decides, in fine, the line of conduct to be followed. In this line of conduct it is not only imperative that nothing should clash with principles and rules of good management, but also that the arrangement adopted should facilitate application of these principles and rules. Therefore, to the divers technical, commercial, financial and other abilities necessary on the part of a business head and his assistants, there must be added considerable managerial ability.

Organizing[42]

To organize a business is to provide it with everything useful to its functioning: raw materials, tools, capital, personnel. All this may be divided into two main sections, the material organization and the human organization. The latter only is to be dealt with here. When equipped with the essential material resources the personnel or body corporate should be capable of fulfilling the six essential functions, viz. of carrying out all the activities embraced by the concern.

MANAGERIAL DUTIES OF AN ORGANIZATION

Between the body corporate of the one-man business, where one man performs all functions, and that of a national concern employing millions of people, there are to be found all possible intermediate stages. In every case the organization has to carry out the following managerial duties:

1. Ensure that the plan is judiciously prepared and strictly carried out.

2. See that the human and material organization is consistent with the objective, resources and requirements of the concern.

3. Set up a single, competent, energetic guiding authority.

4. Harmonize activities and co-ordinate efforts.

5. Formulate clear, distinct, precise decisions.

6. Arrange for efficient selection – each department must be headed by a competent, energetic man, each employee must be in that place where he can render greatest service.

7. Define duties clearly.

8. Encourage a liking for initiative and responsibility.

9. Have fair and suitable recompense for services rendered.

10. Make use of sanctions against faults and errors.

11. See to the maintenance of discipline.

12. Ensure that individual interests are subordinated to the general interest.

13. Pay special attention to unity of command.

14. Supervise both material and human order.

15. Have everything under control.

16. Fight against excess of regulations, red tape and paper control.

Such is the mission of management to be fulfilled by the personnel of every business. It is simple in the one-man business, more complex as the enterprise grows more important and its personnel more numerous.

We shall first establish that despite infinite variety of businesses every body corporate of similar numerical strength shows strong external resemblances to every other one and differs chiefly in the nature and relative value of the constituent elements. Then we shall consider the functioning parts of the body corporate together with the individuals composing such parts, and we shall seek to discover what conditions both must fulfil for the body corporate to be soundly constructed. Finally, we shall concern ourselves with the selection and training of business personnel.

COMPOSITION OF THE BODY CORPORATE

... The same framework is appropriate for all industrial concerns, of whatever kind, employing the same number of people.

In industrial concerns it is the technical aspect which is of greatest importance; were it a case of commercial concerns then it would be the commercial aspect, or in the army the military aspect, in the school the teaching aspect, in the church the religious aspect. The most highly developed organ is that of the professional function which is characteristic of the enterprise. But, regarded as a whole, the body corporate, given the same stage of development, always retains the same general appearance.

The same general appearance, however, does not imply the same detailed structure nor the same organic quality. Of two organizations similar in appearance, one may be excellent, the other bad, depending upon the personal qualities of those who compose them. If it were possible to ignore the human factor it would be easy enough to build up a social organic unit. Any novice could do it, provided he had some idea of current practices and could count on the necessary funds. But to create a useful organization it is not enough to group people and distribute duties; there must be knowledge of how to adapt the organic whole to requirements, how to find essential personnel and put each where he can be of most service; there are in sum numerous important qualities needed.

The body corporate of a concern is often compared with a machine or plant or animal. The expressions, 'administrative machine', 'administrative gearing', suggest an organism obeying the drive of its head and having all its effectively interrelated parts move in unison and towards the same end, and that is excellent. But such expressions might also suggest that, like the mechanical gearing, the administrative one is incapable of transmitting movement without losing power. And that is a false concept: the administrative gearing – i.e. every intermediate executive – can and must be a generator of power and of ideas. In each of these gearings, that is in each intermediary, there exists a power of initiative which, properly used, can considerably extend the supreme authority's power of action. So it is not merely in dissipation of initial power through the multiplicity of transmission mechanisms that limits must be sought for the activity within an administrative whole. It is rather to be sought in the inadequacy of higher authority. When power at the centre is weak, centrifugal force holds sway.

Plant life too has served for numerous comparisons with social units. In the realm of growth there spring from the young single trunk branches which spread out and grow leaves, and the sap brings life to all branches, even the slenderest twigs, just as higher authority transmits activity right down to the lowest and farthest extremities of the body corporate. Trees 'do not grow right up into the sky' and corporate bodies too have their limiting factors. Is it insufficient climbing power of the sap in the first instance and insufficient managerial capacity in the second? But a measure of strength which the tree cannot attain by its isolated growth may result from grouping and juxtaposition – namely the forest. That is what business obtains by agreements, agencies, trusts, federations. Each industrial unit, keeping a fair measure of autonomy, makes to the common whole a contribution which is largely returned to it.

Over and above a certain size – only exceeded with difficulty – grouping by juxtaposition is the means whereby powerful associations are formed and strong units and collective organizations developed with the expenditure of minimum administrative effort.

But it is to the animal sphere that the social organism is most often compared. Man in the body corporate plays a role like that of the cell in the animal, single cell in the case of the one-man business, thousandth or millionth part of the body corporate in the large-scale enterprise. As the development of the organism is effected by the grouping together of elemental units (men or cells) the organs appear, they are differentiated and perfected in proportion as the number of combined elements increases. In the social organism, as in the animal, a small number of essential functional elements account for an infinite variety of activities. Countless approximations may be made between the functions of the two kinds of organic units. The nervous system in particular bears close comparison with the managerial function. Being present and active in every organ, it normally has no specialized member and is not apparent to the superficial observer, but everywhere it receives impressions which it transmits first to the lower centres (reflexes) and thence, if need be, to the brain or organ of direction. From these centres or from the brain the order then goes out in inverse direction to the member or section concerned with carrying out the movement. The body corporate, like the animal, has its reflex responses or ganglia which take place without immediate intervention on the part of the higher authority and without nervous or managerial activity the organism becomes an inert mass and quickly decays.

ORGANIZATION CHARTS

Summarized charts . . . facilitate considerably the building up and supervising of an organization. They enable the organic whole, departments and lines of demarcation and the line of authority, to be grasped at a glance better than could be done by lengthy description. They draw attention to weak points, such as overlapping or encroachment of departments, dual command, functions unstaffed or with no clearly indicated single head. This mode of representation is suitable for all types of concern, large establishments as well as small, expanding or declining, as well as newly-formed businesses. In the latter case the organization chart is a frame divided into compartments in which employees' names are to be written as and when they are selected and the departments decided upon. The use of the summarized chart is not confined to the period of formation of a business, for scarcely is that task accomplished when modifications, as a result of changes in circumstances or people, become necessary. Now, any modification in one part of the organization can have wide repercussions and influence the general running of the whole. The chart offers particular facilities for discovering and providing against those repercussions, but it must always be kept up to date. Granted such a condition, it is a precious managerial instrument.

On the organization chart the whole of the personnel is shown, the constitution and demarcation of each department, who is in each position, the superiors from whom an employee takes orders, and the subordinates to whom he gives them, but it cannot be required to show the individual value of employees nor their functions, nor the physical limits of their responsibility, nor who shall deputize for them. For these various facts special lists must accompany the organization chart. The composition of the staff too must be indicated apart from the chart.

SCALAR CHAIN

The scalar chain is the chain of superiors ranging from the ultimate authority to the lowest ranks. The line of authority is the route followed – via every link in the chain – by all communications which start from or go to the ultimate authority. This path is dictated both by the need for some transmission and by the principle of unity of command, but it is not always the swiftest. It is even at times disastrously lengthy in large concerns, notably in governmental ones. Now, there are many activities whose success turns on speedy execution, hence respect for the line of authority must be reconciled with the need for swift action.

Let us imagine that section F has to be put into contact with section P in a business whose scalar chain is represented by the double ladder G-A-Q, as in Diagram 1 below.

By following the line of authority the ladder must be climbed from F to A and then descended from A to P, stopping at each rung, then ascended again from P to A, and descended once more from A to F, in order to get back to the starting point. Evidently it is much simpler and quicker to go directly from F to P by making use of FP as a 'gang plank' and that is what is most often done. The scalar principle will be safeguarded if managers E and O have authorized their respective subordinates F and P

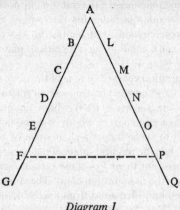

Diagram 1

to treat directly, and the position will be fully regularized if F and P inform their respective superiors forthwith of what they have agreed upon. So long as F and P remain in agreement, and so long as their actions are approved by their immediate superiors, direct contact may be maintained, but from the instant that agreement ceases or there is no approval from the superiors direct contact comes to an end, and the scalar chain is straightaway resumed. Such is the actual procedure to be observed in the great majority of businesses. It provides for the usual exercise of some measure of initiative at all levels of authority. In the small concern, the general interest, viz. that of the concern proper, is easy to grasp, and the employer is present to recall this interest to those tempted to lose sight of it. In government enterprise the general interest is such a complex, vast, remote thing, that it is not easy to get a clear idea of it, and for the majority of civil servants the employer is somewhat mythical and unless the sentiment of general interest be constantly revived by higher authority, it becomes blurred and weakened and each section tends to regard itself as its own aim and end and forgets that it is only a cog in a big machine, all of whose parts must work in concert. It becomes isolated, cloistered, aware only of the line of authority.

The use of the 'gang plank' is simple, swift, sure. It allows the two employees F and P to deal at one sitting, and in a few hours, with some question or other which via the scalar chain would pass through twenty transmissions, inconvenience many people, involve masses of paper, lose weeks or months to get to a conclusion less satisfactory generally than the one which could have been obtained via direct contact as between F and P.

Is it possible that such practices, as ridiculous as they are devastating, could be in current use? Unfortunately there can be little doubt of it in government department affairs. It is usually acknowledged that the chief cause is fear of responsibility. I am rather of the opinion that it is insufficient executive capacity on the part of those in charge. If supreme authority A insisted that his assistants B and L made use of the 'gang plank' themselves and made its use incumbent upon their subordinates C and M, the habit and courage of taking responsibility would be established and at the same time the custom of using the shortest path.

It is an error to depart needlessly from the line of authority, but it is an even greater one to keep to it when detriment to the business ensues. The latter may attain extreme gravity in certain conditions. When an employee is obliged to choose between the two practices, and it is impossible for him to take advice from his superior, he should be courageous enough and feel free enough to adopt the line dictated by the general interest. But for him to be in this frame of mind there must have been previous precedent, and his superiors must have set him the example – for example must always come from above.

Unity of command[43]

For any action whatsoever, an employee should receive orders from one superior only. Such is the rule of unity of command, arising from general and ever-present necessity and wielding an influence on the conduct of affairs which, to my way of thinking, is at least equal to any other principle whatsoever. Should it be violated, authority is undermined, discipline is in jeopardy, order disturbed and stability threatened. This rule seems fundamental to me and so I have given it the rank of principle. As soon as two superiors wield their authority over the same person or department, uneasiness makes itself felt and should the cause persist, the disorder increases, the malady takes on the appearance of an animal organism troubled by a foreign body, and the following consequences are to be observed: either the dual command ends in disappearance or elimination of one of the superiors and organic well-being is restored, or else the organism continues to wither away. In no case is there adaptation of the social organism to dual command.

Now dual command is extremely common and wreaks havoc in all concerns, large or small, in home and in state. The evil is all the more to be feared in that it worms its way into the social organism on the most plausible pretexts. For instance:

(a) In the hope of being better understood or gaining time or to put a stop forthwith to an undesirable practice, a superior S^2 may give orders directly to an employee E without going via the superior S^1. If this mistake is repeated there is dual command with its consequences, viz. hesitation on the part of the subordinate, irritation and dissatisfaction on the part of the superior set aside, and disorder in the work. It will be seen later that it is possible to by-pass the scalar chain when necessary, whilst avoiding the drawbacks of dual command.

(b) The desire to get away from the immediate necessity of dividing up authority as between two colleagues, two friends, two members of one family, results at times in dual command reigning at the top of a concern right from the outset. Exercising the same powers and having the same authority over the same men, the two colleagues end up inevitably with dual command and its consequences. Despite harsh lessons, instances of this sort are still numerous. New colleagues count on their mutual regard, common interest and good sense to save them from every conflict, every serious disagreement, and, save for rare exceptions, the illusion is short-lived. First an awkwardness makes itself felt, then a certain irritation and, in time, if dual command exists, even hatred. Men cannot bear dual command. A judicious assignment of duties would have reduced the danger without entirely banishing it, for between two superiors on the same footing there must always be some questions ill-defined. But it is riding for a fall to set up a business organization with two superiors on equal footing without assigning duties and demarcating authority.

(c) Imperfect demarcation of departments also leads to dual command: two superiors issuing orders in a sphere which each thinks his own, constitutes dual command.

(d) Constant linking up as between different departments, natural intermeshing of functions, duties often badly defined, create an ever-present danger of dual command. If a knowledge-able superior does not put it in order, footholds are established which later upset and compromise the conduct of affairs.

In all human associations, in industry, commerce, army, home, state, dual command is a perpetual source of conflicts, very grave sometimes, which have special claim on the attention of superiors of all ranks.

Co-ordination[44]

To co-ordinate is to harmonize all the activities of a concern so as to facilitate its working, and its success. It is giving to the material and social, functional, organic whole such proportions as are suitable to enable it to play its part assuredly and economically. It is to bear in mind in any activity whatsoever, technical, commercial, financial or other, the obligations and consequences such action involves for all the functions of the business. It is to keep expenditure proportionate to financial resources, equipment and tools to production needs, stocks to rate of consumption, sales to production. It is to build the house neither too small nor too big, adapt the tool to its use, the road to the vehicle, the safety precautions to the risks. It is to relegate the secondary to second place after the principal. It is, in a word, to accord things and actions their rightful proportions, and to adapt means to ends.

In a well co-ordinated enterprise the following facts are to be observed:

1. Each department works in harmony with the rest. Stores knows what has to be supplied and at what time; Production

knows its target; Maintenance keeps equipment and tools in good order; Finance procures necessary funds; Security sees to the protection of goods and persons, and all these activities are carried out in sure, orderly fashion.

2. In each department divisions and sub-divisions are precisely informed as to the share they must take in the communal task and the reciprocal aid they are to afford one another.

3. The working schedule of the various departments and sub-divisions thereof is constantly attuned to circumstances.

Such result demands intelligence and experienced, active direction. It must be conceded that these three requirements are not always fulfilled, for in some concerns the following signs of unmistakable lack of co-ordination are apparent:

1. Each department knows and wants to know nothing of the others. It operates as if it were its own aim and end, without bothering either about neighbouring departments or the business as a whole.

2. Water-tight compartments exist between the divisions and offices of the same department as they do also between different departments. Each one's prime concern is to take cover from personal responsibility behind a piece of paper, an order or a circular letter.

3. No one thinks of the general interest; initiative and loyalty are non-existent.

This attitude on the part of the personnel, so disastrous for the concern, is not the result of pre-concerted intention but the culmination of non-existent or inadequate co-ordination. A good personnel will not take long to be weakened if it is not constantly reminded of its duties towards the firm and towards all members of the body corporate. One of the best methods of keeping the personnel in trim and making the execution of its duties easier is the conference of departmental heads.

Control[45]

... For control to be effective it must be done within reasonable time and be followed up by sanctions. It is quite obvious that if the conclusions derived from checking activities, however efficient, come to hand too late to be of possible usefulness, then control will have been a futile activity. It is no less clear that control is useless if the practical outcome of it is wilfully neglected. These two mistakes are those which good management does not allow to be made.

A further danger to avoid is infiltration of control into management and departmental running. This encroachment makes for duality of management in its most formidable aspect: on one side there is irresponsible control, but capable at times of doing widespread harm; on the other is the operating department, bereft of all but weak means of defence against hostile control. The tendency to encroach on the part of control is fairly common in large-scale affairs especially and may have most serious consequences. To offset it, powers of control must be defined at the outset as precisely as possible with indication of limits not to be exceeded, and then higher authority must watch carefully the use which control makes of its powers.

Management teaching and management theory[46]

We have seen that the ability most essential in the case of higher grades of employee is managerial. So we are certain that an exclusively technical education fails to answer the general needs of undertakings, even industrial ones. Now, whilst the greatest effort is being made, and profitably so, to spread and perfect technical knowledge, nothing, or almost nothing, is being done in our training establishments for industry to equip future leaders for their technical, financial, managerial, or other functions. Management does not even figure in the syllabuses of our colleges of civil engineering – why? Is it that the importance of managerial ability is misunderstood? No. Whether it be a case of choosing a foreman from among workmen or superintendent from among foremen, or a manager from among engineers, it is never, or almost never, technical ability which governs the choice. Naturally care is taken to see that the requisite degree of technical ability is present, but that done, preference is given, when considering candidates of roughly the same technical standing, to the one who seems superior in bearing, authority, orderliness, organization and other characteristics which are the very elements of managerial ability. Does the reason for this lie in the fact that managerial ability can only be acquired in business practice? I can well believe that this is the reason put forward, but it will be seen that it carries no weight and that managerial ability can and should be acquired in the same way as technical ability, first at school, later in the workshop.

The real reason for the absence of management teaching in our vocational schools is absence of theory; without theory no teaching is possible. Now there exists no generally accepted theory of management emanating from general discussion. There is no shortage of personal theorising, but failing any accepted theory each one thinks that he has the best methods and everywhere there may be observed – in industry, the army, the home, the state – the most contradictory practices under the aegis of the same principle. Whereas in the technical sphere a head would not dare to infringe certain established rules without risking total loss of prestige, in the managerial one the most undesirable practices may be indulged in with impunity. The methods used are judged not on their own merits but on their results, which often are very remote and mostly difficult to relate to their causes. The situation might be quite otherwise were there an accepted theory, that is to say, a collection of principles, rules, methods, procedures, tried and checked by general experience. It is not principles which are lacking: were it sufficient to proclaim them to have them prevail we should enjoy the best possible management everywhere. Who has not heard proclaimed a hundred times the need for the grand principles of authority, discipline, subordination of individual interest to the common good, unity of direction, co-ordination of effort, foresight, etc.? It must be admitted that proclamation is not enough. The fact is that the light of principles, like that of lighthouses, guides only those who already know the way into port, and a principle bereft of the means of putting it into practice is of no avail.

Nor is there any lack of methods: their name is legion, but

good and bad are to be found side by side at the same time in the home, workshop and state, with a persistence only to be explained by lack of theory. The general public is not in a position to pass judgement on managerial activity, hence the importance of establishing a theory of management as soon as possible.

NOTES

1. He was the originator of the organization chart, according to T. Burns and G. M. Stalker, *The Management of Innovation*, Tavistock, 1961, p. 106; see also W. H. Norman, *Administrative Action, the Techniques of Organization and Management*, 9th edition, Pitman, 1958.

2. H. Fayol, *General and Industrial Management*, trans. C. Storrs, Pitman, 1949.

3. A list of his published work appears in Fayol, op. cit., Storrs trans., pp. xiii–xx.

Fayol's paper, *The Administrative Theory of the State*, delivered to the Second International Congress of Administrative Science, Brussels, 1923, was also published in English in L. Gulick and L. Urwick, Eds., *Papers in the Science of Administration*, Columbia University, 1937.

4. Fayol's conclusions were published in a pamphlet, *La réforme administrative des postes et télégraphes*, 1921, and later in book form by Dunod.

5. Foreword, Fayol, op. cit., Storrs trans., pp. xii–xvii.

6. M. B. Brodie, 'Henri Fayol: "Administration industrielle et générale" – a re-interpretation', *Public Administration*, Vol. 40, Autumn 1962, pp. 311–7.

7. ibid.

8. Fayol, op. cit., Preface, Storrs trans., p. xxi.

9. *The Administrative Theory of the State*, loc. cit.

10. H. Fayol, *L'Eveil de l'esprit public*, Dunod et Pinet, 1918, p. 6.

11. E.g. 'A Discourse on Higher Education', *Société des Ingénieurs Civils de France*, 1917.

12. M. B. Brodie, *Fayol on Administration*, Administrative Staff College Monograph, Lyon, Grant & Green, 1967, ch. III.

13. Lectures on Administration at the *Ecole Supérieure de Guerre* and at the *Centre des Hautes Études Militaires*, 1920.

14. *The Administrative Theory of the State*, loc. cit.

15. Fayol, *General and Industrial Management*, Storrs trans., p. 45, Pitman, 1949.

16. D. Waldo, *Perspectives on Administration*, Alabama University, 1956.

17. T. Burns and G. M. Stalker, op. cit., p. 108.

18. E.g. A. W. Gouldner, *Patterns of Industrial Bureaucracy*, Routledge, 1956; H. A. Simon, *Administrative Behaviour*, Macmillan, 1957.

19. Fayol, *General and Industrial Management*, Storrs trans., p. 20n., Pitman, 1949.

20. And to a lesser extent, economic thinking, e.g. the Physiocrats of the eighteenth century.

21. E.g. E. Haunt, *L'Entreprise, Unité Cybernetique Vivante, Editions de l'Entreprise Moderne*, Paris, 1960.

22. Fayol, *General and Industrial Management*, Storrs trans., pp. 5, 6, Pitman, 1949.

23. E.g. L. Urwick, *The Elements of Administration*, Pitman, 1947, 2nd edition, p. 19; L. F. Urwick, *The Pattern of Management*, Pitman, 1956, p. 75.

24. E.g. L. Urwick, *The Elements of Administration*, pp. 19, 43, 119–29; L. F. Urwick, *The Pattern of Management*, p. 48.

25. And others, e.g. F. W. Taylor.

26. L. F. Urwick, *The Pattern of Management*, p. 50.

27. H. Fayol, *Administration industrielle et générale*, Dunod, 1916, p. 48.

28. Fayol, *General and Industrial Management*, Storrs trans., p. 20, Pitman, 1949.

29. ibid., p. 33.

30. ibid., p. 20 *et al.*

31. Brodie, 'Henri Fayol: "Administration industrielle et générale"— a re-interpretation', loc. cit., p. 315.

32. E.g. J. D. Mooney, *The Principles of Organization*, Harper, 1947, pp. 14, 15.

33. V. A. Graicunas, 'Relationship in Organisation', *Bulletin of the International Management Institute*, March, 1933.

34. Fayol, *General and Industrial Management*, Storrs trans., pp. 102, 103, Pitman, 1949.

35. ibid., p. 103.

36. W. W. Rostow, *The Stages of Economic Growth*, Cambridge, 1963, facing p. 1.

37. For a view of the relationship between French senior managers,

civil servants, and the Plan, see D. Granick, *The European Executive*, Weidenfeld and Nicolson, 1962, ch. XI.

38. Interview published in *Chronique Sociale de France*, January, 1925.

39. Burns and Stalker, op. cit., pp. 119–22.

40. Brodie, *Fayol on Administration*, ch. IV.

41. Fayol, *General and Industrial Management*, Storrs trans., Pitman, 1949.

42. ibid., pp. 34–6, 53, 54, 57–60, 77, 78.

43. ibid., pp. 24, 25.

44. ibid., pp. 103, 104.

45. ibid., pp. 108, 109.

46. ibid., pp. 14, 15.

2.5 Operational Research; a new discipline

MICHAEL MARTIN

A DISCERNING historian can discover a number of antecedents to Operational Research (O.R.). For instance, Gedye[1] has pointed out that Sir Rowland Hill performed what we would now regard as a typical O.R. investigation, before the introduction of the penny postage system in 1840. Furthermore, during World War I, several studies of military operational problems were made by scientists, and it is of interest briefly to mention these.

F. W. Lanchester performed a mathematical analysis of aerial combat, deriving what became known as Lanchester's equations. He also applied the analysis with some success to the Battle of Trafalgar. Lanchester's work was important for two reasons. Firstly, it showed that a mathematical analysis of combat situations could be performed. Secondly, although his equations were far too simple to form the basis of a total analysis of the complex of combat situations present in a major battle, they could be used to analyse selected parts of such battles and to evaluate the performance of weapons.

During World War I, the anti-aircraft experimental section of the Ministry of Munitions was established, led by a physiologist, Captain (later Professor) A. V. Hill. Working with him were a number of scientists turned soldiers, including four who were later to become Fellows of the Royal Society. As the name of the section implies, it was concerned with the utilization of A.A. guns and can be regarded as a forerunner of the military O.R. groups of World War II. Indeed, Professor Hill played an invaluable part in developing the role of science in defence during the two world wars and the years between, and can be regarded as one of the 'founding fathers' of O.R.

Another man who could also lay claim to this title, though in his case for his work in the U.S.A., is Professor Morse. After the U.S.A. entered the war in 1917, Morse analysed the pattern of losses from transatlantic convoys. Once more, this work was a forerunner to many similar analyses performed in World War II, especially in the U.K., and Professor Morse has led the development of O.R. in the U.S.A. and was co-author of one of the earliest books on the new science. However, these early studies are best regarded as preliminary courtship dances and most O.R. scientists would agree with Zuckerman[2] that their profession was 'the bastard born out of a secret liaison of scientists and airmen' just before the beginning of World War II.

The discipline was born of radar. The pioneer of radar, Sir Robert Watson-Watt,[3] explaining the title of his autobiography *Three Steps to Victory*, said '. . . the three steps were, in chronological order of conception, the Instantaneous Visual Radio Direction Finder, which became Huff-Duff; and Operational Research'.

Let us now consider how this conception and birth occurred.

PRE-WAR AND WAR-TIME DEVELOPMENT 1935-45

In 1935 the Air Ministry set up the Committee for Scientific Survey of Air Defence with Mr H. G. (later Sir Henry) Tizard as chairman. This Committee, through one of its members (Mr Wimpiris), was told of Watson-Watt's belief that aircraft could be detected by radio waves. It was sufficiently impressed with his ideas to authorize him to set up a research unit to prove them in practice. The unit's rapid successes soon led the R.A.F. to adopt radio location as the primary means of detecting the approach of aircraft; and by 1938, a chain of radar stations had been set up round the south-east coast of England.

However, the integration of the new radar systems with existing aural methods of aircraft detection also presented organizational and operating problems which the average R.A.F. officer, because of his rather specialist service experience, was ill-equipped to solve. To help overcome this problem, in 1936, Sir Henry Tizard set up at Biggin Hill a small team of R.A.F. officers, together with one scientist, to study how the radar chain might be used for the interception of aircraft. This team developed the technique of interception of hostile aircraft by fighters which was ultimately adopted by Fighter Command. It also identified the need to develop operations room equipment and techniques for using it. Because it was felt that the civilian scientist's knowledge of radar might help the fighting man in its proper use, this work was continued at Bawdsey Manor, Suffolk (where Watson-Watt's research unit was located). Some scientists there studied the variations in performance of radar stations already in use. From this analysis, they were able to recommend improvements in the methods of operating these stations. At the same time, others looked at the overall performance of the reporting and aircraft control system of Fighter Command, as carried out in the chain of operations rooms and radar stations. The changes these scientists recommended were mostly accepted by the R.A.F. The significant features of all these studies were:

(a) they were performed by civilian scientists in close collaboration with serving officers, on the problem of operating the new weapon, as against improving the design of the weapon itself;

(b) most of the work involved making observations at radar stations and operations rooms where radar was in operational use.

For these reasons the work of these scientists was described as Operational Research by Mr Rowe (Superintendent, Bawdsey Research Unit) in 1938. The R.A.F. valued the work of these scientists so highly that, by the outbreak of war, they had been transferred to H.Q. Fighter Command at Stanmore to form a permanent O.R. group. By 1941, O.R. was recognized by the Air Ministry to be sufficiently important for sections to be set up very widely in the R.A.F.

To illustrate this early work it is of value to look at a specific example. The activities of the war-time groups in the R.A.F. were too varied for it to be possible to choose a representative example. Therefore a study of aircraft maintenance problems has been chosen, since such problems bear direct relation to problems of equipment maintenance in industry.

In 1942, during the Battle of the Atlantic, a number of studies were made of the effectiveness of depth charge attacks by aircraft and U-boats. The studies showed that these attacks were very useful weapons against U-boats. (At one stage of the Battle, it was estimated that one merchant ship was saved from sinking for every three sorties made by a convoy escort aircraft.) Therefore it was most important that the limited number of aircraft available for this purpose should be used as efficiently as possible. Dr C. Gordon (formerly a geneticist) of Coastal Command O.R. section studied the utilization of aircraft performing these duties.[4] He concluded that aircraft can be in one of three states:

(a) serviceable but not flying;
(b) flying;
(c) undergoing repairs and maintenance.

Because of its complexity and the tragic consequences of failure in flight, an aircraft requires continual maintenance, and the R.A.F. had paid considerable attention to planning efficient maintenance effort for squadrons on active service. A simple, but at first sight quite reasonable, criterion of maintenance efficiency called the 'Serviceability Percentage' was chosen. This was the number of aircraft serviceable whether flying or not (that is, the sum of (a) and (b) above), expressed as a percentage of the total number of aircraft in the squadron.

Gordon questioned the validity of this criterion since it does not distinguish between aircraft in state (b) (when they are useful) as against state (a) (when they are not). Aircraft passed through a cycle going from (a) to (c) and then back to (a) again, and Gordon saw the analogy between this and biological life cycles. By an investigation into the interactions of aircraft sorties, manpower available and maintenance effort, he was able to suggest that the operational effectiveness of a squadron would be increased if all aircraft were flown whenever they were available. Since an aircraft requires more maintenance when flying regularly, such a policy would reduce the serviceability percentage.

To test Gordon's hypothesis No. 502 Squadron was ordered to disregard the serviceability percentage and to fly as much as it could, whenever aircraft were available. The flying output of the squadron increased and the serviceability percentage decreased, both considerably, but the maintenance system continued to function satisfactorily.

Following this work, the new overall criteria of efficiency became the proportion of serviceable planes flown on each day that flying was possible and the flying hours per maintenance man. The new criteria were extended throughout Coastal Command and eventually achieved about a 100 per cent increase in its flying output, thus enabling it to make an even greater contribution in the Battle of the Atlantic.

Whilst it was being developed for the R.A.F., radar was introduced in the Army for sighting anti-aircraft guns. In 1940, General Pile (C.-in-C. A.A. Command) requested a scientific study of the problem of co-ordinating radar with other equipment at A.A. gun sites. Again it was clear that the problem would require observations to be made on the sites during action. Professor P. M. S. Blackett, F.R.S., was asked to direct the study and he set up the A.A. Command Research Group consisting of scientists with backgrounds in mathematics, physics, physiology, surveying, and one Army officer. Because of their rather motley academic background they were known as 'Blackett's Circus'. However, Blackett assembled a mixed team by design (though it is likely that the shortage of scientific manpower also affected his choice), as he wanted the problem to be examined from the different 'angles' provided by the different disciplines. The work of this group demonstrated the value of the mixed team approach which has been an important element in many O.R. studies. O.R. in the Army expanded from this start, which subsequently led to an O.R. group being set up later in the war and undertaking studies throughout the British army.

Blackett was also responsible for introducing O.R. into the Navy. In 1941 he moved from A.A. Command to R.A.F. Coastal Command, to study problems associated with the use of aircraft radar to detect ships and submarines. This work brought him into direct contact with Naval problems, and later in 1941 he became director of Naval O.R. at the Admiralty. Thus by 1942 O.R. was established in each of the fighting services.

Unfortunately World War II was also a civilian's war and O.R. had a civilian role to play. Under the supervision of Professors J. D. Bernal and S. Zuckerman, the human injuries and material damage caused by enemy bomb attacks were analysed. Experiments were also performed on animals to evaluate the effects of explosives, particularly blast, on living organisms. On these studies, Bernal and a co-worker predicted what would be the effect of a raid by five hundred enemy bombers on Coventry. Later, as is well known, such a raid took place and their predictions were exactly confirmed. Their analyses, with their tragic confirmation by 'experiment', were to prove invaluable when used in reverse, to help plan the allied bomber offensive against Germany later in the war.

When the U.S.A. entered the war, their armed services were quick to recognize the value of O.R. and such functions were rapidly set up. As in the United Kingdom, some of the early O.R. work in the U.S.A. centred round the introduction of new radar equipment, but the scope of problems studied quickly expanded to cover a wide range of service activities. War-time O.R. work was also performed in the Commonwealth and French armed services, but there is no record of the equivalent of O.R. having been performed in the armed services of either Germany or Japan.

We have seen that the war years saw the development of a new applied science. Up to that time, it had been commonplace for scientists to develop new weapons of war, but World War II saw scientists advising servicemen on the operational use of these weapons and on the conduct of the strategy and tactics of war. A military commander has to make decisions in very complicated circumstances with a limited amount of information relevant to the decision available. He makes these decisions by means of judgement based on experience. The war-time development of O.R. showed that the scientist, using his professional skills, could analyse operational problems and offer an alternative basis on which to make decisions. He discovered that the training he had received in his own discipline could be used to analyse operational problems of war. Equally important, many scientists discovered that these problems offered an intellectual challenge equal to that of traditional science. One eminent war-time O.R. scientist, the late Professor E. J. Williams, is reported[5] to have confessed that he had found the study of U-boat warfare of comparable intellectual interest to his own specialist field as a physicist, which was the quantum theory of atomic collisions.

Williams's recognition of the similarity between his work as a physicist and as an O.R. scientist gives us an important insight into two intrinsic elements of O.R. A physicist performs investigations into various phenomena of the physical universe, establishing theories and building what are known as 'models' of these phenomena. The physicist's model is rather different from the layman's concept of the term. To the layman the word model implies a scaled-down physical replica of the 'real thing', for example, a model of an aeroplane used in wind tunnel experiments. To the physicist a model is an abstract representation of the physical phenomenon being studied, which should provide a unified conceptual description of that phenomenon. The scientific method in physics is essentially concerned with validating these models by experiment, so that they can become part of the 'theory' or body of knowledge of physics. Because the physical universe must be described in mathematical language, these models must inevitably be mathematical in character. A typical model, which the reader may have come across in his school-days, is the so-called kinetic theory of gases.

The war-time O.R. scientists were concerned with investigating problems of military operations and quantifying the factors affecting their outcome. They quickly realized that these problems could only be represented and solved by constructing mathematical models analogous to those of the physicist. These models were constructed to represent the factors involved in the problem and the interrelation between them. By manipulating these models, as against the 'real life' problems which they represented, the O.R. scientists were able to provide military leaders with a prediction of the outcome of alternative policies. Thus, in the example we considered earlier, by constructing a 'life cycle' model, Gordon was able to show that the flying output of squadrons could be increased by a change in operational policy.

We have seen that an intrinsic element in O.R. is the measurement and quantification of factors in a problem and their incorporation into a mathematical model. A second intrinsic element arises from the nature of the quantitative measure. Within the limits of observational error, many physical quantities can be measured with certainty. For example, given an accurate thermometer, we can measure the temperature of water in a glass with certainty. However, this 'temperature' really represents the aggregate of the motions of all the atoms making up the water, which individually are much less predictable in their behaviour. Just as an actuary may observe and predict the pattern of deaths of a large group of men and women (which he uses in fixing life insurance premiums) but cannot predict the life span of a single individual, a physicist can measure the aggregate of the motions of all the atoms making up the water, but cannot measure the motions of the individual atom. Both the life spans of individuals and the motions of individual atoms are indeterminate quantities because they are subject to variability from a large number of causes. Fortunately for the actuary and the physicist, however indeterminate individual behaviour may be, the science of probability and statistics has been developed specifically to handle such problems. Thus mathematical models based on statistics have been developed by both the physicist and the actuary to enable him to observe and predict the behaviour of aggregates of units, which individually are unpredictable.

The problem of the variability and indeterminacy of individual factors exists also in O.R. Obviously the value of factors within a military operation may be affected by many causes which the O.R. man cannot predict. For example, the length of time a particular plane in a squadron would remain in service, or its 'life', could not be predicted individually. However, like the actuary, Gordon was not concerned with the individual but with the aggregate (that is, a squadron of planes), so using probability and statistics he could derive an improved operational policy. Because military operational problems almost always contain a large element of variability, the science of probability and statistics has played, and will continue to play, a vital role in O.R. We conclude this section by considering some of the basic concepts of this science and by examining a second example of wartime O.R. work which specifically illustrates the use of statistics.

The theories of probability and statistics have been developed mainly since the seventeenth century, when mathematicians like Fermat and Pascal were invited by gambler friends to determine the odds in various games of chance. Probability theory is concerned with events in which the outcome is determined by chance, or when enormous numbers of causes combine to produce the final outcome. A simple example is the outcome from tossing a coin. If a coin is unweighted, then the outcome of the toss (that is, whether it lands 'heads' or 'tails') will depend on a number of factors such as the degree of force and spin imparted to the toss, air movement, position of the hand when the coin is caught, etc. However, if we toss the coin many times we find that an approximately equal number of 'heads' and 'tails' appear. Because, in the long run, heads occur for 50 per cent or half the tosses, we can say that the probability of a head occurring is 50 per cent or half. We measure the probability of the outcome of events on a scale ranging from 0 to 1. Where a probability of '0' means that an outcome is certain not to occur, a probability of '1' or 100 per cent means that it is absolutely certain to occur. For example, if we tossed a double-headed penny the probability of a tail occurring is 0, since the coin can never land tails, and of a head occurring is 1 or 100 per cent, since the coin must always land heads.

Obviously in many situations there are more than two possible outcomes to an event. For example, if we throw an unweighted die there are six possible outcomes (1, 2, ... 6 spots on the uppermost face), but we can say that the probability of a particular number (say 4) being thrown is $\frac{1}{6}$th or $16\frac{2}{3}$ per cent.

Using the example of the die, we can also show how the probability of combinations of events can be evaluated. Suppose we wish to know the probability of observing a 3 or a 4 in the single throw of a die:

Probability of outcome being $3 = \frac{1}{6}$

Probability of outcome being $4 = \frac{1}{6}$

Probability of outcome being either 3 or 4 = the sum of the constituent probabilities $= \frac{1}{6} + \frac{1}{6} = \frac{1}{3}$

Similarly suppose we wish to know the probability of obtaining a 4 in two successive throws:

Probability of outcome being 4 on the first throw $= \frac{1}{6}$

Probability of outcome being 4 on the second $= \frac{1}{6}$

Probability of outcome being 4 on both throws $= \frac{1}{6} \times \frac{1}{6} = \frac{1}{36}$

These simple addition and multiplication theorems of probability are two basic bricks with which very elaborate mathematical models may be built.

For example, in the nineteenth century Bortkewitch performed an analysis of the pattern of deaths from horse kicks of cavalry men in the Prussian army. He analysed the records of 10 cavalry corps over 20 years, thus obtaining 200 corps-years of observations. From these records, he was able to construct the following table showing the number of corps-years in which 0, 1, 2 . . . etc. deaths occurred:

Table 1

Deaths	0	1	2	3	4
Number of years this number of deaths occurred	109	65	22	3	1

The total number of deaths is 122 so the average number of deaths is 0·61 per corps-year ($\frac{122}{200}$). However, as the above table shows, this average is spread out over sets of years in which 0, 1, 2 . . . etc. deaths occur because of all the chance influences that are present. Since there were a large number of men in a cavalry corps and on average only 0·61 men were killed per year, the probability of a fatality per man at risk was small. This type of situation can be represented by a mathematical model known as a Poisson process,[6] which is basically an extension of the two theories of probability we have just examined. Using this model and the average number of deaths (0·61) Bortkewitch derived predictions for the number of years in which 0, 1, 2 . . . etc. deaths occurred. These predicted values are compared with observed values in Table 2 below.

Table 2

Deaths	0	1	2	3	4
Actual number	109	65	22	3	1
Predicted number	109	66·3	20·2	4·1	0·6

It can be seen that the agreement between prediction based on the mathematical model and observation is almost exact. Thus it is possible to build a model which produces the same spread as occurs in practice by chance.

We now turn to a similar study that was performed in World War II by O.R. scientists. As many readers will doubtless be aware, in the summer of 1944, shortly after the Allies' Normandy landings, Hitler released the first of his long-awaited secret weapons which, in the event, proved to be the V.1 bomber or 'doodle-bug'. These pilotless aircraft, fired from launching sites in northern France and the Low Countries, were directed towards south-eastern England and, after their engines cut out, crash-landed and exploded.

Most of these bombs crashed in the London area and the Allies wondered whether they were being aimed accurately at the centre of the capital, or whether they were being fired towards the large London conurbation and crashing in it at random. This knowledge was important to strategic planning in Normandy, since it affected the degree of urgency to be attached to the task of capturing or destroying the V.1 launching sites. Fortunately this knowledge could easily be extracted from the pattern of location of V.1 bomb incidents, using the Poisson process.

A large map of the London area was taken and divided into 576 equal areas using appropriate grid lines. The locations of 537 incidents were placed on the map and the number of areas with 0, 1, 2 ... etc. incidents was tabulated. The average number of incidents per area was $\frac{537}{576}$ or 0·93. If the bombs could not be aimed at the centre of London, then it could be argued that their point of impact could be affected by a large number of factors and that they landed at random anywhere in the area under study. Thus, it was argued that the pattern of incidents would follow a Poisson process analogous to the one discussed by Bortkewitch. In this case an event was a V.1 bomb incident, as against the death of a cavalryman from a horse kick, and the pattern of events was distributed over a space (that is, the London area) rather than time. Bortkewitch's calculations were repeated with 0·61 replaced by 0·93, and the number of areas containing 0, 1, 2 ... etc. incidents were predicted. These were compared with the observed number of incidents. This comparison is shown in Table 3 below.

Table 3

Number of hits		0	1	2	3	4	5
Number of areas this number of hits occurred	Actual number	229	211	93	35	7	1
	Predicted number	227	211	99	31	7	1·6

It can be seen that agreement between the two was good. Thus it was shown that Hitler could not aim his V.1 bombs accurately, and the Allies could plan their strategy in Northern Europe secure in that knowledge.

So far as the author is aware, no one knows how many Allied scientists worked, at one time or another, in O.R. during World War II. It seems likely that the figure amounted to 2,000 at least. The operational problems of the military commander at war are not totally dissimilar to those of the industrial manager at peace, so in 1945 not surprisingly some of the 'demobbed' O.R. scientists turned their attention to industry.

In the U.K., the immediate post-war situation offered a good opportunity for the introduction of the new science into peace-time civilian affairs. The British economy, strained and distorted by six years of war, needed renovation. This renovation required planning at national level. The Board of Trade therefore set up a research unit to apply the techniques used by war-time O.R. scientists to the broader problems of peace-time industry and trade. Furthermore, the return of a Labour government in 1945 led to the nationalization of several large industries. Nationalized industries which introduced O.R. as a management aid soon after their birth were coal, railways, air transport and electricity. At the national level, also, a number of the cooperative research associations, responsible for providing a service to a particular type of industry, set up O.R. functions. For example, the British Iron and Steel Research Association has a unit which has made an outstanding contribution to the development of the science. Early development was not confined to the national level or to enterprises publicly controlled. Private enterprises played their part too and individual firms in the textile, steel and oil industries also began to employ O.R. scientists. By the early 1950s, at least forty organizations had an O.R. function, over half of them belonging to private firms.[7] It can be said with Rivett and Ackoff[8] that the decade 1945–55 saw the seed of O.R. sown and germinated in British industry. The next decade (1955 to the present) saw that seed mature into flower with the establishment of O.R. as an important branch of management science.

In the U.S.A. after the war, O.R. was slower to develop in industry. However, the late 1940s and early 1950s saw the rapid development of automation and computers. As with the R.A.F. in connection with radar, this presented American industrial management with an implementation problem which they were too inexperienced to solve. This gave O.R. scientists an opportunity to establish their worth in U.S. industry, and as in Britain, the last decade has seen O.R. blossom into a major activity in the U.S.A. Indeed, as with most other sciences, the U.S.A. is easily the largest contributor to the field.

In many other countries, too, the O.R. approach is well established. It is active in several Commonwealth countries, including Australia, Canada and New Zealand. O.R. can help strengthen the economies of under-developed countries, and this type of work has been notable in India, particularly under the guidance of Sir Charles Goodeve. Readers who would like to learn of this work are referred to *Management Sciences in the Emerging Countries*, by Barish and Verhulst.[9] Most Eastern and Western

European countries are also active in the field and in France *Recherche Operationelle* has been closely associated with *Le Plan*. Japan also has made contributions to the science.

During the war O.R. scientists used only their own analytical skills and the mathematics and statistics they had learnt in their parent disciplines in tackling operational problems. Since the war, parallel with the growth of O.R. in industry there has been the invention and development of a large number of specialized mathematical techniques which aid the solution of operational problems. In fact, during the war a scientist with good mathematical aptitude and analytical ability could enter O.R. and do useful work immediately. Nowadays, a period of specialist training is required and many universities and other educational institutions run courses of training for prospective O.R. scientists. A number of the large O.R. groups in this country also run their own courses for new entrants.

O.R. AS A SCIENCE

As we have seen, an O.R. scientist performs an investigation in a manner analogous to a traditional scientist, both using the scientific method. However, a traditional science, for example physics, is made up of two parts:

(a) the activities of physicists engaged in investigating various phenomena of the physical universe, establishing theories and building models of the phenomena under study; and the experimental and analytical techniques they use,

(b) the body of knowledge known as physics, which is (in principle anyway) a synthesis of the individual models of the various phenomena to form a conceptual unity which embraces the whole of the physical universe.

At present, O.R. is not attempting to build up a unified body of knowledge like physics. The O.R. scientist is concerned with solving the immediate problems at hand, employing the techniques, mainly mathematical, at his disposal. Work on new, and improving existing, techniques is continuous and constitutes an important area of development of the science. What O.R. has discovered is that in industry operational problems, however varied their context, can be reduced to an individual or combination of a few simple conceptual structures. It has been suggested that at present only eight types of structure have been discovered and it is of value to examine these.

INVENTORY CONTROL

In this context inventory is defined as idle resources. A company usually needs to maintain some of its resources (e.g. raw materials or finished goods stock, men or money) in reserve and therefore idle. The function of inventory control is to determine the best level for these reserves. Taking raw material stock as an example, we may say that some costs increase and some decrease as the level of stock is increased.

(i) Tied-up capital, storage space, taxes and insurance costs, together with risks of obsolescence and spoilage, all increase as stock-holding increases.

(ii) Shortage, ordering and purchasing costs generally all decrease as stock-holding increases.

An accurate assessment of how demand for stock items varies, using the mathematics of probability, can identify the stock level and order policy required to keep the total stock-holding costs minimal. The minimum cost may be as much as 40 per cent lower than that obtained by 'rule of thumb' methods and so substantial cash savings can be made.

Problems of similar logical structure arise when deciding on:

(a) how many items to make in a production run, so as to minimize the total of production and finished goods stock-holding costs;

(b) how often to hold training courses for air stewardesses and how large the classes should be, to ensure that an airline has adequate but not excessive supplies of trained stewardesses;

(c) how much operating capital a company should carry.

154

ALLOCATION PROBLEMS

A company may manufacture a number of different products and there may be a 'best' way of making each product. However, the company may have insufficient resources available to make each product in its 'best' way. The problem is to decide on which allocation of resources provides the 'best' way of making all the products taken together. A number of mathematical techniques have been developed to solve this problem (the best known being linear programming) and the answer thus obtained is usually a minimum 5 to 10 per cent better than that given by commonsense.

As well as in production planning, allocation problems also occur when deciding:

(a) where to build a new plant;

(b) how to allocate workers to jobs;

(c) how to plan the distribution of finished products from factories to customers, so as to minimize transport costs.

The last example above will now be used to illustrate the use of O.R. in a hypothetical problem, which is a simplified version of one occurring commonly in industry.

Suppose that a company has 5 factories (A, B, C, D and E) located in different parts of the country, which all make the same prefabricated housing units which can be assembled on site at 10 different housing developments. Suppose the outputs from the 5 factories are as follows:

	Units/Week
A	150
B	170
C	130
D	200
E	220
Total	870

These units are sent to 10 building sites (1, 2 . . . 10), where the contractors require the following number of units per week, as shown in Table 4.

Table 4

1	2	3	4	5	6	7	8	9	10	Total
60	80	50	110	80	50	70	120	140	110	870

The cost of transporting housing units from manufacturing point to site is high and obviously dependent upon the distance travelled. In Table 5 below is listed the scheduled rate per unit in £ (there is no quantity reduction, because each unit is hauled on a single trailer):

Table 5

	1	2	3	4	5	6	7	8	9	10
A	63	21	6	14	59	92	96	99	4	35
B	18	57	83	83	46	22	35	74	81	58
C	49	38	80	54	86	75	1	11	79	52
D	6	15	49	82	7	25	59	34	15	43
E	71	33	98	43	96	76	66	9	46	98

Since the housing units are indistinguishable from each other, the building site managers do not mind which factory they obtain the units from, therefore the manufacturer desires to allocate the units from factories to sites so as to minimize the total transport costs. There are 5 × 10, that is 50 possible routes that can be used, so it is by no means immediately obvious which set of routes minimizes this cost. Fortunately, what is known very appropriately as the transportation technique of linear programming can be used to solve the problem. A table, such as the one shown below, may be set up with 5 rows representing the 5 factories and 10 columns representing the 10 sites. There are 50 'cells' in this table, each cell representing a particular route from factory to site (analogous to the table of mileages between major cities given in many motoring handbooks). In the bottom right-hand corner of each cell the transport cost per unit for that route is given. An allocation of units from factories to sites may now be made so as to satisfy the weekly needs of each building site, and using the total production capacities of all the factories. An allocation of units is shown below, in Table 6.

Table 6

	1	2	3	4	5	6	7	8	9	10	Total
A	60 | 63	80 | 21	10 | 6	| 14	| 59	| 92	| 96	| 99	| 4	| 35	150
B	| 18	| 57	40 | 83	110 | 83	20 | 46	| 22	| 35	| 74	| 81	| 58	170
C	| 48	| 38	| 80	| 54	60 | 86	50 | 75	20 | 1	| 11	| 79	| 52	130
D	| 6	| 15	| 49	| 82	| 7	| 25	50 | 59	120 | 34	30 | 15	| 43	200
E	| 71	| 33	| 98	| 43	| 96	| 76	| 66	| 9	110 | 46	110 | 98	220
Total	60	80	50	110	80	50	70	120	140	110	870

This particular allocation costs a total of £51,140 in transportation costs. It is not the cheapest way of allocating units from factories to sites (which is obvious since it has been obtained by starting in the top left-hand corner and working through the table), but by manipulating this table by a set of mathematical rules, it is possible to find the cheapest or minimum cost allocation of units.

The cheapest cost allocation is £17,480, and it is left to the ingenuity of the reader to discover how this can be made. The allocation which gives this cost will be found at the end of the chapter.

As this problem is a very small one with only 50 possible routes which can be used, readers may be able to find the answer quite easily by trial and error. In real life such problems may typically contain several thousands of possible routes that may be used, and it is beyond human ingenuity to find the cheapest allocation on a trial and error basis. With the aid of the transportation technique of linear programming and a large computer, it is possible to solve a problem containing several thousand routes within five or ten minutes! Equally important, when an answer is obtained this way, the mathematical method used ensures that it is the cheapest allocation; whereas when the trial and error approach is adopted one can never be certain how good (that is, near the minimum cost allocation) one's own allocation is.

QUEUEING PROBLEMS

Here also it is required to balance conflicting sets of costs. Housewives waiting to 'check out' at a supermarket, patients waiting at a hospital for Out-Patient treatment, partly manufactured products awaiting completion at a stage – these are queueing situations, where time and therefore money is being wasted. On the other hand, if service facilities (cash-desk, doctors or machines) are increased too much they will wait or queue for customers also (like taxis waiting at a rank) so money will be wasted in this way.

Again a careful analysis needs to be made, to balance the costs associated with generating a queue against those associated with increasing the service facilities.

SEQUENCING PROBLEMS

Very often on a shop floor, a number of products needs to be made, each of which must be processed in sequence by a number of machines. Even with a few jobs and machines, the number of combinations in which the products may be put through the machine rapidly becomes astronomical. Each combination may have an associated cost in terms of money or time different from the others and it is most important to identify those combinations for which the cost is approximately minimal. There are no rigorous mathematical techniques for dealing with a reasonably sized problem of this nature, but the technique known as computer simulation usually can identify a very low cost combination. In this technique the problem is simulated logically and numerically on a computer and the costs of the alternative combinations are systematically evaluated on the computer. From this analysis a near ideal combination can be chosen.

Recently new techniques have been developed for handling sequencing problems as they occur in planning and scheduling complex projects. Most readers will by now be fairly familiar with these, known under a variety of names (e.g. network analysis, critical path method, and P.E.R.T.).

ROUTING PROBLEMS

The routing of delivery and collection services (e.g. postmen, meter readers, refuse collectors and school bus rounds) so as to minimize the total cost of providing the service, has received increasing attention recently. Again it is difficult to obtain a rigorous mathematical solution but, using mathematical techniques, routes have been designed which have been better than the ones in current use. Routing problems also occur in production planning.

REPLACEMENT PROBLEMS

Many firms have planned maintenance schemes for machinery on the floor, but fewer know when it is the right time to replace it. Basically it is the same problem as deciding when to buy a new car.

A machine deteriorates and its secondhand value depreciates with the passage of time. As it deteriorates, the machine falls off in efficiency and requires increased expenditure on repairs and maintenance. The time occurs, before the machine has worn out, when the increased capital investment required to buy a new one less the secondhand value of the old one, is more than offset by the savings in maintenance and repair costs.

An alternative replacement problem is with a part (such as an electric light bulb) with an efficiency which remains constant throughout its life, but which fails unpredictably. Again analysis may show a pattern of replacement which is cheaper than replacing each item as it fails.

An interesting replacement problem is that concerned with the planning of labour recruitment to balance labour wastage.

COMPETITIVE PROBLEMS

In many business situations, the outcome of a decision taken by a given company may be affected by the decision taken by its competitors. Examples of competitive situations are the bidding for the specific contract, and the pricing and advertising of one's products in the open market. The theory of games has been developed to provide a useful conceptual framework for considering these problems, but unfortunately its development has been too limited to solve any real-life problems. An extension of this theory, known as the statistical decision theory, has been of greater value.

A technique which has been of value in both the military and the business context is known as Operational Gaming. This is a variant on the simulation technique described earlier and the nineteenth-century German *Krieg Spiel* (War Game). Two or more teams play each other in a game. The structure of the competitive situation, or rules of the game, is built into a computer programme. The interactions between the plays (i.e. strategies pursued by the teams) are evaluated by the computer and reported back to the teams. As the game develops, using the experience built up, the teams try to improve their strategies in an effort to reach a winning position. Although the games lack psychological realism (e.g. a manager playing a game will know that a serious mistake will not really 'bankrupt' his 'firm'), it is believed that they can be of value in determining the possible outcomes in novel competitive situations. For example, this technique has been used to try to predict the introduction of a new product into a market. Two teams were formed, one representing the sponsors of the product and the other representing their competitors. The sponsors tried to pursue strategies which maximized the product's share of the market and their competitors tried to prevent this. Operational Gaming is used considerably by military O.R. workers to analyse hypothetical conflict situations

SEARCH PROBLEMS

These problems were first identified during the war when tactics for searching the oceans for hostile submarines were developed. An oil company faces similar problems in searching an area of desert for oil deposits. In both cases with the resources available (aircraft or money) a decision must be made on what search tactics to use. A large area can be searched quickly, thereby increasing the chances of passing over a submarine, but reducing the chances of spotting it should the searcher pass over it. Alternatively a smaller area can be searched slowly, thereby reducing the chances of passing over a submarine, but increasing the chances of spotting it should the searcher pass over it. Probability theory and statistical analysis have been applied to this problem to determine the optimum search strategy.

Account auditing is a similar type of search problem and these techniques have been applied to auditing in large organizations.

It is likely and indeed hoped that this list of problem types will not prove to be exhaustive. In recognizing the essential similarity of operating problems in diverse contexts and in resolving them into a few different types, it can be claimed that O.R. is making a most valuable contribution to the fuller understanding of problems of business administration.

O.R. is playing an increasing role in the public sector of the economy and the educational, social and health services. In these services decisions must be based on criteria of social benefit rather than profitability. O.R. scientists have borrowed from the economists the concept of cost-benefit analysis, where the costs of alternative policies are set against their respective benefits. A useful review of cost-benefit analysis can be found in reference [10]. This approach was used as a basis for the decision to build the Victoria Underground line in London.[11]

It must be remembered that the science was born in a military context, and here also many problems cannot be analysed against the profitability of the enterprise. In evaluating the usefulness of weapons, an analogous technique to cost the benefit, namely cost-effectiveness, has been developed. This approach is self-explanatory and compares the cost of alternative weapons with their relative effectiveness at fulfilling their military purpose.

THE CONTRIBUTION OF O.R. TO INDUSTRY

In many areas of industry O.R. can by now claim to have established itself as a powerful means of decision making, based on the scientific analysis of operational problems. The establishment and rapid growth of very many O.R. groups provides sufficient evidence of this success. The implications of this, however, are even more important when considered in association with another outstanding scientific invention of the war years – the electronic computer.

The introduction of O.R. into British industry was rapidly followed by that of the computer. The computer has received a somewhat mixed reception so far. On the one hand it has been received rapturously by some people, who claim that it heralds a second industrial revolution, giving immense supplementary power to the human brain, as the machine of the first industrial revolution gave immense supplementary power to human brawn. On the other hand, some computer users are less enthusiastic, having found that the introduction of a computer installation into their organization has brought considerably less benefits than expected. Just as the introduction of radar required that the

R.A.F. should re-examine the organizational system designed to detect hostile aircraft, so the introduction of a computer requires that a similar investigation be made in the organizational system in which it is to be installed. Disappointments experienced by computer users can usually be attributed to the failure to make an adequate preliminary analysis of this kind. This fact in turn can be partially attributed to the absence in a firm's senior management of any one able to appreciate what the computer can (and cannot) do, or to perform the more sophisticated numerical thinking required about organizational systems. If the considerable potential of the computer is to be fully explored the capacity for this type of thinking must be developed. An important role of an O.R. function in such a firm should be to perform this thinking.

So far O.R. has been mainly developed by scientists who have received their primary training in the pure or applied physical sciences, or mathematics. These scientists have extended the concept of the mathematical model as a means of describing a physical system or organization, to a means of describing an industrial system or organization. Most of these models have concentrated on determining the best arrangement of the physical and financial resources (that is, the mathematical variables – materials, machines and money) of the organization. An industrial organization, however, is a human organization (that is, it includes men as one of its 'mathematical' variables) and ideally models should be able to incorporate effects attributable to human behaviour. Up to the present, O.R. scientists, probably because of their backgrounds in the exact sciences, have not seriously attempted to incorporate human factors in their models.

In later chapters, the reader will be introduced to the human factors movement and the work of industrial psychologists and sociologists (that is, behavioural scientists). At the moment O.R. and behavioural scientists are less than enthusiastic about each other's work. The O.R. man thinks that the behavioural scientist is unable to establish verifiable and usable models of problems in industrial organizations; whilst the behavioural scientist thinks that the O.R. man is prepared to ignore or over-simplify human factors in order to build a viable mathematical model. Ideally, these 'two cultures' should be synthesized into one, possibly by the establishment of interdisciplinary teams of behavioural and O.R. scientists to study industrial problems, or by the recruitment of behavioural scientists into industrial O.R. groups. There is some evidence to suggest that this kind of activity is beginning.[12]

ANSWER TO CASE STUDY

Output from A goes to
$\begin{cases} 3 & 50 \text{ units} \\ 4 & 100 \text{ units} \end{cases}$

Output from B goes to
$\begin{cases} 1 & 60 \text{ units} \\ 6 & 50 \text{ units} \\ 10 & 60 \text{ units} \end{cases}$

Output from C goes to
$\begin{cases} 7 & 70 \text{ units} \\ 8 & 10 \text{ units} \\ 10 & 50 \text{ units} \end{cases}$

Output from D goes to
$\begin{cases} 5 & 80 \text{ units} \\ 9 & 120 \text{ units} \end{cases}$

Output from E goes to
$\begin{cases} 2 & 80 \text{ units} \\ 4 & 10 \text{ units} \\ 8 & 110 \text{ units} \\ 9 & 20 \text{ units} \end{cases}$

NOTES

1. G. R. Gedye, *Scientific Method in Production Management*, Oxford University Press, London, 1965.

2. Sir Solly Zuckerman, 'In the Beginning – and later', *Operational Research Quarterly*, December, 1964.

3. Sir Robert Watson-Watt, *Three Steps to Victory*, Odhams Press, London, 1957.

4. 'Operational Research in the R.A.F.', H.M.S.O., London, 1963.

5. P.M.S. Blackett, *Studies of War*, Oliver & Boyd, Edinburgh and London, 1962.

6. M. J. Moroney, *Facts from Figures*, Penguin Books, 1951.

7. Sir Charles Goodeve and G. Ridley, Survey of O.R. in Great Britain, *Operational Research Quarterly*, 1953.

8. Patrick Rivett and Russell L. Ackoff, *A Manager's Guide to Operational Research*, Wiley, London, 1963.

9. N. M. Barish and M. Verhulst, *Management Sciences in the Emerging Countries*, Pergamon, London, 1965.

10. 'Cost-Benefit Analysis: A Survey', *Economic Journal*, December, 1965.

11. C. D. Foster and M. E. Beesley, 'Estimating the Social Benefit of Constructing an Underground Railway in London', *J. R. Statist. Soc.* A, 126, pp. 46–78.

12. J. R. Lawrence, ed., *Operational Research and the Social Sciences*, Tavistock Publications, London, 1966.

FURTHER READING

The early development of O.R. is amply described in the literature. Readers who wish to know of this development in more detail should consult:

P. M. S. BLACKETT, *Studies of War*, Oliver & Boyd, Edinburgh, 1962.

R. W. CLARK, *The Rise of the Boffins*, Phoenix, London, 1962.

J. G. CROWTHER and R. WHIDDINGTON, 'Science at War', H.M.S.O., London, 1947.

'Operational Research in the R.A.F.', H.M.S.O., London, 1963.

J. F. MCCLOSKEY and F. N. TREFETHEN, *Operations Research for Management*, vol. 1, Johns Hopkins Press, Baltimore, 1954.

A book which provides an admirable introduction to O.R. as a whole and which is completely non-technical is:

PATRICK RIVETT and RUSSELL L. ACKOFF, *A Manager's Guide to Operational Research*, Wiley, London, 1963.

Alternatives which are a little technical, but still accessible to the general reader, are:

E. DUCKWORTH, *A Guide to Operational Research*, Methuen, London, 1962.

N. L. ENRICK, *Management Operations Research*, Holt, Rinehart & Winston, New York, 1966.

D. W. MILLER and M. K. STARR, *Executive Decisions and Operations Research*, Prentice-Hall, New York, 1960.

M. J. SARGEANT, *Operational Research for Management*, Heinemann, London, 1965.

PART THREE

THE CRITERION OF WELFARE

3.1 Introduction: the Criterion of Welfare

WELFARE is more difficult to identify than efficiency in the management of the firm. Decisions about welfare cannot be made by management in isolation; they are affected by society. What may be termed the 'positive' approach to welfare is a concern for the 'whole' man, that is his social as well as his economic well-being, and a concern with the dignity of labour and the social good that can be achieved through business. The 'negative' approach includes attempts to diminish waste, to make the workforce more content, and hence more stable, and to accept the standards set by society in order to preserve the independence of the business. These two approaches are not always easily distinguishable, although 'positive' welfare obviously involves a moral dimension. Seebohm Rowntree in the introduction to his book, *The Human Factor in Business*, observes:

that under any satisfactory industrial system two conditions will always be observed.
(i) in the process of wealth production, industry must pay the greatest possible regard to the general welfare of the community, and pursue no policy detrimental to it.
(ii) the wealth produced must be distributed in such a manner as will best serve the highest ends of the community.

These abstractions did not, of course, preclude Rowntree from emphasizing the importance of good work and efficiency, but he widened the goals of his business to include not only profits and efficiency but also harmony and welfare.

Management welfare is more usually associated with easily identified items such as fringe benefits, medical schemes and social facilities, all of which make the conditions of work, if not the work itself, more pleasant.

Where business has been unwilling to accept the obligations of providing minimum standards of welfare, society has usually enforced these standards. The growth of interest in welfare in industrial countries can be demonstrated by the increase in laws dealing with social standards, the role of government in promoting and encouraging these standards and the special position accorded to unions, both legally and socially, to protect these standards. Social legislation has increased so much over the last thirty years that it now forms one of the most important branches of law.

3.2 The Development of Personnel Management

IAN McGIVERING

THROUGHOUT the nineteenth century, the machine was dominant. Technical invention and the enterprise of its exploiters were producing miracles of productivity, creating material wealth at a rate that challenged the imagination, and transforming, both by accident and by intent, the very basis of society. And as society changed, so did the beliefs which explained and justified it.

The traditional conception of the proper relationship between master and man was expressed in the phrase *noblesse oblige*. It was a relationship of mutual obligations in which the man was to labour and to serve and the master was to provide and to protect. It was an ideology suited to a stable era and for many generations it had served as a guide, both socially and legally, to the regulation of employment relationships. To be sure, it was not always a reliable guide to what was, for its tenets were not always strictly observed, but it served its social purpose by providing a generally understood indication of what ought to be. But the economic transformation of society created new relationships and brought a need for a new set of beliefs to justify them. The justification was provided in the writings of the political philosopher, Edmund Burke, and of economists such as David Ricardo and Thomas Malthus. No longer was the master deemed to have social obligations to his men or to their families; instead, his obligations were to himself and to his business, for only if the master succeeded in a harsh, competitive world in finding a market for his product could he provide his labour force with the employment which constituted their livelihood. So ran the argument. Wages and, indeed, employment itself, were determined by economic laws, and economic theory demonstrated the impossibility of any employer paying more for labour than the rate at which the bare subsistence of the labourer was possible. Moreover, as wages, employment and working conditions were fixed by economic laws, it seemed to follow that any attempt to interfere with this natural process would be socially harmful if not downright wicked. The good of all could only be served if the controllers of the new industry were free to use their enterprise as they thought fit, untrammelled by any consideration other than personal gain.

Yet even in the first half of the nineteenth century when social unrest and repression were at their height, there were employers who stood out from their contemporaries by their stubborn refusal to accept the prevailing economic, medical and religious views that the appalling working and living conditions of the time were not only necessary but desirable. Josiah Wedgwood, Matthew Boulton and James Watt, Samuel Oldknow, Richard Arkwright, Robert Owen, Samuel Courtauld and Titus Salt are known to us today for more than the industrial empires they founded. Each left behind a record of humanity in his practice of management that was in marked contrast to the standards and practices of his competitors. In each there was a deep concern for the well-being of employees, manifest in a willingness to accept a responsibility for the quality of their lives not only whilst at work but also at home and in their village and urban communities. It is to these men that the modern personnel manager turns when he contemplates the origins of his profession.

As the century wore on, society began to adjust to the fact of its industrialism. The Factories Act of 1833 established the Factory Inspectorate, a move of the greatest significance because the four men appointed under the Act not only provided a means for ensuring that its requirements were likely to be met but by travelling through their assigned districts, visiting mills and factories, they made widely known amongst the managers the success of the welfare practices of the best. Much of the subsequent slow but steady spread of factory legislation was due to the dedicated work of the gradually increasing band of inspectors, who through their reports and personal contacts maintained a continuous pressure for the betterment of conditions.

During the second half of the century, a comparatively stable pattern of industrial relations began to emerge. The erratic and disorganized unions of the previous generation, with their nebulous and hopeless aims, gave way to the so-called 'New Model' trade unions, the prototype of which was the Amalgamated Society of Engineers, founded in 1851. These unions, almost entirely organizations of craftsmen, possessed adequate funds, a competent leadership and a stable organization. They established a system of collective bargaining both with individual employers and with the employers' organizations which developed in response. The conditions of employment they secured compared favourably with the minimal conditions for women and children laid down by the Factories Act.

These developments were supplemented by legislation as Parliament gradually departed from the strict application of the principles of *laissez faire*. The circumstances and the manner in which industrial disputes were to be conducted and the role of the government if disputes became obstinate were defined (the Trade Union Act, 1871; the Conspiracy and Protection of Property Act, 1875; the Conciliation Act, 1896); attempts were made to deal with some of the victims of industrialism (Employers' Liability Act, 1880; Workmen's Compensation Acts, 1897 and 1906; Unemployed Workmen Act, 1905; Trade Boards Act, 1909); and the Factories Acts continued to be made more rigorous and their coverage more extensive. Nevertheless, progress was slow and the period was marked by considerable industrial unrest, for although Britain could claim to be the richest nation in the world, the wealth of the upper classes, the affluence of the middle classes and the reasonable comfort of the artisans, tended to distract attention from the wretched situation of the unskilled men and women – the 'labouring classes'.

A survey of people in working class districts of London, conducted by F. D. Hyndman in 1885, revealed that 25 per cent of the population were living in conditions of extreme poverty.[1] Charles Booth's survey shortly afterwards, undertaken to refute Hyndman's 'illfounded and exaggerated claims', suggested a figure of 30·7 per cent[2] and B. S. Rowntree, investigating conditions among the population of the city of York in 1899, estimated that 43·4 per cent of the wage-earning class (equal to 27·84 per cent of the total population of the city) were living in poverty.[3]

Given these figures, the reasons for social unrest were not hard to understand and the spread of unionism among the unskilled in the last two decades of the century gave their discontent the means of practical expression. Their trades unionism reflected an anger born of a deep sense of social injustice. They were not disposed to copy the policies of the older established craft unions and to seek agreements with employers but sought the betterment of their conditions in the radical restructuring of society, believing that popular control of the means of production was a necessary first step towards a less inequitable distribution of wealth. The militancy of the new unions under the leadership of men like Will Thorne, Tom Mann, Ben Tillett and John Burns spread to the more conservative elements of the T.U.C. The exclusive craft membership of many of the old unions began to break down as unskilled men were admitted to their ranks, often, however, with inferior membership status.

Lacking, as yet, any effective political power, the trade unions resorted to industrial action to achieve their aims. There were many who sympathized with the plight of the underprivileged but not all who did so could accept with equanimity the uncompromising radicalism of the unions or the degree of industrial conflict which the country was enduring. Alternatives were sought, therefore, whereby the conditions of wage earners might be improved and the relations between managements and men stabilized without a major modification of the existing industrial system. Two such alternatives, co-partnership and profit-sharing, attracted many adherents and by the turn of the century a third began to make its appearance – the welfare movement.

The general apprehension over the state of relationships between management and men coincided with a growing concern among socially conscientious employers that the increasing size of factories was making it impossible to maintain the close personal contact with employees that they wished to maintain. Some saw a solution to this problem in the appointment of Wel-

fare Workers or Social Secretaries* who would act as inter-
mediaries, representing the directors to the work people and the
work people to the directors. Probably the first to be appointed
in Britain was Miss Mary E. Wood, a former teacher, who commenced welfare work at Rowntrees in 1896.[4] So successful was
her appointment that she was joined in October 1900 by a settlement worker, David S. Crichton.[5] The work expanded rapidly
and within a few years the Welfare Department at Rowntrees
had acquired a national reputation and was setting the standard
for others to emulate.

The work of the department has been described in these words:

As the representatives of the Directors, the Social Secretaries are
expected to suggest and advise any improvements in conditions of
work, etc. that may be helpful, to initiate and control extensions of
social work and to assist in keeping the personal element prominent in
their relations with the employees.

As the representatives of the employees, it is the duty of the Social
Secretaries to be constantly in touch with them, to gain their confidence, to voice any grievances they may have, either individually or
collectively; to give effect to any reasonable desire they may show for
recreative clubs, educational classes, etc.; and to give advice and assistance in matters affecting them personally or privately.

Their specific duties include the engagement of employees other than
the skilled workmen and clerks, the suggestion of improvements in the
terms and conditions of employment, etc.; the supervision of dining-
rooms and dinner-hour arrangements, the initiation and supervision of
clubs, societies, etc.; for the benefit of employees when such are not
independently successful – all being self-governed – and the fostering
generally of a spirit of unity and good fellowship amongst all connected
with the firm.

In other words:

It is the aim of the Social Secretaries to make employees feel that they
are more than mere parts in an industrial machine; that someone in

---

*The office, Social Secretary, was suggested by the American Institute of
Social Service. It was first adopted in 1889. The idea spread so rapidly that
in 1893 it was possible to hold a conference of Social Secretaries. (Budgett
Meakin, *Model Factories and Villages*, T. Fisher Unwin, 1905, p. 41.)

the factory cares for them as human beings – cares whether they get on well, whether they behave ill or well.[6]

At the time of the outbreak of World War I, about two dozen firms were known to have established specialized Welfare Departments charged with responsibilities broadly similar to those of the department at Rowntrees, and there were certainly several other firms who were applying the principles of welfare work without having made specialist appointments for the purpose.[7]

In 1909, Edward Cadbury convened a conference at Bournville for all who were interested in welfare work in order that experiences could be shared and general policies discussed. An attempt was made to form a permanent association, and Mary Wood was elected secretary. But it was not until June 1913, when Rowntrees organized a similar conference at York attended by some sixty people, that a permanent body, the Welfare Workers' Association, was founded. Miss Wood was its first Honorary Secretary.[8]

The war gave welfare work a tremendous impetus. The sudden demand for unlimited production from hastily adapted factories and the recruitment to the industrial labour force of many thousands of women quite unused to factory work, presented the managements of the day with unprecedented problems. The very long hours of work and the makeshift conditions which both workers and managements patriotically accepted, failed to lead to the increased output on which national survival depended. It was a clear demonstration of the fact that paying due regard to the human factor in production was not a philanthropic luxury but an economic necessity. Robert Owen had said it a hundred years earlier but not, apparently, sufficiently loudly.

But it was one thing to know that one must pay due regard to the human factor and quite another to translate that need into practical policies. In what circumstances were employees most productive? What hours of work were optimal in what circumstances? How was fatigue affected by temperature, ventilation and the spacing of rest pauses? These were just some of the questions to which answers had to be found, but knowledge on these and similar topics was woefully lacking. The first important step, therefore, was to deal with the productivity problems with which the country was faced. This required the establishment of a research organization to investigate the effect on the workers of different aspects of the physical environment. This organization, the Health of Munition Workers Committee, was appointed under the chairmanship of Sir George Newman in 1915, and issued an informative series of reports, first under its original name and later over the next thirty years under its subsequent names, the Industrial Fatigue Research Board and the Industrial Health Research Board.

A few weeks after the establishment of the Health of Munition Workers Committee, Seebohm Rowntree suggested to the Minister of Munitions, Lloyd George, that there was an urgent need to improve working conditions and welfare facilities in the munitions factories. The Minister immediately invited him to undertake the task and on 3 January 1916, Rowntree's appointment as Director of the newly created Welfare Department of the Ministry of Munitions was announced.* Employers did not take kindly to the idea of the manager of a cocoa works teaching them their business but gradually, by patience, personal ability and the example of the steadily improving conditions in the munitions factories, Rowntree wore down the ignorance and hostility with which he had been faced.

In April 1916, the appointment of welfare workers in all 'national' factories was made compulsory if women or young persons were employed. However, although it is possible to create

---

* Asa Briggs, *A Study of the Work of Seebohm Rowntree*, ch. V, Longmans, 1961. Among the distinguished staff whom Rowntree gathered around him were Dorothea Proud and the Rev. Robert Hyde. It is difficult to exaggerate the importance of Rowntree's contribution to the development of British management. There was hardly a development of any importance in the first half of the present century in which Rowntree did not play a significant part. In 1918 he was closely concerned with the foundation of the Industrial Welfare Society, of which Robert Hyde was secretary for some thirty years. He was also involved in the creation of the National Institute of Industrial Psychology in 1921 and served on its executive until 1949, being chairman for seven years.

appointments by the stroke of a pen, it is not possible in the same facile way to create a supply of suitably qualified people. Those entering the work did so from a wide variety of backgrounds,* and with different conceptions of the role they were to play. Thus, despite the setting up of short training courses at several universities and a careful screening of applicants by a Central Interviewing Board, not all the appointments were successful and some were disastrous.

In too many factories the welfare workers were guilty of exceeding the bounds of acceptability by an officiousness and an over-concern for the well-being of their charges of a kind that is nowadays occasionally attributed to elderly headmistresses. The trade unions viewed the great expansion in welfare activity with growing suspicion. They expressed the resentment of their members at the interference with their private lives that welfare work too often entailed. They saw the welfare worker as an informer paid by management although masquerading as a friend. They feared, too, the danger that welfare work might develop along the lines of co-partnership and profit-sharing as an employer-sponsored alternative to trades unionism,† keeping the employee in a state of dependence and enabling the employer to exercise unilateral control over conditions of work, particularly wages.[9]

With the return to peacetime conditions, it was to be expected that the need for welfare work would diminish. Not only were there the closures of munitions factories and the return to domestic life of many of the women who had worked in them, but there

---

* Dorothea Proud reports that 'Clergymen, teachers, organists, doctors, gymnasts, overlookers, cooks, ex-constables are some of those who are found engaged in the work. Such variety in personnel is bound to produce variety in practice.' E. D. Proud, *Welfare Work*, Bell, 1916, p. 67.

† In fairness to the pioneers of welfare work, it must be emphasized that all of them saw welfare work as complementary to a strong trade union movement. See, for example, E. Cadbury, *Experiments in Industrial Organisation*, 1912, particularly pp. 269–70. Where they differed from the trade union leaders was in their belief that if all employers were 'good' employers, social justice could be achieved. The trade unionists took a more cynical view and the student of social history would find it difficult to blame them.

were also those employers who regarded welfare workers as they regarded food rationing: a wartime expedient to be accepted under duress and to be dispensed with as soon as it was legally or socially possible to do so. Yet it is doubtful if even the most pessimistic prophet would have foreseen the rapidity with which the wartime developments disappeared. Some indication of the decline in the number of firms employing welfare staff may be gained from the membership figures of the Welfare Workers' Institute.*

The decline was certainly accelerated by the economic depression following the war, but other factors may have contributed. With the development of 'scientific management', particularly that branch most influenced by Frank Gilbreth, attention was directed to those numerous aspects of the physical environment that have a bearing on the fatigue and efficiency of the operative. The best possible working conditions were urged as a prerequisite of the attainment of the greatest efficiency. Scientific management was thus joining forces with, and in this respect, perhaps supplanting welfare work in advocating the importance of industrial betterment. Managers were now being pressed, not by social workers but by efficiency engineers, to make proper provision, not only 'in the shops themselves, but such direct installations as the provision of a room in which to take food, the provision of food itself, of a rest-room, of proper lavatories and cloak-rooms'.[10]

Yet to the practitioner, welfare work was a moral principle. Its importance to efficiency was conceded almost reluctantly, and those engaged in it seemed to believe that it would wreak changes in the souls of men. This evangelical approach persisted throughout the inter-war period. Thus, the Foreword to a publication by members of the Institute of Industrial Welfare Workers proclaimed that 'Others are coming to believe that the remedy [to our industrial problems] will be found, not in any one reform, but in the gradual readjustment of our relations with each other, with

*The Welfare Workers' Association changed its name several times in the process of becoming the Institute of Personnel Management. Its various titles and its annual membership figures are given in Appendix B.

the physical world around us and with God'. Welfare work was not simply a set of techniques for improving working conditions. More important than what was done was the spirit in which it was done. 'The authors would here emphasize their belief that it is only in so far as these material devices are the expression of a spiritual outlook on life that they will secure any permanent improvement in general conditions.'[11]

As late as 1938, it was possible for a writer to declare:

When the great 'Money-God' calls to his disciples, thousands run blindly on, climbing over any obstacles, even human ones, which may be in their way. When a man is out for profit, why should another, however innocently, stand in his way, he asks. The only answer, of course, is nothing more than a common spiritual truth, the fact that being the children of one Father, we are all brothers, set upon the earth to reap and to sow, to enjoy and to share.[12]

Yet despite the moral values of the welfare worker, during the 1920s and, particularly, during the 1930s, the emphasis was changing. The need for welfare work in the old sense was declining as social and economic conditions gradually improved and as the militancy of the trade union movement died away after the fiasco of 1926 and the Mond-Turner conferences presaged the future pattern of industrial relations. Welfare work had always included elements of employment management in that the welfare worker had been involved in the selection and placement of new labour, in the maintenance and, in some cases, the analysis of personnel records, and in questions of transfer, promotion and dismissal. This employment management aspect of the work assumed greater importance as the welfare aspect diminished. The change was signalled in 1931 by the change in name of the professional body from the Institute of Industrial Welfare Workers to the Institute of Labour Management.

This shift in emphasis occurred much earlier in the United States, where the term 'welfare' was short-lived, being replaced before World War I by the terms 'employment management' and 'personnel management'. Although there is a danger that too much importance may be attached to the difference in terminology, it seems clear that the difference is more than semantic. The general shortage of labour in the United States concentrated attention on its most efficient use and on the associated problems of recruitment and wastage. The welfare worker in Britain was, of course, concerned with questions of labour wastage, but for quite a different purpose and in quite a different way. In the United States, the purpose was to prevent the loss to the company of a valued employee, whereas in Britain the purpose was to prevent the unjust dismissal of a man who was thereby being doomed to unemployment. Magnus Alexander successfully turned his attention to the problem of costing labour turnover in 1913, and much of the American literature of the period is concerned with the expense of turnover and with the importance of careful selection, placement and even exit interviewing.[13]

The extent of the American problem may be judged from the following brief report: 'Mr Boyd Fisher, after analysing the employment figure for the last year in 57 Detroit plants, found that the average turnover for the group was 252 per cent. The Ford Co. from October 1912 to October 1913 hired 54,000 men to maintain an average working force of 13,000. This was a labour turnover of 416 per cent for the year.'[14]

In these circumstances it is not surprising that employment management spread more rapidly in the United States than did either welfare work or employment management in Britain. Indeed, in this country, the American preoccupation with efficiency was considered to be sordid and was generally deplored. For example, 'Two distinct motives, however, have led to specialization [in the care of the workers] – the motive of pity and the motive of profit. Undoubtedly the former has been the more powerful in England; the latter, it would seem, is the only one tolerated in America,'[15] and virtuous disapproval is apparent in these comments: '. . . Welfare Work in America is as anti-philanthropic as may be. There is no question of the welfare of the worker as such; it is the welfare of the business which demands that workers be as fit as possible physically, mentally and morally. Few workers should be "fired", because of "the loss arising from the introduction of new men". All workers should be well treated, because "the contented employee has a positive money value". It is a matter of dollars right through."*

Employment management spread slowly in Britain and gained ground chiefly in the new, consumer industries. Membership of the Institute of Labour Management gradually expanded and both the Institute and the Industrial Welfare Society painstakingly disseminated knowledge of modern techniques and principles of personnel work through publications and conferences. Techniques improved as knowledge was gained from research data on human needs and potential, on selection and training methods, on the effectiveness of different payment systems and on problems of fatigue and productivity. The research data derived mainly from University departments in this country and in the United States, from the National Institute of Industrial Psychology and the indefatigable Industrial Health Research Board, and from the published results of research and investigations conducted by industrial firms themselves.

These developments, coupled with the spread of workshop bargaining, were gradually producing an Employment, or Labour, Manager who differed substantially from the welfare worker of the previous decades. Knowledge was accumulating which would form the basis of a technical expertise, and changing social circumstances were causing the expertise to be very different from the social case-work skills of the welfare worker. Yet even though a growing number of employment managers were supplementing the ranks of the welfare workers, the total number of firms who employed specialists in the general field of personnel work was still extremely small when war again broke out in 1939.

* E. Dorothea Proud, op. cit., pp. 72–3. Similar sentiments are expressed elsewhere in the British literature. (See, for example, E. T. Kelly, ed., *Welfare Work in Industry*, p. 2, and A. G. Woodward, 'Personnel Management', *Efficiency Magazine*, 1938, p. 11.) Woodward found himself in some difficulty because Seebohm Rowntree, whose work he admired and for whom, personally, he had an obvious respect, said that the better he treated his workpeople the more profits he made. Woodward explained, 'Fortunately for him his reputation saves him from being misunderstood' (p. 10). Although Rowntree said it, to Woodward apparently, he did not really mean it.

World War II brought employment problems similar to those of World War I and caught the country almost equally unprepared. During the crisis of 1940, culminating in the dramatic June exodus from Dunkirk, British industry was frantically exhorted to attempt impossible feats of productivity. For a few months industry struggled to meet the challenge and both managements and workers alike put the short-term needs of war production above any other consideration. But the pace was impossible to maintain and in due course could only have resulted in collapse. Fortunately, the lessons of 1914 and 1915 were re-learned in time and by the end of 1940 the industrial war effort was being rationally organized to maximize production in the long term.

The need for welfare and medical supervision was probably as great as, if not greater than, that in World War I, and for the same reasons. Thousands of men and women entered factory work for the first time, many of them having to live away from home, separated from their families and presenting a variety of personal problems.

Nevertheless, although the special circumstances recreated a need for welfare activities, the personnel function was stimulated to develop along a broader front. The number of employers who could be described as sophisticated in matters of labour administration may have been disgracefully low but it was certainly larger than in 1914. Not only was there available much more information concerning techniques and principles but bodies like the Institute of Labour Management and the Industrial Welfare Society had helped to make it more widely known. And in addition to rather more sophisticated managements, there was a more sophisticated labour force so that many of those firms untouched by the work of the above organizations were made aware of, and forced to take into account, the standards and practices of the most advanced firms through pressure from the trade union movement.

The developments described briefly above were already taking place when, late in 1940, the mobilization of the nation's manpower on a full war footing began to get under way. The organization of this tremendous task was entrusted to a trade union leader who was not even a member of parliament, Ernest Bevin, General Secretary of the Transport and General Workers' Union. Bevin became Minister of Labour and National Service in Winston Churchill's coalition government in May 1940 and an elected M.P. shortly afterwards.

The powers needed by the government to control the full range of national resources necessitated the passage of a great deal of legislation, Statutory Rules and Orders. The consequent legal labyrinth is too complex to be disentangled here but mention must be made of some of the measures most important to the development of personnel work.

Shortly after taking office, Bevin transferred the Factory Department from the Home Office to his own Ministry and set up a Factory and Welfare Department charged with the stimulation of welfare activities both inside and outside the factory. Later Orders required the Chief Inspector of Factories to make arrangements, where he considered it necessary, for welfare and medical provision in war factories, for canteens, and the compulsory appointment of personnel or welfare officers. The Factory Inspectors were encouraged to give advice and assistance to any employer who needed help with labour problems. Later, in 1945, this role was to become separated from that of inspector with the establishment of the Personnel Management Advisory Service staffed by experienced personnel officers.

In 1940, the Conditions of Employment and National Arbitration Order (No. 1305) made strikes and lock-outs illegal and established a National Arbitration Tribunal to which all disputes reported to the Minister were to be referred. The Order also laid down that conditions of employment in any factory should be no less favourable to the worker than the conditions agreed at national or district level by trade unions and employers' representatives.

Probably the most far-reaching in their effects were the Essential Work Orders, the first of which was introduced in January 1941. The provisions of the Order were designed to restrict the freedom of employer and employee to terminate their relationship at will: no employee could quit his job nor could any employer dismiss an employee (except for 'serious misconduct') without the permission of a National Service Officer. Employees who were absent or persistently late without reasonable excuse were to be reported to the appropriate Works Committee for consideration. In some mitigation of the restrictive nature of the Order, it was also laid down that an employee who was 'capable of and available for work' and who was willing to undertake whatever alternative work he was reasonably asked to perform, would receive a wage guaranteed to be not less than that which he normally received. The E.W.O.s eventually covered nearly nine million workers.

The effect of the E.W.O.s was extensive and, in many cases, long-lasting. Employers accustomed to basing their relationship with employees on the use of authority backed by the sanction of dismissal now found the use of such a sanction denied them and were impelled to find other means of influencing employee behaviour. To some employers, of course, a cooperative relationship based on reason, discussion and consultation was nothing new but to many others the change from an authoritarian system of management involved changes in attitudes and behaviour which were not easy to achieve. Throughout 1941, trade unions, particularly in the engineering industries, pressed employer representatives to establish joint consultative committees in member firms so that managements and workers could meet regularly to discuss production problems and any other matters of common interest not covered by the existing negotiating procedures. The idea was hardly novel, having been advocated by the Whitley Committee more than twenty years earlier and, in retrospect, it seems extraordinary that such a suggestion should have been so strongly resisted. The employers' reasons for resistance are not entirely clear but it may, perhaps, be conjectured that the maintenance of managerial authority was a prime concern and that this preoccupation with authority, which has bedevilled industrial relations for so long, was underlaid by vague fears that the establishment of production committees with their wide terms of reference might constitute the first step on the downhill road to workers' control – the thin end of the Bolshevik wedge!

In February 1942, however, the Ministry of Supply established Joint Production Committees in all factories for which the Ministry was responsible, and the following month agreement was reached between the engineering unions and the Engineering Employers' Federation for the establishment of 'Joint Production Consultative and Advisory Committees' in federated establishments.[16]

Sir Stafford Cripps was appointed Minister of Aircraft Production in November 1942 and the following month the Production Efficiency Board was set up. In July 1943, the Board commenced the issue of a series of pamphlets addressed to all those engaged in personnel work in the aircraft industry. In his Foreword to the series, the Minister wrote, *inter alia*, 'Personnel management is not a hobby or a fad: it is an essential element in the proper management of industry and has now become recognized as such by the majority of the more enlightened employers. It is, moreover, a profession which demands a high degree of training and skill coupled with a thorough knowledge of labour problems of every kind.'

By the end of 1943, the change-over of the economy to a war footing had been largely accomplished. Of the total adult population available for work, over two-thirds were 'gainfully employed', the vast majority of the remainder being women engaged in necessary domestic tasks such as the care of dependants. The proportion of women in the labour force had risen sharply: in the aircraft industry, for example, from 12 per cent in 1940 to 40 per cent, and in the munitions industries generally, including shipbuilding, women constituted a third of the labour force.[17] To correct an over-enthusiastic call-up of miners to the armed forces, young men were permitted to opt for 'war service' in the mines as an alternative to service in the armed forces. They were dubbed 'Bevin Boys' for obvious reasons and although the scheme was introduced to redress a miscalculation of the manpower needs in coal mining, it was hoped by Bevin that it would have beneficial social consequences by helping to break down class barriers.[18]

The number of people engaged in personnel management was

estimated to have increased from '1,500 at the outside' in 1939 to '5,759 early in 1943'[19] decreasing slightly to 5,478 in January 1944.[20] It would be too much to expect that all the appointments made at a time of increasing manpower shortage would be outstandingly successful. Undoubtedly there were mistakes, but it seems reasonable to suppose that, generally speaking, the standard of the appointments was higher than it had been in World War I. There was firstly, a greater understanding of the nature of the job and hence of the type of person most suited to fill it, and secondly, the introduction of systematic training courses planned jointly by the Institute of Labour Management and the Joint Universities Council for Social Studies. The courses were held in the social science departments at the universities of Birmingham, Edinburgh, Liverpool and the London School of Economics and consisted of a highly concentrated three months in applied social science subjects followed by four weeks' practical experience in a personnel department. Approximately 800 students passed through the twenty-five courses held between 1940 and 1949.[21] In addition, lecture courses were provided at a number of industrial centres throughout the country: and Liverpool University, by arrangement with the Ministry of Supply, experimented with a six weeks' course for Royal Ordnance Factory Labour officers. The experiment was sufficiently successful for the Ministry of Aircraft Production later to make a comparable arrangement with Edinburgh University.

This extensive development of personnel work was received by the trade union movement in a spirit rather different from that with which it had greeted the spread of welfare work a generation earlier. The strong hostility of 1917 had faded to a watchful suspicion by 1945. The General Council of the T.U.C. had presented a memorandum to the Congress of 1932 in which they expressed the view that welfare schemes were acceptable provided that they were run in conjunction with trades unions,* and this

---

*64th Annual Report of Trades Union Congress, 1932, p. 149. The memorandum notes a number of developments which appear hostile to trade union interests. For example, 'One of the rules for membership of a new Friendly Society which has been organized by the employers in the wool

attitude had not basically changed. The ambiguous definition of the welfare worker's role – 'representing the worker to the Board and the Board to the worker' – no longer applied, but there was still a sensitivity to any expression of patronization or paternalism on the part of employers. Where the personnel manager was plainly a part of management, not constituting a threat to the development of trades unionism but providing a formal channel in the firm for facilitating the creation, and the subsequent handling, of day-to-day relationships with employee representatives, then his role was acceptable. To a trade union movement no longer wishing to overthrow management but desiring a closer, cooperative relationship with it, the personnel manager could even appear as an ally.

The developments in personnel management theory and practice, although apparent during the 1930s, had been greatly accelerated by the needs of full manpower utilization during the war. The change in emphasis from welfare work inspired by sympathy to labour management necessitated by the demands of efficiency had been so rapid as to leave the practitioners with problems of adjustment. The moral force which had sustained the work from its inception was suddenly revealed as being apparently invalid, almost something to be ashamed of. The Institute of Labour Management asked in the editorial columns of its journal the question, 'What is personnel management?' and invited its members to contribute their thoughts so that their purpose might be redefined.[22] The resultant definition appeared on the front page of the journal just over a year later.[23] It is worth repeating in full for it has changed little over the last twenty years.

Personnel Management is that part of the management function which is primarily concerned with the human relationships within an

---

textile industry is that Trade Union membership must be lapsed, and as the Unions concerned are in a very bad way financially, they have lost many members to the Friendly Society, which has all the capital of the employers behind it. This is an example of the most dangerous development of welfare work . . .'

organization. Its objective is the maintenance of those relationships on a basis which, by consideration of the well-being of the individual, enables all those engaged in the undertaking to make their maximum personal contribution to the effective working of that undertaking.

In particular, personnel management is concerned with: methods of recruitment, selection, training and education and with the proper employment of personnel; terms of employment, methods and standards of remuneration, working conditions, amenities and employee services; the maintenance and effective use of facilities for joint consultation between employers and employees and between their representatives, and of recognized procedures for the settlement of disputes.

The inclusion of the phrase 'by consideration of the well-being of the individual' reflected the values of the old school whilst the extension of the function to include 'methods and standards of remuneration' and 'the maintenance and effective use of recognized procedures for the settlement of disputes' embodied the developments of recent years.

The second post-war period has been very different from the first. In the last twenty years there has been a continuing labour shortage, a phenomenon hitherto unknown in Britain's peacetime industrial history. With a labour force in regular and, for the most part, secure employment and wage levels generally above subsistence level the need for welfare work amongst those in employment has virtually vanished. Also, welfare work has itself become specialized – probation, child care, almoning, family case work – each branch with its own professional training, so that even were an employee to report a personal problem, the personnel manager would be unlikely to consider himself competent to handle it but would be disposed to refer the employee to the appropriate specialist agency for help. The labour shortage has also awakened employers to the need for its most effective use, and the labour shortage has not been confined to the hourly paid. For manual, clerical, supervisory, technical and executive personnel demand has exceeded supply and, accordingly, the focus of personnel work has moved away from the hourly paid to the organization as a totality. Once again, the shift in emphasis was signalled by a change in name of the professional body, and in

1946 the Institute of Labour Management became the Institute of Personnel Management.

The post-war period has been marked also by a heightening of industrial relations activity at shop-floor level. The reasons for this increased activity may be complex[24] but one factor has certainly been the general employment situation. The labour shortage has enabled workers to change employers more easily than employers can change workers. The resultant change in the relative power of the two groups has reduced the effectiveness of formal managerial authority and has created the necessity on the part of managements to come to terms with employees to develop habits of frequent consultation and negotiation as normal management practice. The earlier generation of welfare workers would have warmly approved. This continuous interaction necessitated the nomination of a member of management to whom worker representatives could have ready access, at least in the first instance. The most obvious candidate for this role has been the personnel manager and the importance which the role has assumed, particularly in strongly unionized firms, has further enhanced his status.

Personnel management is now a secure part of the management function, and there has not been the dramatic drop in the number of persons employed in the field that was such a feature of the period following World War I. On the contrary, there has been a steady expansion, as the membership figures of the I.P.M. imply. A further step to consolidate the position was taken in 1955, when the Institute introduced an examination scheme as a necessary qualification for membership for all applicants under the age of thirty-five, with the intention of raising the age limit until eventually all admissions to full membership would be on the basis of formal examination. Yet, the confidence in the future of the profession which prompted this step seems to have waned and the age limit, instead of being successively raised, has been lowered to thirty, provided that the applicant has five years' successful experience in the personnel function of management. This limit may even be reduced to three years if the applicant has sufficient relevant experience in other fields.

The profession, it would seem, is not at peace and personnel managers have been described as an introspective lot.[25] Since the definition of personnel management, published in 1944, hardly a year has passed without either some reappraisal of the nature of the personnel function or the role of the personnel manager, or suggested amendments to the constitution of the Institute, or changes in the examination system and the qualifications required for membership.

To some extent the problem lies in the very nature of personnel work. It seems possible to define the personnel function of management in a manner that is generally satisfactory, but to define the functions of the personnel department and the role of the personnel manager is a much more difficult task. To what extent can the personnel function be centralized under the administrative control of a personnel manager? The process of management inevitably involves the management of personnel and without this responsibility a manager simply would not be a manager. For what then is the personnel manager to be responsible?

The practical answer has not been easy to find and varies considerably in detail from one firm to another. In general terms it may be said that the personnel manager administers those parts of the personnel function which may conveniently be centralized without diminishing his responsibility for the final result. In practice, of course, this is frequently impossible and the personnel manager is constantly brought into relationships with colleagues in which responsibility for some activity is shared, presenting both with the problems to which this sort of relationship is prone to give rise.

Another aspect of the personnel manager's role which is frequently stressed is that of adviser to his colleagues and to higher management when general policy is determined. To perform either properly he requires a high level of expertise and a depth of knowledge of personnel matters greater than that of any other manager in the organization. Yet the most rigorous form of training to which the profession aspires is a course lasting one academic year, together with a period of four weeks' practical experience in each of two personnel departments.

Recently the inadequacy of the personnel manager's training has been the subject of criticism from several sources. Knowledge of organizational behaviour has increased substantially in the last decade and the question has arisen as to the most appropriate means whereby this knowledge can be made available to the industrial executive. It has been cogently argued that the personnel manager is the managerial specialist best suited to fill the role of adviser in the application of the behavioural sciences.[26] It would seem that this suggestion is precisely what personnel managers have themselves been advocating over the years, yet it received a somewhat mixed reception. The explanation lies in the present state of development of personnel management practice. It is misleading to generalize about 'the role of the personnel manager', for the role varies widely from one organization to another. In some, the personnel manager occupies a position high in the organizational hierarchy and plays a full part in the determination of personnel policy; in others, he is responsible for the administration of those centralized services which have been entrusted to him and does so in the light of personnel policies which have been determined at a higher level; whilst in others, the role has hardly developed beyond that of the welfare worker. Personnel managers have long been accustomed to the phrase 'the specialist knowledge of the personnel manager' and hitherto the phrase has not given rise to difficulties, for each has placed upon it an interpretation to suit his own situation. However, when Lupton, in particular, spelled out in detail the nature of the specialist knowledge he considered necessary for the successful performance of the full, professional role, it was clear that the knowledge was possessed only by a small minority of practitioners.

There is a desire among personnel managers to become increasingly professional with the object, presumably, of earning recognition equal to that of an engineer or an accountant. Yet the attainment of such a professional status would necessitate an intellectual and theoretical training considerably more thorough than the majority of personnel posts require.

Personnel managers are now encountering the problem

familiar to every student of the behavioural sciences; namely, the consequences of the low status popularly accorded this particular branch of academic study. Every manager tends to regard himself as an authority on human behaviour and is consequently reluctant to regard this area of knowledge as an adequate basis for a professional specialism. Nor does the limited training of the personnel manager do much to dispel this tendency; indeed, probably the majority of personnel managers have not received any relevant formal training at all.

It would appear, therefore, that the recurrent concern with the role of the personnel manager goes deeper than merely establishing relationships with managerial colleagues that are organizationally satisfactory. Further advances towards professionalization must depend upon the willingness of personnel managers collectively to enforce more rigorous standards of qualification and upon their ability to exert a greater influence on the determination of their role. Whilst they continue to accept the various roles defined for them in practice by their managements, the disjunction of their actual and their potential roles will remain, and introspection will continue.

APPENDIX A

The attitude of women trade unionists to welfare work, 1917

On the 5 May, 1917, the Standing Joint Committee of Women's Industrial Organizations* called a conference on welfare work. The conference is one of the few occasions when trade unionists have collectively and formally committed themselves to a point of view on welfare work, and for this reason alone it is worth reprinting in full the following account of what took place.[27]

Miss Mary MacArthur declared 'that there is no word in the

---

*Women's Industrial Organizations included 'the Labour Party, the Women's Cooperative Guild, the Women's Trade Union League and the Railway Women's Guild'. (Elizabeth D. Newcomb, 'Industrial Welfare Work in Great Britain', *International Labour Review*, April, 1922, p. 556.)

English language more hated amongst the women workers of today than that of "Welfare"'. The chief objection they have to recent developments is that they find it difficult to understand the position of the welfare worker who tells them she is looking after their interests, but yet they know that she is paid by the employer. Necessarily all seek real welfare for themselves, but the workers do not feel that this is secured by the interference of the employers' representatives. It is for the welfare of human beings that they should be independent and be able to combine with their fellows, but most welfare workers discourage organization, and only try to increase output. Besides, welfare workers often interfere outside factory hours, and such interference with home life, leisure, and liberty undermines the workers' independence and self-reliance, and tends to make them forget that it is more important to be a good citizen than a good machinist. The workers have a right to the best conditions obtainable. Trade Unions are necessary to claim and maintain these conditions, and, having secured them and acting in combination, the workers can look after much for themselves which the welfare workers undertake to do.

It was stated that girls object to even a good welfare supervisor, because they think her goodness will not last, and they wonder what the game is. Instances of complaints made to welfare supervisors were given, many being of a most trivial nature, and all being individual complaints for the benefit of the individual, no attempt being made to improve the general well-being, nor was there any encouragement given to mutual action. A good supervisor tries to do everything for the girls, and they do nothing for themselves or each other, and she discourages organization. The bad supervisor disciplines and is always interfering. She interferes if the girls are out at night (especially if they are with a man in khaki), she interferes if boots are dirty, or blouses low at the neck, or stockings thin. But she hardly interferes as thoroughly as it is done in America, where the welfare supervisors fill up charts with particulars about the parents, religion, taste in books, etc., etc. In America this scheme is part of scientific management, where the essence of scientific management is centralization of authority and the subordination of the workers, and the employers take the view that when the workers become independent the welfare supervisor gives them back their authority. It is this unwarrantable interference on the part of the employers or their representatives that is objected to, not to what welfare workers do in looking after food, rest rooms, sanitation, etc. In New York the welfare supervisor has been long hated because she is paid by the employer, and she cannot serve two masters; and the position is becoming the same here. Really good welfare workers can rarely continue in their position. An enthusiastic welfare worker tried to get young girls off heavy machines, and protested against having the rates cut, but her job had to be given up, because supervisors are not expected to use their influence in this direction. A manager or superintendent is accepted by the girls as being for the boss, and being so recognized all is fair and square; but if a supervisor is said to be for the good of the girls, they are at once suspicious of her. Instances were given of places in America and in this country where there are no welfare supervisors, but good conditions are secured by Committees of Trade Union women looking after the shops, and if anything is wrong they see that it is put right. These workers are left free, so there is no more need to supervise the workers than for the workers to supervise the employers; but where welfare work exists some girls have said, 'We have to fight welfare for all we are worth.'

Another speaker emphasized the need for women to supervise the work of women. Frequently the whole control is in the hands of men, and it is most important to have women to refer to about girls' health, etc.; but this need not mean welfare supervisors, but forewomen or women superintendents, as they would understand the workers and the work of the workshop, and would be more satisfactory. It was at one time suggested that a supervisor should qualify by working in a factory; but in appointing supervisors social influence is the most important factor, university degrees are also often demanded, and the result is that many supervisors understand neither the work nor the workers.

It is scandalous that women without practical experience should have such positions (some think it is enough to have had experience managing domestic servants), and in this way the whole system of welfare supervision is discredited. If run by the State it might be satisfactory, if on the same lines as factory inspections; but probably it would be best managed by Trade Unions. There was plenty of evidence that the girls think it is really a dodge to get more out of them, and there is no doubt that welfare pays. For instance, an employer thought of increasing wages to retain the services of his employees, but instead gave them cocoa and a bun in the middle of the morning, and the output was greatly increased at a trifling expense.

It is all right to try and get a big output on the employers' side, but there is no need for hypocrisy and interference. The workers are right in trying to get all possible chances for human interest and a full life, and perhaps there is no need for the mistrust of employers – mistrust which prevents any good relations between welfare supervisors and workwomen. It was suggested that at the present time there is a place for welfare workers, but the best welfare supervisor should try and make herself unnecessary. At present girls are frequently hardly ready to take charge of their own interests, and need help and training to do so, though instances were given where girls are promoted from the bench and make most satisfactory forewomen. From this discussion and that on the other resolutions (factory inspection, housing of the workers, and the health of the younger employees), it was evident that many working women and girls are keen on managing their own concerns. The right Trade Union instinct is working, and they will soon be in line with the most advanced men, if not able to give them a bit of a lead.

The following Resolution was put and carried:

That this Committee declares its conviction that the establishment of a system of welfare workers in the service of employers can never materially increase the wellbeing of the workers as a whole; and that while it advocates the employment of women to supervise the work of women, it does not consider that such supervisors should be regarded as having any other functions than those of management.

It protests against any extension of control over the private lives of the workers, and asserts that in every factory the welfare, social and physical, of the workers is best looked after by the workers themselves.

With this object in view this Conference urges that in every workshop and factory there should be a Trades Union Committee, not only to look after wages and similar conditions, but to interest itself in all the concerns of the workers under their direction and to make representations thereupon, when necessary, to the management.

APPENDIX B

Changes in title of the association of welfare/personnel officers

1913 Welfare Workers' Association.
1917 Central Association of Welfare Workers.
1918 Central Association of Welfare Workers (Industrial).
1919 Welfare Workers' Institute.
1924 Institute of Industrial Welfare Workers.
1931 Institute of Labour Management.
1946 Institute of Personnel Management.

Annual membership of the Institute of Personnel Management, 1913–67[28]

1913	35	1934	546
1917	600	1935	616
1921	528	1936	616
1922	398	1937	613
1923	476	1938	725
1924	454	1939	779
1925	478	1940	812
1926	455	1941	1053
1927	423	1942	1725
1928	478	1943	2283
1929	487	1944	2812
1930	496	1945	2881
1931	509	1946	2896
1932	508	1947	2786
1933	513	1948	3036

1949	3239	1959	4308
1950	3337	1960	4497
1951	3536	1961	4938
1952	3086	1962	5362
1953	3807	1963	5730
1954	3767	1964	6084
1955	3905	1965	6510
1956	3979	1966	7298
1957	3993	1967	8163
1958	4119	1968	9302

NOTES

1. T. S. and M. B. Simey, *Charles Booth*, Oxford University Press, 1960, p. 69.

2. ibid., p. 116.

3. B. S. Rowntree, *Poverty: a Study of Town Life*, Macmillan, 1902, rev. ed., p. 117.

4. Mary M. Niven, 'The Beginnings of the Institute', *Personnel Management*, vol. XXXIX, No. 339, March, 1957, p. 28.

5. Rowntree & Co. Ltd house journal, *Cocoa Works Magazine*, March, 1921.

6. Budgett Meakin, *Model Factories and Villages*, Unwin, 1905, pp. 45–6. Meakin was quoting a Rowntree report. A fuller discussion of the work of a welfare department is given by E. Dorothea Proud, *Welfare Work*, Bell, 1916.

7. Notably Cadburys. See E. Cadbury, *Experiments in Industrial Organisation*, Part II, ch. V, Longmans Green, 1912.

8. Mary Niven, loc. cit., p. 30.

9. For a vivid and contemporary description of the trade union viewpoint, see Appendix A.

10. M. and A. D. McKillop, *Efficiency Methods*, Routledge, 1917, pp. 155–6.

11. Eleanor T. Kelly, ed., *Welfare Work in Industry*, Pitman, 1925, p. v.

12. A. G. Woodward, 'Personnel Management', *The Efficiency Magazine*, 1938, p. 10. Later (pp. 157–8) the author expresses some advanced thoughts on sex education and its place in personnel work.

13. See Daniel Bloomfield, ed., *Employment Management*, Pitman, 1920.

14. Paul H. Douglas, 'The Problem of Labor Turnover', *American Economic Review*, June, 1918. (Reprinted in Bloomfield, op. cit.) See also Sumner H. Slichter, *Turnover of Factory Labor*, Appleton, 1919.

15. E. Dorothea Proud, op. cit., pp. 59–60.

16. A. Marsh, *Industrial Relations in Engineering*, Pergamon Press 1965, p. 109. The attitudes and policies of the Federation are discussed in Chapter III. The unions continued to press, unsuccessfully, for the representation on the J.P.C.s of clerical and administrative workers.

17. G. R. Moxon, *The Growth of Personnel Management in Great Britain during the War 1939–1944*, Institute of Labour Management, 1945, reprinted from the *International Labour Review*, vol. L, No. 6, December, 1944.

18. Francis Williams, *Ernest Bevin*, Hutchinson, 1952, p. 227.

19. Annual Report of the Chief Inspector of Factories for the Year 1942, Cmd. 6471, H.M.S.O.

20. Annual Report of the Chief Inspector of Factories for the Year 1943, Cmd. 6563, H.M.S.O.

21. G. R. Moxon, op. cit., p. 29.

22. *Labour Management*, Institute of Labour Management, vol. XXV, No. 266, February–March, 1943.

23. *Labour Management*, Institute of Labour Management, vol. XXVI, No. 274, June–July, 1944.

24. For a useful summary discussion of the factors affecting the influence of shop stewards, see W. E. J. McCarthy, *The Role of Shop Stewards in British Industrial Relations*, Research Papers, No. 1., Royal Commission on Trade Unions and Employers' Associations, H.M.S.O., 1966, pp. 58–70.

25. See, for example, Anne Crichton, 'A Persistent Stereotype?', *Personnel Management*, Institute of Personnel Management, Vol. XLV, No. 366, December, 1963, pp. 160–7.

26. See, for example, M. P. Fogarty, 'An Independent Comment', *Personnel Management*, Institute of Personnel Management, Vol. XLV, No. 363, March, 1963, pp. 23–5.
T. Lupton, *Industrial Behaviour and Personnel Management*, Institute of Personnel Management, 1964.
Allan Flanders, 'The Future of Personnel Management', *Personnel Management*, Institute of Personnel Management, Vol. XLVI, No. 370, December 1964, pp. 137–41.

27. The account is quoted in S. Webb, *The Works Manager To-Day*, Longmans, 1917, pp. 142–6. A footnote gives the source as the *Journal of the Confederation of Iron and Steel Workers*, June, 1917.

28. The figures have been kindly supplied by the Institute of Personnel Management. Annual reports were not prepared until 1921 and figures before then are incomplete. For a full history of the Institute see Mary M. Niven, *Personnel Management, 1913–1963*, Institute of Personnel Management, 1967.

3.3 Seebohm Rowntree and Factory Welfare

DENNIS CHAPMAN

WHEN the contribution of a great man is assessed, the assumption is made that the world would have been a different, generally a worse, place without his work. This is almost impossible to demonstrate. In most fields of science there are often many working to the same end and chance may decide who will get the credit in popular histories: in our culture we seek heroes rather than social processes. Moreover, few men work alone and many more owe their fame to the work of their colleagues, their contribution having been to select able men to assist them. In such cases we tend to remember the leader and forget the rest. Again, we like our heroes to be all of a piece, consistent, virtuous and successful in all fields: they rarely are.

Here, it will be argued that in one field at least, Rowntree's contribution was unique. No other social scientist in 1899 was looking at the problem of the consequences of inadequate wages in the same practical way as he was, and his analysis of the consequences brought about some important social changes earlier than might otherwise have happened. In other fields he was sometimes a leader in this country, often through being the most persuasive member of a group. In some cases his contribution was to describe or formulate a practice which was already known and to advance it as a policy or social movement. In others his skill was to create an institution which gave permanent life to an idea. Much of his success was in choosing able collaborators and assisting them to develop new knowledge through experiment and then encouraging them to publish the results.

In most sciences, progress is made by specialists attacking problems in a well-defined field. This is true in management also; the work of Taylor, Gilbreth, Urwick and many others displays this fact. With Rowntree the situation was quite unlike this. He was a member of the Society of Friends and he was a Liberal. His father was a social reformer and social investigator in his own right and a relative on his mother's side, Frederick Seebohm, was a distinguished economic historian. In his family business he was subject to many, but not conflicting, pressures and presented with a wide range of problems. His great gift was an ability to see the total industrial and commercial situation as an organic unity.

This is not to say that he was always successful or consistent or that he approached all problems as a scientist. His policies in some fields derived more from his experience in the Rowntree family than from an objective appraisal of the situation, and in other matters Quaker influences were dominant. In yet others the policies of the Liberal party which he helped to create tended to direct his thinking.

His approach to problems was eclectic and he often lacked discrimination. He was most able where the problem could be dealt with in the relatively simple physical and mechanical terms of 19th century natural science. His brief period at Owens College, Manchester equipped him for this, yet he was compelled to make his greatest contribution in the vague field of what is now called 'human relations'. This in spite of two contradictory features in his intellectual equipment: a lack of knowledge of statistical method and a fear that sentiment might prevent a rational appraisal of a situation.

In his practice he could be perceptive, recognizing the importance of power in relation to trade unions; yet he did not see so clearly the problems created by the struggle for power within the management structure of his own company. In his social surveys he recognized the primacy of the family as the unit of discourse and realized its implications for wages policy and social legislation, yet he failed to perceive the problems of the family, even the Quaker family, in management structure. He spent much of his energy in demonstrating the importance of consultation and frankness in industrial relations, yet was involved in complex cloak-and-dagger negotiations with trade union leaders in the railway strike of 1919, and in the coal dispute and the general strike of 1926. He regarded this last situation as contradictory; had he a theoretical sociology rather than an intuitive grasp of sociological processes, he might not have been so concerned. Indeed, discussion with him made it evident that he had the capacity to describe the role of power in the trade union leadership in such a way that the theoretical implications were clear. At the same time his feeling that these processes were 'wrong' from an ethical standpoint caused him to destroy many important documents and letters which would have displayed these processes, lest they fell into the hands of his biographer. (The author of this essay spent a melancholy fortnight feeding the precious raw material of social history into the stove at the Homestead, York, under the eagle eyes of Rowntree and his collaborator and friend, Frank Stuart.)

He was remarkably fortunate in his choice of collaborators and co-directors, of whom many worked with him throughout his life, yet he was restrained in his emotional relationships with them because these were more important to him than he was willing to admit. Thus his disappointment with the remarkable I. T. Trebish Lincoln made him leave untouched for a quarter of a century the schedules of what would have been the most extensive and probably most remarkable social survey in history – a study of European agriculture, holding by holding – and finally destroy the records because they had been the work of this extraordinary but venal man.

Most writers on Rowntree's contribution to the sciences of industrial production treat his poverty studies as marginal to their interests, but to Rowntree himself they were central and he saw his life's work as evolutionary, a steady expansion towards the study of all those factors which contribute to man's capacity to produce. The rough order of his studies was the influence of nutrition and shelter on the capacity to work, then problems of morale, problems of health and fatigue, social influences on work, the physical organization of the task, selection training and education, the social structure of the factory, the special problems of juveniles and women, the functional organization of management, the professions of management and their organization, and the trades union movement. Once a topic had been developed it remained a continuous interest. To this list of subjects of interest must be added practice as the head of the largest organization in the field of what would now be called personnel management – Director of the Welfare Department of the Ministry of Munitions from 1916 – and the rebuilding and expansion of the family business. At the same time, from the 1920s onwards, through visits abroad, correspondence, the organization of conferences, the introduction to Britain of other pioneers in management and above all a continuous process of innovation and experiment in the cocoa works at York, he created in effect a university of management.

For most of the 19th century, poverty had been regarded as a moral problem. The influence of Malthus had helped to create a stereotype of the poor as being morally inferior to the middle classes and likely, if given material aid, to revert to idleness or to breed to excess. Charles Booth's great study of London was written in the atmosphere of the beliefs of the latterday Malthusians, the Charity Organization Society, and his main findings, a classification of the population of London by income, were overlaid with moral criticism. In consequence he turned to the study of the practice of religion in London as holding the key to the moral problem and proposed as his principle administrative solution, pensions for those whose age made it impossible for them to support themselves at work and who by definition could not have their will to work undermined by assistance.

Rowntree began his study *Poverty: a Study of Town Life*[1] by following Booth both in his classification and in his appraisal of worthiness of the families he visited. He likewise studied church attendance and the public house. Having done this he was profoundly dissatisfied with the value of the evidence as a guide to action and he described to the author when he was working on his second great York study *Poverty and Progress*[2] how he rethought the whole problem in terms of the chemistry he had learned at Manchester. Quite dramatically he turned away from 19th century philanthropy and piety to the chemistry of Justus von Liebig (1803–1873). Liebig's influence was twofold: not only had he studied the chemical and physical laws of animal life, but equally he had elucidated the physiology of plants. He laid the foundations of a scientific agriculture. Rowntree determined to break through the ideological barrier by treating human beings for the purpose of study simply as animals and measuring input and output as a physical problem in calories. This approach made it impossible for his findings to be refuted on 'moral' grounds. At the same time, with Liebig in mind, he noted for future study the problem of the nutrition of the urban worker as dependent upon scientific agriculture and an efficient transport system.

Rowntree based his examination of the condition of the working classes of York on the latest data about human nutritional needs and on some controlled experiments of the effects of different quantities of food on the weight and morale of prisoners who were engaged on manual work in Peterhead Prison. He established that 43·4 per cent of the working class in York had incomes insufficient to provide for mere physical existence at the 'animal' level. He found that the main causes of poverty were low wages of men in regular work and the burden of large numbers of children. He not only showed this as a problem at a moment of time, but he also demonstrated the effects of differences in income and maintenance costs through the life cycle of the family. For the first time were revealed the minimum costs of the production and reproduction of labour.

In his published study he was content to leave the discussion at this point but in private and in his political life, which was almost always behind the scenes, he demonstrated that wages below the poverty line made it impossible for the worker to make physical effort except at the expense of his body weight or his health, that income above this line produced a vastly increased output of energy per unit of income and that it was certain that increases of wages far above those thought to be desirable would be profitable, if only manufacturers could understand the simple physiological processes involved. Eventually, he persuaded the Liberals to introduce, in 1909, minimum wage legislation to compel employers to pay higher wages that would make their businesses more profitable and that would ensure the security of the supply of labour.

Although in *Poverty* Rowntree had adopted the criterion of

'mere physical efficiency', he had, by listing the factors that he had specifically included, indicated those he believed contributed to the effectiveness of labour. The list included the concept of morale. These factors he explored in a family budget study made in 1918, *The Human Needs of Labour*,[3] and in what was in essence a manifesto for the reorganization of his business, *The Human Factor in Business*,[4] published in 1921. The second of these was revised in 1925 and 1938 and new editions became progress reports on his experiments in the cocoa works. The first was redone in 1937 to take account of the change in social conditions. This practice, which extended to Rowntree's poverty studies and his investigations into housing and agriculture, shows his belief that scientific study of human affairs must be continuous and must respond to every change in social conditions: there can be no dogmatic or final solutions.

In the period after *Poverty* had been published, Rowntree continued his social investigations publishing his study of Belgian agriculture and industry, *Land and Labour: Lessons from Belgium*,[5] in 1910 and commencing his monumental enquiry into European agriculture. In 1911 he published with Bruno Lasker a descriptive study of unemployment in York in which, again following the line he had taken in *Poverty*, he stressed the importance of maintaining the capacity of the unemployed man for work and the necessity of training for new skills.

Rowntree differed from other students of industrial problems in that he saw strong trade unions as an essential part of the functioning structure of industry, advocated collective bargaining and deplored the relatively narrow craft basis of British Trades Unionism. Later, in his practice at the cocoa works, he regarded the shop steward as an essential part of the social structure of the factory. In this he was not concerned to replace 'conflict' with 'peace' but recognized that different interests could be accommodated in a continuous process of dialogue, in which, subject only to the effects of outside social and economic pressures, a near optimum solution of problems could be achieved, independently of the wills of the different parties. This attitude was in direct contrast to the authoritarian practice of most employers, including many 'philanthropic' or 'model' employers, and to many exponents of management theories based upon 'rational' or 'mechanical' beliefs.

In his working life, Rowntree was the first labour director to be appointed in his father's new model factory opened in 1890. Here he had the task of interpreting his father's social policies. The policies of Joseph Rowntree were liberal and enlightened but by no means unique: much of his philosophy and his practice had been anticipated by Robert Owen and others like him in the first quarter of the 19th century. Titus Salt in 1851 had perhaps an even more comprehensive vision and Lever and Cadbury had pioneered practices that he later followed. The works had the 48 hour week, a suggestion scheme, a works doctor and dentist, a sick club, a pension scheme and, before long, a model village. In only one feature was it distinctive; it had in addition to supervisors mainly concerned with production, 'social helpers', first women and then men and women to care for the health, welfare and social behaviour of the operatives. These were in due course put into the charge of an experienced and qualified man and woman who reported to Seebohm Rowntree as labour director. This pattern of having direct representation of the personnel staff on the board avoided many of the problems that personnel departments experienced in firms where Rowntree's practice was initiated without his understanding of the nature of the social structure of the firm.

The emphasis on social behaviour may in the present context appear strange but it was regarded by both father and son as important, and later during World War I, Rowntree made it an issue of vital national importance. In discussing this matter Rowntree argued that the woman in domestic service was receiving training not only in household management, but in dress, speech, manners and morals. She lived in a regulated and protected environment and her health and nutrition were safeguarded by the family of which she was part; he contrasted this with the kind of life in industry depicted by the journalist Robert Sherard in his book *White Slaves of England*.[6] The social helper was to provide for the factory girl some part of the protection and education that the domestic servant enjoyed in the Rowntree home.

In 1915 the Lloyd George administration had established a 'Health of Munition Workers Committee' and its first reports showed the need to add to the factory inspectorate a new body to protect the interests of the vastly-increased numbers of women who had entered industry, a high proportion of whom had moved away from their homes and families. Rowntree was appointed the director of the new body, the welfare department of the Ministry of Munitions.

His work in this new department took many forms, two of which at least are notable. Firstly, he extended the work of the committee that had given birth to his department, by creating a unit to conduct scientific research into industrial productivity, and he took measures to prevent the demoralization of women and young persons who were divorced from their homes, working long hours, and earning high wages. Some of the results of the researches appeared in a now almost forgotten classic, *The Health of the Munition Worker*,[7] which he edited. Most striking amongst its many findings was the demonstration that the increase in working hours, undertaken from motives of the highest patriotism, reduced the output of munitions, increased their cost and injured the health of the operative. Rowntree lived to see the same misguided policy repeated in World War II with identical results. The inquiries made under his direction led to the creation of a permanent research organization, the 'Industrial Fatigue Research Board' (later the 'Industrial Health Research Board'), and to a widespread awareness of the importance of Industrial Psychology. In turn this awareness was channelled with Rowntree's aid into the creation of the 'National Institute of Industrial Psychology'.

Secondly, Rowntree began the task of introducing provisions for the welfare of women and young workers into industry. One of the appointments he made was that of the Reverend Robert Hyde who at the end of the war founded with Rowntree's support and guidance, the 'Industrial Welfare Society'.

The existence of a large munitions factory and its associated hostels near Gretna outside Carlisle presented a problem and the possibility of an experiment. High wages, social isolation and lack of supervision had created conditions in which the weekend saturnalia had reached the dimensions of a national scandal. Central in the situation was the public house. Joseph Rowntree in his *The Temperance Question and Social Reform*[8] had shown how under suitable management the Inn could be a positive influence for good and bodies like the People's Refreshment House Association and the Trust Houses had shown in practice that refreshment need not be synonymous with debauchery. The government, under pressure from Rowntree's department, took over the licensed premises from the brewers, appointed managers whose salaries did not depend on sales, instructed them in social responsibility, improved the amenities of the houses, widened the variety of refreshments sold, and in months transformed the situation – an act of nationalization which has not been criticized or repealed in the near half century which has followed.

In this period Rowntree extended his interests in the scientific study of work, maintained his interest in welfare but extended it further into the community and began the process of promoting the institutionalization of aspects of management specialization which might in turn create the professional practitioners that industry would need. This process included the creation of university courses for welfare workers. Always he made his case by demonstration rather than by exhortation.

As the war ended, Rowntree began to return to the cocoa works where his father had begun to develop processes of consultation which were later to develop under Rowntree's control into the distinctive characteristics of his management theory.

A phase in his career ended in 1921. He had published in 1918 a slight, popularly written exposition of minimum wages designed to provide the basis for a civilized life, under the title of *The Human Needs of Labour*,[3] and in 1921 had written *The Human Factor in Business*[4] which described the policy of father and son in the cocoa works. *The Human Factor* was written at a time of great industrial and political conflict and was addressed to employers to urge them to recognize the need for social change.

He wrote 'it is well to remember that much social legislation consists in making generally compulsory what voluntary experiment has shown to be desirable', and amongst the influences responsible for the changing attitude of the working classes to bad industrial conditions, he noted 'they have exchanged notes upon industrial conditions with Americans and men from the dominions, and now they ask why they should submit to conditions which compare unfavourably with those of other workers'. Soon after the publication of *The Human Factor* Rowntree himself went to the United States 'to exchange notes upon industrial conditions with Americans'.

The Human Factor epitomized Rowntree's beliefs and experience at the end of the first war. His chapter headings were in this order: wages, hours, security of life, good working conditions and the joint control of industry. He had established the importance of adequate wages to efficiency and morale. He had investigated the effectiveness of financial incentives. In wartime he had discovered the approximate level of optimum working hours but had willingly and in consultation with his workers, reduced hours at the cocoa works below this and had reaped the advantages of the incentive of leisure. From this time he had an increasing interest in the importance of leisure, both as a moral and as an industrial problem. The provisions for security anticipated those of the modern welfare state, and included unemployment insurance to supplement that of the state but conditional upon the employee making provision through his trade union. The scheme was particularly impressive in that the unemployed man could draw up to 75 per cent of his normal earnings. Rowntree had no fear that men would prefer idleness to work. Other benefits were paid in sickness, in old age and to widows.

On working conditions, he describes all the features of the working environment which we should now accept as best practice – colour, light, ventilation, noise reduction, etc. He dealt with selection, training and recruiting policy. Here and there, however, the Victorian peeps through: 'great care is taken to avoid putting boys into blind alley jobs. Where it seems likely to occur we try to arrange for the work to be done by girls.' Again 'married women are not employed, save in very exceptional circumstances'. It is worth noting that the policy on blind alley jobs broke down in the thirties when, under the influence of the very pattern of wage regulation that Rowntree had pioneered, juveniles were dismissed at 18 when they became eligible for higher wages. In spite of his intentions, Rowntree could not opt out of the great depression.

Rowntree's system for joint control in industry was in part a response to demands from the trade unions, in part a protective response to socialism and in part an expression of his 'conviction' of the importance of status and valuation as a motive force in the industrial worker. This was a development of the concept of morale and was associated in his mind with both education and morality – the concept of the 'dignity of labour' was very real to him. Joint control in the cocoa works had two features which are worthy of note; firstly, in practice, the elected members were all trade unionists, and shop stewards were members of departmental councils ex-officio, thus the joint control was trade union based; and secondly, the scope of the business extended beyond the familiar subjects of safety, working conditions, complaints and the like to such matters as piece rates, the length of the working week, annual holidays, the appointment of overlookers and the proposed appointment of a works psychologist. The system was organized after experiment, with departmental councils and a central council.

Summarizing this experience, Rowntree concluded that he believed his policy to be 'the only way in which business can be successfully carried on under modern conditions'.

The problem of modernizing the cocoa works, however, raised other issues which presented personal as well as practical and theoretical problems. Control was still substantially in the hands of Joseph Rowntree who saw the future of the business as essentially family-based in its management, relatively small and run on personal rather than policy lines; moreover the war reduced the effectiveness of both management and the operative force.

Rowntree's visit to America was a preparation for the organizational changes he knew would be essential when he took over from his father. This took place in 1923. Rowntree felt so strongly about the differences of view he had had with his aged father that he made a rule that the chairman of the cocoa works must retire on his 65th birthday. It was ironic that it was this rule which compelled Rowntree himself to relinquish control at the very height of his powers.

Rowntree's first visit to the United States was important in many ways. Most important was that he made the acquaintance of pioneers in management, some of whom had approached the problem of human relations in the same comprehensive way. Henry Dennison became a lifelong friend and correspondent as did Mary Parker Follett.[9] From the visit Rowntree learned much about technical efficiency in management although much that he saw in mass production horrified him. He was reinforced in his conviction of the need for specialist, professional functional management and above all he realized the possibility of the conference as a method of management education. The conference, combined with the exchange of experience and the result of experiment, was to be a major activity for the rest of his working life.

Although the visit to the United States crystallized these ideas in Rowntree's mind, they were part of a pattern which was already well established. From his earliest days Rowntree had participated in adult education. He had introduced lectures into the running of the cocoa works, and conferences within the plant on specific problems had led to their institutionalization in the works councils. In politics, housing and in agriculture he was the master of the symposium and many excellent reports were produced by this means. He had in 1918 and again in 1919 organized conferences and schools of employers and managers.

Upon his return, Rowntree began the work of modernizing the management of the cocoa works. He replaced the family-based structure with functional specialists who were without experience in the confectionery industry, and who would decide policy on the basis of research and experiment, rather than by reference to what Joseph Rowntree would have done in the circumstances. These specialists, who included Oliver Sheldon, William Wallace,

C. H. Northcott and, above all, Colonel Lyndall Urwick, were not only experts in their fields, but had the capacity to write about their experiments and their practice. The cocoa works became in their hands a laboratory of management as well as a centre for the diffusion of knowledge by being open to visitors and critics. It was the base for two allied activities, the Oxford Management Research Conferences which settled down to two meetings a year at Balliol College, and the Management Research Groups, a means of exchange of experience between non-competing firms.

These two activities pioneered the development of management studies and education which brought about the establishment of the British Institute of Management in 1948.

The influence of the cocoa works publications was equally far reaching and was especially important in personnel management. The publication of *Personnel Management: its Scope and Practice*[10] by C. H. Northcott in 1945 marked the beginning of a new chapter in what had been known up to that point as 'labour management' – the change from the economist's 'labour' to the 'person' of the sociologist and psychologist was a major achievement of the Rowntree school. The book became a manual of practice and a textbook for training and in due course the Institute changed its name to acknowledge the change of outlook.

After this phase in Rowntree's activities the pattern was largely set: from then on it was to proceed by expansion. Two new provisions were ultimately introduced, family allowances and profit sharing, neither of which had the direct relevance to productivity of the earlier schemes, but were introduced in the context of social justice.

In only one matter was there activity outside the established factory-based process; this was industrial conciliation in the great strikes of the twenties. Rowntree believed that it was possible by rational discussion with neutrals and by exposition and persuasion to find a common basis for agreement. This brought him into the quasi-political field again and he was involved in many negotiations, often secret, and sometimes dubious, from which he was unable to create anything of lasting value or of theoretical interest.

The final stages of Rowntree's long intellectual life saw him returning to the study of the standard of living. A new edition of *The Human Needs of Labour* published in 1937 paved the way for a new survey of York on classic lines – *Poverty and Progress*[2] (1941). This work, which stands comparison with his masterpiece *Poverty*, returned to the problems of leisure and contained echoes of the temperance-demoralization ideas that he took from his father and found relevant in World War I; he foresaw the approaching adjustment problems of affluence.

Unhappily the extension of this interest in *English Life and Leisure*[11] (1951) was disastrous. For 'rational' reasons Rowntree had, on leaving York, dispersed all his research team except F. D. Stuart, one of the greatest social investigators of this century. Stuart died and there was no one to maintain the continuity of method and thought or to insist on a scholarly discipline. The result was a largely unrepresentative and anecdotal picture of Britain in moral decline.

It would be impossible to summarize Rowntree's contribution; there is almost nothing in the modern practice of business in which his influence is not present and every feature of the welfare state owes much to his research and advocacy. I acknowledge the debt I owe to Professor Asa Briggs's writings in the preparation of this chapter.[12]

READINGS FROM SEEBOHM ROWNTREE,
The Human Factor in Business

Democracy and efficiency[13]

Broadly, it may be said that in framing that policy our objective has been to raise the status of the workers of all ranks from that of servants to that of cooperators; in other words, to introduce into the management of the business, in all matters directly affecting the workers, as great a measure of democracy as possible without lowering efficiency. But as one of the questions considered in this book is whether, in the matter of status, as in other matters, it is possible to afford to the workers conditions as good as they might reasonably expect under any other industrial system, let us, before describing the steps we have taken to improve the workers' status, ask what kind of status workers might reasonably expect to enjoy under a socialist or communist system of industry, for it is one of these which they have in mind when they think of alternatives to capitalism. Not until we know this can we say whether it would be possible to give them as good a status under capitalism.

In seeking an answer to our question, we cannot divorce a claim for a good status from the necessity for efficiency in industry, for if industry is inefficiently conducted the standard of life of the workers will necessarily be low. They will not be satisfied with an industrial system unless it affords them both a good status and a satisfactory standard of living. Bearing this in mind, I suggest that most thoughtful workers would accept the following propositions:

(1) Under any system of industry, every enterprise must be conducted efficiently. This involves that, so far as possible, every employed person, whether an executive or a manual worker, shall work at the task and under the conditions which will enable him to make his greatest contribution to the success of the enterprise.

(2) No business can be efficiently managed by mass meetings of the workers. The workers must be divided into those whose duty it is to give orders and those whose duty it is to obey them. Orders must be given by individuals, not by committees.

(3) The 'order givers' should be selected by those best qualified to do so, and they should be chosen because among all the available candidates for the posts they are those who can make the greatest contribution to the success of the enterprise.

(4) Managerial policy should be devised by those best qualified to do so. Thus in the case of large enterprises the financial policy should be devised by financial experts, the marketing and sales policies by marketing and selling experts, the labour policy by experts on labour questions, and so on. It will be noted that in framing these propositions I assume that the organization of industry must be such as will enable it to function efficiently.

Role of the unions[14]

While unions, quite naturally and rightly, seek to secure the best terms they can for workers in matters of wages, hours, and general working conditions, I have almost invariably, and always in the case of the National Union of General and Municipal Workers, found them willing to look at both sides of a question. We have succeeded in discussing any differences that might arise between us in a friendly and reasonable spirit, and hope that both parties have always felt that fair and reasonable decisions had been reached.

Of course, if reason is expected from a trade union, reason must be offered first. An employer who does not recognize the right of the workers to negotiate with him about any matter concerned with their wages or working conditions on even terms through their union officials, or who seeks to dictate terms to the workers, either individually or through their unions, cannot expect them to show a reasonable spirit in negotiation.

To summarize the part which trade unions play in building up a spirit of cooperation between capital and labour, it may be said that they help to lay the foundations on which the structure of cooperation may be built. But after they have done all that is possible, an enormous amount remains to be done in each individual factory, and the extent to which this is successful will depend, first of all, upon whether the methods adopted are wisely chosen, and, secondly, on whether those seeking to operate them are actuated by a truly cooperative spirit. I pass, therefore, from the work of the trade unions to that of steps taken in our own factory to develop democratic methods of management.

As already stated, the object of the directors is and has for long been to introduce as much democracy into the management of the business as can be done without lowering efficiency. They want to reach a point where every one employed, no matter in what position, not only regards himself as a cooperator in a joint effort to render the business successful, but regards every one else in the same light. It is an ideal which is difficult of attainment, but both the management and the rank and file workers have for years been striving together to advance on the road to its attainment, and they are encouraged by the results so far obtained.

The first essential to the creation of a spirit of cooperation is full and frank consultation on all matters affecting the workers' daily life within the factory. This is not only desirable in itself, but forms a preliminary step to any more specific sharing of responsibility.

Can industry afford higher real wages for low-paid workers?[15]

It is true that, in many cases, to raise minimum wages tomorrow by a substantial amount would be impossible, since industry could not adapt itself to so sudden a change. But I suggest that all employers should definitely set before them, as an end to be achieved with the least possible delay, the payment of such wages as will allow their lowest paid workers to live in health and reasonable comfort. It is a mistake for them to leave all the pressure in connexion with wages advances to be made by the workers. Of course, there are already many employers who are not in favour of low-paid labour, and who pay all they can, but this should be the policy not only of individuals, but employers as a class. The adoption of such an attitude would revolutionize industrial relations, and do much to allay labour unrest.

There is no single specific which will render generally possible the payment of adequate minimum wages. The desired end may be achieved by adopting one of three courses, or, more often, by adopting more than one of these at the same time. The three courses are to increase selling prices, to reduce profits, and to reduce costs.

The first method tends to defeat its own end, for it raises the cost of living, and thus lowers the value of wages. It is justified, however, when selling prices in a particular industry are too low in relation to other costs and services produced in comparable conditions of efficiency. In such circumstances there is a case for joint effort by the different employers in the industry to raise wages. With regard to the second, the only fund available is the 'surplus profits': i.e. profits over and above what are necessary to keep the business financially sound. Of course there are industries which habitually make surplus profits, but I think that unprejudiced persons will agree that the problem of how to raise real wages cannot be solved merely by reducing profits. Turning now to the third method, the wealth produced per worker depends partly on his own exertions and partly on those of others. So far as his own exertions are concerned, there is no doubt that they represent a potential source of increased wealth which varies greatly from worker to worker and from trade to trade. Many workers are not doing their best and will tell you so quite frankly. It is the task of those who are responsible for the administration of industry on its human side to seek out the causes for this, and to find appropriate remedies. I refer to this question frequently in succeeding chapters, and will only say here that the causes are often deep-rooted. Among them are the fear of 'working oneself out of a job', the risk of rate-cutting in the case of piece-workers, and the belief that no advantage will accrue to the worker as a result of increased effort.

Turning to the possibility of increasing the production of wealth by means other than the exertion of the wage-earners, it will not be disputed that many factories are still running on inefficient lines. Much of the machinery is antiquated, the buildings are badly planned, the staff and workers are ill-trained, and the work badly organized. In such cases the profits earned are often inconsiderable, even when wages are low, and any request for higher wages is met by the argument that the industry cannot afford them. What is here needed is a critical examination of each process, and of the organization of the factory as a whole to see whether the profit margin can be increased. Only after a minute examination, on these lines, is an employer really in a position to say whether his industry can or cannot afford to pay higher wages. I suggest that the aim of every employer should be to provide equipment and organization which will enable every worker to earn good wages, and to establish a relationship with the workers which will encourage each of them to take the fullest advantage of these opportunities. I have not been a lifetime in business without realizing how difficult this is, but if experience has made me conscious of the difficulty, it has also impressed on me the importance of overcoming it, and has strengthened my belief that it is possible to do so. I must refer the reader to other books for a discussion of methods of business efficiency. The matter is only mentioned here because I want to press home the fact that failure to render a business thoroughly efficient injures not only the shareholders but the workers.

Labour department[16]

Although it is important to surround workers with good material conditions, it is even more important to create and maintain what perhaps I can best describe as a 'personal environment' which will encourage each individual to be and to do his best. The ideal at which we should aim is that every one should work with as much enjoyment, energy, and intelligence as if he were working on his own account. This, of course, is a very high ideal, which probably has never been realized, though I have occasionally visited factories which very nearly attained it. In seeking to create such a spirit, the first thing is for those in positions of responsibility to recognize that the workers are something more than profit-producing instruments. They are not simply a means to an ulterior end. On the contrary, their personal welfare is an important end in itself, though not the only one for which the factory exists. Much, probably most, of the unrest from which industry has suffered for so long, and is suffering so acutely at present, is due to the failure on the part of employers to recognize this fact. Largely through lack of clear and independent thinking, we have been inclined to look upon those working in our factories in the mass, and to speak of them as 'hands'. We have not had imagination enough mentally to separate the mass into its constituent units. We have failed to realize that 500 'hands' are really 500 individuals, each with a personality as sensitive to its environment as yours or mine.

Now it is just as fatal an error to treat workers in the mass as it would be to treat machinery in the mass – a thing no one would dream of doing. Quite apart from the human aspect of the question, and for the moment considering the workers solely as instruments of production, such an impersonal way of regarding them is a serious flaw in our method of business administration. Every worker should be looked upon as an individual and encouraged to contribute his individual quota to the success of the firm. This is the policy we naturally adopt when we work with two or three persons, but can it be carried out in a large factory where hundreds or thousands are employed? Yes, it can, but only as the result of a considered policy supported by an adequate organization. The managing director, or works manager in a large factory, cannot give the necessary detailed attention to this side of the business any more than he can personally attend to each machine, and so, if it is not to be neglected, adequate steps must be taken to look after the labour force, just as they are taken to look after the function of production or sales.

In our factory all labour matters, and by that I mean almost all the matters discussed in this book, are under the control of one of the directors. He is responsible for seeing that the 'human factor in business' is not neglected and that a progressive labour policy is adopted. On him devolves the responsibility for thinking out and developing the company's labour policies, and after he has secured the approval of the board, it is for him to see that they are carried out.

But although the post of labour director is by no means a sinecure, he has other duties to perform, and it necessarily follows that the day-to-day management of the department must be undertaken by its manager. The labour manager should be a man having true sympathy with the workers, but he must not be a sentimentalist. He must see the point of view of the management as well as that of the workers, for if he is to succeed in his work, he must win the confidence not only of the workers but also of the management. Indeed, these qualities are required by all those in the labour department who have to deal with the workers. Having regard to the importance which the directors attach to labour matters, it follows that the labour manager's position is one of real authority. He ranks as one of the half-dozen or so functional managers outside of the York Board.

He is responsible for all wage and labour questions in the works, and for all educational and recreational activities. By reason of his expert knowledge, he is the responsible officer associated with the labour director in all specially important negotiations with trade unions, and he himself deals with the unions on ordinary matters. His two chief assistants are the men's and women's employment officers, who are responsible among other things for the engagement and dismissal of all labour, and its transference, when necessary, from one department to another. In addition, he controls the wages section, all recreational and educational activities, the medical and psychological departments, and the canteen.

Education[17]

The adoption of an up-to-date policy will depend on at least two factors for its success: one is the capacity of its administrative staff to rise to the demands made upon it, and the other is the degree of intelligent understanding shown by the rank and file workers. The education of administrative officials and of the more ambitious or responsible rank and file workers has, therefore, become a necessity in a well-equipped factory. The former have been termed the fourth agent of production. As a result in the increase in the size of business, they have come to play an increasingly important part as an intermediary between employers and workers. They have thus the difficult function of interpreting a firm's policy so as to maintain the highest possible efficiency, and at the same time to promote a spirit of goodwill and loyalty in the workers. Leadership is thus an essential quality in an administrator. I venture to think that in the past not enough stress has been laid on the value of the art of leadership when appointing administrative officers, nor have employers been sufficiently anxious to develop that art after their appointment. It has been too often assumed that a thorough knowledge of the technical processes involved was the supreme necessity, and that if this were associated with the power to hustle, little more need be asked. Much of the unrest in industry today is due to a lack of tact and of a nice sense of justice on the part of the staff, from charge-hands to directors. They have sought to drive when they should have been leading, and they have been satisfied with rough justice instead of insisting on as complete justice as possible in each case. The somewhat rough-and-ready method of handling labour which has so often done duty in the past will not serve us in the future, any more than will the old rule-of-thumb industrial processes where science is ignored and costing systems are unknown. Both are becoming relics of the past. Just as we must give science a more prominent place in the development of industrial processes, so we must learn to handle the human problems of industry with more intelligent sympathy and tact. We must induce men to do their best by encouragement, inspiration, and example.

But here we are face to face with a practical difficulty. It is comparatively easy to find foremen with good technical qualifications and the capacity to 'hustle', but it is difficult to find men who can inspire and lead. Yet such men must be found or made, for the plain fact is that workmen nowadays refuse to be driven. Unless we can learn to lead them industry will suffer severely. I suggest, therefore, that those responsible for the administration of business should realize the great importance of surrounding themselves with a body of administrative officers possessing not only the necessary technical qualifications but the power of leading men. Obviously the first essential in securing this end is to select for administrative posts those men who, besides the necessary technical qualifications, have tact and sympathy. But that is not enough. They should be told quite clearly what are the ideals of the directors as to the way in which the business should be administered, and the relations which should be established and maintained between the management and the men. Emphasis should be laid on the need for absolute justice and the importance of courtesy, and a high ideal held out regarding the part which a foreman or other officer may play in creating a right 'atmosphere' in the works. The great changes which have come over industry during the past few years should be explained, and the staff made to realize how much greater are the claims made upon it now than formerly.

Authority and participation[18]

I think our experiments do show that it is possible, without lowering efficiency, to accord to the workers a status as good as they would enjoy under any alternative system, and if I am right, then I think this is a matter of real importance, for I am convinced that the workers attach far more importance to the question of their status in industry than is generally supposed. As I pointed out in a preceding chapter, no industry can be efficiently administered by mass meetings, nor indeed by committees. There must be 'order givers' and 'order takers', and discipline must be maintained. The beliefs at present held by many as to the measure of industrial democracy which would be enjoyed under a socialistic or communistic system would prove, in practice, to be illusory.

With regard to remuneration and working conditions, I am satisfied that it is *possible* under capitalism to provide conditions which compare not unfavourably with those which could be expected under any other system, but it is no satisfaction to the workers to know that a given system of industry is *capable* of providing good conditions unless, in fact, it does so. Taking industrial conditions as a whole, they fall far short of what they might and should be, and it is this fact which is rightly causing discontent among the workers.

NOTES

1. *Poverty: a Study of Town Life*, Macmillan, 1901.
2. *Poverty and Progress*, Longmans, 1941.
3. *The Human Needs of Labour*, Nelson, 1918.
4. *The Human Factor in Business*, Longmans, 1921.
5. *Land and Labour: Lessons from Belgium*, Macmillan, 1910.

6. R. H. Sherard, *White Slaves of England*, Bowden, 1897.

7. *The Health of the Munition Worker*, H.M.S.O., 1917.

8. Joseph Rowntree, *The Temperance Question and Social Reform*, Hodder & Stoughton, 1899.

9. See Part 4.2 for a fuller description of the work of Mary Parker Follett.

10. C. H. Northcott, *Personnel Management: its Scope and Practice*, Pitman, 1945.

11. *English Life and Leisure* (with G. R. Lavers), Longmans, 1951.

12. A. Briggs, *A Study of the Work of Seebohm Rowntree*, Longmans, 1961.

13. Seebohm Rowntree, *The Human Factor in Business*, Longmans, 1921, pp. 1–3.

14. ibid., pp. 8–9.

15. ibid., pp. 40–43.

16. ibid., pp. 98–101.

17. ibid., pp. 155–6.

18. ibid., p. 187.

3.4 Consumption and Welfare; Caveat Emptor to Caveat Vendor

GORDON WILLS

THE attitudes of producers of goods and services in advanced industrial nations, toward the disposal of their outputs, have undergone dramatic changes in this century. The effect can be clearly seen in the shift in the balance of power between emptor and vendor in the market-place. Analysis of the causes of this shift, however, presents considerable problems of which the most formidable is the dynamic nature of the process. The study of the interrelationship of technological and economic growth, which has already generated a literature in its own right, is essential to an understanding.[1] Equally important is an understanding of consumption behaviour within a given economic setting. The writings and actions of academics and businessmen in the first forty years of this century constitute an inevitable development in the face of changing demand conditions. It was the changes in these conditions which brought an increasing interest in the marketing process to North America in the 1930s and to Europe in the 1950s.

During those years teaching and writing met the emerging needs, normally on a basis of functional analysis. At the turn of the century it was advertising, then selling, then market research, which took the main attention. Few of these functional pioneers held a total concept of marketing, and their work was substantially empirical. It was, of course, carried on almost entirely in North America.

It would be wrong to decry the functionalism of these early writers, for their behaviour is quite normal in an area of operational business management. The synthesis of a total marketing concept was not required in the earlier years of this century. Critics of functionalism would do well to visualize the modern synthesis of the marketing concept as no more, perhaps, than the appropriate functionalism for our present economic and technological climate.

In this examination, therefore, the continual empirical nature of thinking will be emphasized. Side by side with an examination of economic and technological growth in the twentieth century will be laid the mainstream of ideas and concepts. As the problems of disposing of outputs grew, the attention of businessmen naturally turned more and more towards their solution.

A greater and greater proportion of total demand in the economy was made up of what could be termed 'discretionary' items. One of the most significant results of this trend was the proliferation of competitive alternatives for the consumer to choose between. A manufacturer was no longer solely in competition with manufacturers of similar products. This trend in consumption patterns itself led to increasingly complex problems in meeting the needs of manufacturers in industrial markets.

It would, of course, be unjust to suggest that no businessmen had used marketing techniques prior to this time, but little objective evidence has yet become available. Two important studies, however, have recently examined the marketing practice of Josiah Wedgwood and Matthew Boulton[2] in the eighteenth and early nineteenth centuries. Both these entrepreneurs demonstrated quite clearly an understanding of the modern concepts involved in marketing management. Boulton, for instance, developed the use of direct mail for the sale of 'toys' in the fashion goods trade, and Wedgwood had a clear idea of the possibilities of market segmentation and the introduction of fashion in pottery; he also consistently traded up the market in terms of price as a competitive weapon.

PRODUCTION ORIENTATION

In the industrialized nations of the world, the major problems of business management at the turn of the twentieth century were those concerning increased productivity and volume output. The leading influences in management thinking were the schools of

Frederick Taylor[3] and the Gilbreths.[4] Supply was generally the problem rather than the disposal of outputs, and all efforts were bent to optimize production. Such a direction of activity was both timely and successful. Demand was of a basic nature and almost insatiable. The problem for the user or consumer was not whether or not to choose this or that brand of shirt or food, but to obtain the required quantity of the commodity.

Such an age was quite obviously propitious for unscrupulous producers, hence the prevailing attitude of *caveat emptor*. The balance of power in the market-place undoubtedly lay with the producer or supplier rather than the consumer. Only professional pride stood between the bad producer and the consumer. The philosophy towards the disposal of outputs on the part of producers of goods and services was formulated accordingly – 'Make a good product you can be proud of and sell it at a reasonable profit'.

Robert Keith has summarized the philosophy of his firm of millers at this time as follows: 'As professional millers, blessed with the finest supply of wheat, and with excellent milling machinery, we turn out flour of the highest quality. We know our product is good because it meets our standards of quality. Our function is to mill flour, and, of course, we must hire salesmen to sell it.'[5]

The precise time scale for the change of business attitudes from this production orientation to a consciousness of sales management in the disposal of outputs varied between nations. In many developing countries of the world, production orientation still indeed prevails. In the U.S.S.R. the striving towards an appreciation of consumer needs began under Nikita Khrushchev; it co-incided with a spontaneous movement in Italy. In Britain and much of Western Europe the crucial years were the 1950s; in North America the 1930s. In each case, however, the evolution was the logical outcome of economic growth factors which transformed the nature of demand, and began to reverse the balance of power in the market-place.

The main dimension on which the shift took place was first detected and discussed by Arch Shaw at Harvard as early as 1912.

It concerned the logistics of distribution within a sellers' market.

Shaw perceived that the advances in manufacturing capacity, and the economies of scale, meant that the problems of sheer distribution of output were going to become more and more complex. He was writing at a time before the internal combustion engine was in full commercial use. At that time he foresaw, not problems of actually selling the produce, but of creating the time and place utilities. Shaw wrote:[6]

> The most pressing problem of the businessman today is systematically to study distribution, as production is being studied. He must apply to this problem the methods of investigation that have proven of use in more highly developed fields of knowledge.
>
> While we are on the threshold of the possibilities of efficiency in production, the progress thus far made has outstripped the existing system of distribution. If our producing possibilities are to be utilized, the problems of distribution must be solved.

It has been emphasized that within different countries the time scale for the shift of attitudes differed. The same is equally true at an industry and firm level. Certain markets advanced more rapidly towards a saturation position for immediately apparent demand, thereby focussing attention much earlier on the problems of sales management. The most noticeable example in the U.S.A. was agriculture.[7]

The pressures of sustained economic depression in the 1920s and 1930s accentuated the problems of the production orientated approach in both North America and Britain, and focussed attention on the manner in which the salesmen who had been hired could be assisted in disposing of the output.

Vergil Reed, writing in 1929, observed: 'Only a few years ago industry was necessarily production minded. Today it has become market minded. Production has so far outdistanced marketing that there is no longer a problem of increasing production but of profitably disposing of the capacity available.'[8]

Robert Keith[5] could now summarize the position of his company's philosophy: 'As a flour milling company, manufacturing a number of products for the consumer market, we have a first-rate sales organization which can dispose of all the products we can make at a favourable price. To accomplish this objective, our sales force must be backed by consumer advertising and market intelligence.'

SALES MANAGEMENT ORIENTATION

The step from production to sales management orientation in business attitudes was blurred. It involved no drastic rethinking of the philosophy of business, but rather a reflex action to a slowing down of sales; more resources came to be diverted to a major problem area. The habit still involved implicit arrogance in the selection of what was to be produced. The addition to the formula as before was more pressure on the consumer. Hence thinking during this period was predominantly concerned with the effectiveness of discrete functional aids to the selling effort. Advertising was the first to come in for close scrutiny, and latterly sales methods, retailing and credit were put under the microscope.

In the universities of America – particularly Wisconsin, Ohio State, Illinois and Harvard – research and development in these areas preceded business realization and acceptance by a decade or more. Robert Bartels has traced the origins and development of marketing teaching in the North American universities.[9]

Advertising

Walter Scott, a psychologist, made the first major contribution to a theory of advertising in the first decade of the century.[10] Working at Northwestern University he developed a statement of the principles of psychology related to advertising. He achieved an explanation of the mental processes of advertising communication which could be applied, for example, to the creation of advertising copy. The ideas he introduced are valid and familiar for practitioners today – attention, association of ideas, perception, illusion and mental imagery. Henry Adams, working at Michigan, concentrated more on the measurement of advertising effectiveness.[11] By the 1920s economists and businessmen, as well as psychologists, were writing on the subject and its use in support of salesmen. Paul Cherington was their most outstanding spokesman; he was mainly concerned with the relation of advertising to physical distribution. He coincided with a period of consolidation by men such as Otto Kleppner[12] who formulated not just a theory of advertising communications but strategy. Kleppner was the forerunner of the product life cycle concept with his concept of the advertising spiral. He identified distinct selling phases when different advertising strategies were appropriate. By 1933 George Hotchkiss was able to integrate advertising thinking in a way which remains satisfactory to this day even though the emphasis has changed in areas such as media.[13]

Britain was not completely left out of such developments however. Thomas Russell, lecturing at the London School of Economics in 1919, dealt with the subject of 'Commercial Advertising' in a special series of lectures. He demonstrated a high degree of awareness of the implications of psychology for the whole field of communications, as was apparent in his treatment of copywriting. Also worthy of note was his spirited economic justification of advertising, particularly the way it 'cut out the middleman'.

Credit

Credit as a function in marketing is normally overlooked in discussions today. If it does crop up it will normally concern hire purchase terms designed to stimulate consumer demand. In the period of sales management orientation it was an important and much discussed weapon to assist the hired salesman dispose of output. The history of lending to finance trade, of course, has roots in antiquity, and has long been a subject for economic and moral disputation. Practice and thinking in the first two decades towards mercantile credit were summarized by Ettinger and Golieb,[14] in a credit equation based on the three C's of credit – character, capacity and capital. The 1920s, however, saw the realization of the economic implications of personal instalment selling[15] as well as the expansion of mercantile credit to boost distribution.[16]

Salesmanship

Whilst scientific methods of analysis were being applied to many of the functional aids to hired salesmen, many were fighting a rearguard action in the area of salesmanship over whether it was an art or a science. In the field, the nature of representation was changing from order-taking for staples to competitive representation in speciality goods. Sales practices were therefore changing. Nonetheless, it was not until the substantial reverses in business of the 1930s that scientific method won its way into selling in those areas where it had a substantial contribution to make, for example in preparation, communications effectiveness and follow-up.

Once again the literature had preceded it.[17] By the time Canfield wrote,[18] in 1940, of the application of rigorous training in scientific selling and applications of work study, the wheel had come full circle.

Inside salesmanship, i.e. in the retail outlet, had a parallel development with thinking on salesmanship. It came, however, at a time when retailing already had institutional and technical streams of development in full flood. The Herculean contribution to retailing thought of Paul Nystrom in a succession of works from Wisconsin cannot go unmentioned.[19] The improved technical and managerial efficiency of retail outlets had a crucial part to play in the distribution of production. Following Nystrom came further technical development in consumer credit, buying, merchandising and accounting procedures.

Marketing research

As in our discussion of each of the other functional areas which were called to assist the sales effort in the period of sales management orientation, marketing research was also called into service.

It had begun in the second decade as a commercial tool for the collection of facts for the better direction of sales effort. Accordingly, its greatest contribution was made in the area of setting sales quotas on the basis of market potentials.[20] Research, however, did not take its base in sampling methods common today so much as in the objective, analytical approach to problems facing sales management. Charles Parlin was the manager of the first commercial research department in America, and his work in 1915 on departmental store shopping habits is one of the earliest classics.[21]

We must not be blind, however, to the fact that many of the functionalists were employing scientific method in their own areas without consciously seeing marketing research as a separate function of business.

We have demonstrated the manner in which the major functional areas of marketing activity emerged and developed in response to the salesman's need for assistance during the first twenty to thirty years of the twentieth century. It has inevitably been an over-simplification in many ways. Throughout the period there were, as we shall see later, a great number of contributors to the general theory of marketing. Nonetheless, our analysis is based on the overall stance taken by business managements. Nowhere in their management organizations was there to be found a marketing function as such, mixing or co-ordinating the various elements we have considered. The operating philosophy remained firmly that of supplementing salesmen with various promotional devices in order to sustain the previous pattern of production. The weight of advertising ever increased in the hope that the additional impact of a message would generate sales. Of course, it sometimes could. Yet just as the ailing role of the salesman in the production orientation phase inevitably led to sales management orientation, so the intolerable role of the sales manager led to a new concept of marketing management. The co-ordination of the growing diversity of elements of marketing activity within the firm was normally a general management function during our period of sales management orientation. As early as 1929 Vergil Reed had held the sales manager responsible for profitability, but the new attitude of marketing concept orientation was summed up for General Electric as follows:

Under the traditional sales concept, engineering designed a product, manufacturing produced it – and then the sales people were expected to sell it. Under the modern marketing concept, the whole business process starts with marketing research and sales forecasting to provide a sound, factual, customer-orientated basis for planning all business operations, and the business function which has sales responsibility now participates in all stages of the business planning process.[22]

The emergence of marketing concept orientation in business has also had a further significant effect on operating philosophy, because it has completed the transfer of profit responsibility to the marketing function. The distribution of the output of goods and services is no longer seen as a struggle for volume sales, but as navigating a course of mutual benefit for consumer and producer.

MARKETING CONCEPT ORIENTATION

The continuing acceleration of economic and technological development enabled first one and then another advanced industrial nation to reach the age of mass consumption. Income levels rose to a point where staple requirements could be satisfied and leave considerable margins of discretionary income in consumer hands. It was this stage of development in the U.K. economy which was reached in the 1950s (after the delays inevitable from the war and the post-war period of recovery) and which finally tipped the balance in the market-place from vendor to emptor. Business had to begin to adjust to these new circumstances. To win a part of discretionary consumer disbursements a much wider concept of the purpose of business had to be embraced, and the necessary organizational structure introduced to ensure the effective implementation of the appropriate concept. In its simplest expressions business began to see its role as meeting consumer needs and wants, and the competitive situation as a struggle to satisfy such needs and wants most effectively.

Hence business management of necessity required a new range

of techniques, of which perhaps the most significant arose from a new formulation of marketing research. Further, however, it detected the paramount importance of identifying within the firm a complete function concerned with ensuring the maintenance of continuous contact with the market-place. The company's market offering had to meet the requirements of the market-place. Within this marketing function was lodged responsibility for determining the optimum mix of ingredients in the market offering on three major dimensions – product, distribution and communications.

Thus marketing was perceived as a social institution by which society communicated its needs and wants to business and by which business satisfied such social requirements. At the macro level, marketing management became concerned with understanding its social environment; at the micro level, the concept of the marketing mix postulated a co-ordinative and integrative activity for product distribution and communication.

Each of these major ideas can be traced to earlier contributions than those in which the most substantial developments have been made but it is once again true to say that it was the march of economic and technological events which ushered these concepts to the fore.

Opinion, however, has by no means been unanimous in viewing marketing concept orientation as such a satisfactory expression of the social function of business. The leading critic has been John Kenneth Galbraith,[23] who depicts the modern corporation as the usurper of consumer sovereignty which is supposedly implicit in marketing concept orientation. The range of product offerings made by a company is seen as the outcome of policy decisions in the field of technological development, taken with scant regard to the social objectives often seen as appropriate for business. Finally, what is termed the 'dependence effect' in the modern economy and the consequent planned obsolescence of outputs, are construed as positively anti-social. Galbraith has certainly injected into the discussion of customer orientation of business a number of issues which had hitherto tended to be overlooked in the rush to improve the social 'image' of business, on the basis of the marketing concept.

Managerial marketing

The perception of marketing as a management function was set out in 1940 by Alexander, Surface, Elder and Alderson.[24] They saw the role of the marketing manager as a planner of total marketing activity with the use of research and budgeting. Duddy and Revzan took such thinking a stage further in trying 'to think of the marketing structure as an organic whole made up of inter-related parts, subject to growth and change and functioning in a process of distribution that is co-ordinated by economic and social forces'.[25]

Within the firm such views grew stronger as the 1950s and 1960s progressed and the significance of the total marketing function within many companies grew enormously. The consumer viewpoint became the starting point for all marketing planning and administration, and the marketing plan the starting point for all company activity.[26]

In the face of these new ideas the marketing concept was formulated to conceptualize the process by which marketing management and the market-place maintained contact. Its most adequate formal statement is from Robert King,[27] whose model is reproduced below (Diagram 2). Peter Drucker, writing from the standpoint of general management, is perhaps the foremost exponent of the marketing orientation which total integration of the concept into a business produces.[28] The entire structure of the company must be extrovert, organized to act and react in accordance with customer requirements. Some of the 'business realities' which Drucker lists emphasize this point. He suggests that 'there are no profit centres within the business; there are only cost centres. Results and resources both exist outside the business'. Further, 'results are obtained by exploiting opportunities, not by solving problems'.

King's exposition envisages a continual process of monitoring marketing reactions to the offering prior to the continuance of any offering. Should any shortcomings be detected provision is made for routine adjustments or major modifications. Such a

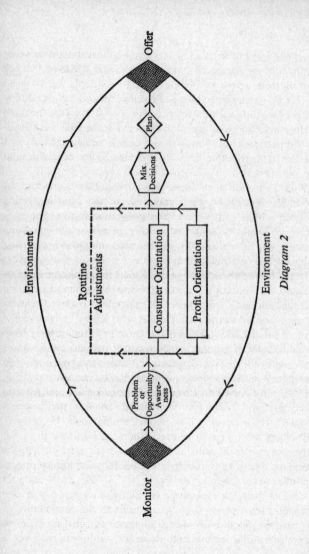

Offer

Plan

Mix Decisions

Routine Adjustments

Consumer Orientation

Profit Orientation

Problem or Opportunity Awareness

Environment

Environment

Monitor

Diagram 2

monitoring process has indeed become a permanent feature of many firms, and the responsibility of marketing research departments. In the work of Crisp[29] we can see the extent to which marketing research techniques have developed to ensure that both the monitoring and the mix management are based on qualitative and quantitative analysis.

The idea that marketing involved the carrying out of all those activities which precede the actual sale of a product was commonly expressed and generally accepted in the 1930s. It was the teaching of Neil Borden, however, which highlighted the extent to which the various possible ingredients in marketing should be managed to arrive at an optimum mixture. His concept did, of course, precede the use of computer models and simulation within marketing, but provided a ready framework for such developments. Borden's exposition grew out of his involvement with research into the marketing costs of a wide range of different companies.[30] No matter how Culliton and the Harvard team doing the research arranged classificatory groups for the companies, no common ground could be found for generalizing about cost patterns in marketing. Borden had already found an identical lack of pattern in his own work on advertising, and had rapidly concluded that advertising costs could only be explained in the context of the total marketing programme:

Advertising is not an operating method to be considered as something apart. An able management does not ask 'shall we use advertising?' without consideration of the product and of other management procedures to be employed. Rather the question is one of finding a formula giving advertising its due place in the combination of manufacturing methods, product form, pricing, promotion, selling methods and distribution methods.[31]

Thus Borden formulated a concept for optimization within the marketing function which took cognizance of the varying nature of a firm's resources at any point in time. But he went further still and introduced the same significance for external environmental forces acting on the company. Most specifically he isolated consumer and trade behaviour, competitive forces, and legal/quasi-legal parameters.

Marketing environment

The growing contribution of psychologists and sociologists to research and development work in marketing led inevitably to a closer examination of the behaviour patterns of humans as consumers or traders. Not only was psychology able to offer explanations of consumer needs and wants, of learning patterns and habit formation, which had immediate relevance to marketing activity: it provided techniques – for example, in deployment in observation, depth interviews, group discussions and projective tests. Sociology likewise made a massive contribution to the marketing man's understanding of social motivation, groups, social psychology, cultural change, human ecology and demography. There has been an ever-widening range of literature since the 1950s which seeks to create awareness of the external environment in which marketing takes place. (It sometimes goes under the title of macro-marketing.) Holloway and Hancock[32] visualize the dynamic environment as consisting of economic, psychological, institutional, technological, competitive, ethical, legal, sociological and anthropological elements. George Schwartz[33] is content with a detailed examination of the economic, sociological and psychological elements. This growing understanding of the dynamic environment in which the marketing process takes place has, of course, sharpened the effectiveness of marketing research in numerous ways. Allied with the substantial advances in operational research, it has also enabled substantial progress in the construction of models of consumer behaviour and of total markets. However, the development of attitude and motivation research has probably had the most considerable influence on the efficiency of marketing practice. In Britain it was Harry Henry[34] who first described the application of motivation research.

More recently still, cultural analysis has become of significance in the screening of export markets, and the processes of innovation by manufacturers and adoption by customers have begun to yield valuable insights for new product development. A further example is provided by the development of recent knowledge of patterns of message diffusion in a society for the improvement of marketing communications systems generally.

Marketing functionalism

In a time of such growing significance for marketing as an integrative function, it was inevitable that rapid developments should also take place within the major ingredients of the marketing mix – product, communications and distribution elements. They have been partly the cause of, and partly made possible by, substantial advances in marketing research, most noticeably in sampling and research design. Berg and Shuchman have given an extremely broad consideration to the product mix.[35] George Fisk pioneered the systems approach which illuminates the subordinate mix level in distribution:

Marketing channels are usually under the control of a single firm in that a single enterprise directs the allocation of resources for all agencies in the channel without interfering with the objectives of independent agencies which participate in the channel flows. These controllers, or decision makers, do not set goals for other firms in the constituent marketing channels, but they do decide what kind of agencies shall be combined to form the distribution network for systems they organize. In this sense the executive controls by optimizing, sub-optimizing, maximizing and minimizing, the work input combinations of micro-marketing systems.[36]

The subordinate integration of the communications mix has been perhaps less adequately tackled, and certainly personal selling is seldom reckoned in. Undoubtedly the runaway development, and phenomenal growth, of the TV and press advertising industries have dwarfed other media of marketing communications. Intermedia comparisons are still relatively in their infancy, and knowledge in media such as posters, packaging, merchandising, public relations, and personal selling is too sparse even now to provide an adequate base for any early improvements. A recent contribution has begun to tackle communications as a sub-mix in earnest.[37]

NEW ORIENTATIONS

It surely seemed unlikely to the mass of the population in Britain in the eighteenth century that the era would dawn when there would be sufficient income for them to secure the standard of living we have today. Today it is almost equally impossible for the mass of people to visualize a cornucopia where technological advances reduce the working week to a few hours, and where the problems of how to spend higher incomes and greater leisure time become major issues. There can be no doubt, however, that this is the inevitable direction in which industrialized nations are moving.[38] Higher incomes and longer leisure periods inevitably mean a further growth in the significance of consumer behaviour for marketing. Accordingly, one can confidently predict further developments in the behavioural science applications to marketing, not just in terms of understanding how to persuade most effectively but also what products and services to develop for the increasingly discriminating consumer. Firms which have not embraced the marketing concept as an opportunity will be forced to embrace it as a defence against competition.

Because of these developments the role of marketing both within the community and within the business, will be strengthened still further. The beginnings of the social function concept of marketing can already be detected in the manner in which the environment is monitored, and in which the wishes of consumers are described as determining (after profit orientation) company behaviour. Society-orientated concepts can be confidently expected to see not only consumer orientation but also profit orientation solely in terms of fulfilling social objectives. The behaviour of marketing groups will be moulded by social norms and values, and as such one can see considerable scope for more attention to ethical and legal dimensions of the marketing environment.

An important corollary to the conceptualization of marketing in this way will be the examination of comparative marketing systems[39] employing particularly the services of the cultural anthropologist. The drawback to such comparative study is, of course, the primitive stage of literature about the facts of the marketing systems in countries other than the U.S.A.

A society-orientated concept of marketing could have wide significance if business can be seen as fulfilling a vital social function in a socially responsible manner. It could provide, and sustain, a philosophy or economic activity which is non-capitalistic, if not to say marxist. It could provide a basis for a reintegration of marxist and capitalistic directions in economic thought. New economic insights which the emergence of such a concept of marketing and business could precipitate must be considered a real possibility.

NOTES

1. See particularly W. W. Rostow, *Stages of Economic Growth*, Cambridge University Press, 1960.

2. *Economic History Review*, 1963, 16, pp. 39–60, and 12, pp. 408–33.

3. See Part 2.2.

4. See Part 2.3.

5. In *Advancing Marketing Efficiency*, A.M.A., Chicago, 1959.

6. Arch Shaw, *Some Problems in Market Distribution*, Harvard University Press, 1915.

7. See F. G. Coolsen, *Marketing Thought in the U.S. in the Late 19th Century*, Texas Tech. Press, 1961.

8. Vergil Reed, *Planned Marketing*, Ronald Press, New York, 1929.

9. Robert Bartels, 'Influences on the Development of Marketing Thought', *Journal of Marketing*, U.S.A., July 1951.

10. Walter Scott, *The Theory of Advertising*, Small Maynard, Boston, 1903, and *Psychology of Advertising*, Small Maynard, Boston, 1908.

11. Henry Adams, *Advertising and its Mental Laws*, Macmillan, New York, 1916.

12. Otto Kleppner, *Advertising Procedure*, Prentice Hall, 1925.

13. George Hotchkiss, *An Outline of Advertising: Its Philosophy, Science, Art and Strategy*, Macmillan, New York, 1933.

14. Ettinger and Golieb, *Credit and Collections*, Prentice Hall, 1917.

15. E. Seligman, *Economics of Instalment Selling*, Harper Bros., New York, 1926.

16. R. Young, *Industrial Credits*, Harper Bros, New York, 1927.

17. H. Whitehead, *Principles of Salesmanship*, Ronald Press, New York, 1917.

18. B. Canfield, *Salesmanship Practices and Problems*, McGraw-Hill, 1940.

19. See particularly *Economics of Retailing*, Ronald Press, New York, 1915; *Economics of Fashion*, Ronald Press, New York, 1928.

20. See P. White, *Sales Quotas*, Harper Bros, New York, 1929.

21. 'The Merchandising of Textiles' 1915, reprinted in *Marketing in Progress*, H. Barksdale, ed., Holt, Rinehart & Winston, 1964.

22. E. S. McKay, 'The Marketing Concept in G.E.' in *Science in Marketing*, G. Schwartz, ed., Wiley, 1965.

23. See particularly the 1966 Reith Lectures, *The Listener*, November and December, 1966, and *The New Industrial State*, Hamish Hamilon, 1967.

24. *Marketing*, Ginn & Co., New York, 1949.

25. *Marketing: an Institutional Approach*, McGraw-Hill, 1947.

26. H. Lazo and A. Corbin, *Management in Marketing*, McGraw-Hill, 1961.

27. In *Science in Marketing*, G. Schwartz, ed., Wiley, 1965.

28. See *Managing for Results*, Heinemann, 1964.

29. *Marketing Research*, McGraw-Hill, 1957.

30. J. W. Culliton, *Management of Marketing Costs*, Harvard Uinversity Press, 1948.

31. Neil Borden, *The Economic Effects of Advertising*, Irwin, Chicago, 1942.

32. *Environment of Marketing Behavior*, Wiley, 1964.

33. *Science in Marketing*, G. Schwartz, ed., Wiley, 1965, chs., 6, 7, 8.

34. *Motivation Research*, Crosby Lockwood, 1957.

35. *Product Strategy and Management*, Holt, Rinehart & Winston, 1963.

36. George Fisk, 'General Systems Approach to the Study of Marketing', in W. D. Stevens, *Social Responsibilities of Marketing*, A. M.A., Chicago, 1961.

37. See particularly E. Crane, *Marketing Communications*, Wiley, 1965.

38. See particularly Ronald Brech, *Unilever's Forecast, Britain 1984*, Darton, Longman & Todd, 1963.

39. R. Bartels, *Comparative Marketing*, Irwin, 1963.

PART FOUR

THE CRITERION OF COOPERATION

4.1 Introduction: the Criterion of Cooperation

THE criterion of cooperation is more a point of view than an operational concept. It focusses on the human aspects of the organization and depends on both the quality of the leadership and the disposition of the members. Of course, what is termed 'cooperation' from the standpoint of the organization is, in fact, 'participation' from the viewpoint of the employees and so the writers described in this section are concerned both with the organization of the employees and with the employees as human beings. The questions which these writers asked about human beings in organizations had been posed in similar terms before by political philosophers about society. They were: how is organization possible when the persons in an organization have many interests that must conflict, and what are the obligations that must be fulfilled by a person entering an organization and by the organization during the period of employment?

Attempts to answer these questions led to a more complex view of the organization and the relationship of the individual to it. The rejection of individualism had been a common theme in writing since the turn of the century. These writers put forward the idea of man as a primarily social being who worked not only for money but also for social prestige and acceptance. One of the major practices in explaining human action was to take the group as the fundamental unit of social activity. One of the concepts of the group taken up by Mayo and Barnard harks back to the ideas of Durkheim, that is that human beings are bound together not only by their self-interest, but also by the values which they hold in common. Furthermore, in the process of getting to know each other people form expectations of each other's behaviour. These mutual beliefs about the actions of others were labelled 'circularity of response' by Follett. Men value and accept the norms of their fellows as legitimate standards, and 'normative' man often replaces 'economic' man. The major discovery during this phase of management thought was that of the 'informal group'. Those who worked in organizations felt loyalty to their workmates, not to the goals of the company or to their employers. The Hawthorne experiments demonstrated the importance to employees of the friendship and good esteem of their colleagues.

The discovery of the 'informal group' led to a new conception of the role of the manager, and the idea of the creation of common values which everyone in the organization could accept. The manager, like any leader, must pay attention to his followers. Constant communication and the establishment of trust were more important than the authority of his position. If people had a choice between working hard or slacking and might either like or dislike their work, they could be influenced by creative managerial leadership and new organizational values. The result was a great emphasis on the worker's morale or, in Follett's terms, the creation of 'common responsibility'.

Many of these approaches were ragged at the edges but they did begin to take into account factors in the organization that needed exploring. Two approaches were particularly important for future theoretical work. The first was to view the organization as a whole and the second was to stress the interdependence of all parts of the organization, and indeed of all social phenomena. In the latter approach the intellectual influence on which Mayo and Barnard depended became very important. These included Pareto, Henderson and Durkheim and they introduced into management studies the concept of 'functionalism'. The inductivism of Taylor was yielding diminishing returns. Specific factors in an organization could no longer be isolated and explained without taking into account the various other factors which made up the organization.

4.2 Mary Parker Follett and the Integration of Business Administration

GORDON WILLS

MARY PARKER FOLLETT is a fascinating example of a person who transferred disciplines, from political science to management studies, and was able through the insights of the former to illuminate the latter. She found business a vital and stimulating subject. Lecturing at the newly formed Department of Business Administration at the London School of Economics in 1933, she summed up her interest and excitement:

Certain changes have been going on in business practice which are destined, I believe, to alter our thinking fundamentally. I think this is the contribution which business is going to make to the world and not only the business world, but eventually to Government and International Relations. Men may be making useful products, but beyond this, by helping to solve the problem of human relations they are perhaps destined to lead the world in the solution of those great problems of co-ordination and control upon which our future progress must depend.

Mary Parker Follett was born in Boston in 1868, and was educated at Radcliffe College, and Newnham College, Cambridge. She studied politics, economics, philosophy and law. Whilst at Newnham she delivered to its Historical Society the paper which became her first published work, *The Speaker of the House of Representatives*.[1] At the age of thirty-two she began a career of public service in the Boston area with the formation of a local debating society which soon extended to a series of social centres in the poor areas. There was a great need for recreational facilities for the young at the time, and she was a prime mover in the campaign for the 'Extended Use of School Buildings in the Evenings'. This participation in social work was an early manifestation of the social conscience which emerged so strongly later in her life. A visit to Edinburgh, where she saw the great need for vocational guidance, had awakened her interest in it, and she soon grafted this on to the social centres in Boston. By 1912 the Boston schools system was ready to try the experiment of a placement bureau for school leavers in partnership with Follett, and she shared half the costs for the first five years until the Municipal Department of Vocational Guidance was established in 1917. She maintained an active interest in this work until she visited London in the closing years of her life. This work gave her the first real contact with administration and the problems of business and industry. It marked a shift in her interests from political analysis to a concern with industrial relations: she brought in her powers of scholarship and reflection to elucidate practical problems.

Her interest in social affairs can be found in her first important book, *The New State*.[2] In this book she argued for a better ordered and controlled society, in which the individual could live a fuller life. Both government and industry, the two main centres of control in society, did not exercise their control arbitrarily but with the acquiescence of the population. The psychology of this acquiescent relationship was to become her life's work. She did not wish to manipulate people, but to encourage better organization through their meaningful participation.

Her second major work, published in 1924, was *Creative Experience*.[3] In this book she developed the idea of the interrelatedness of all psychological phenomena involved in human relations. The problem of conflict became one of her abiding interests. As a solution to conflict she advocated integration, which she defined as the combination of what is best in all viewpoints but accepts neither view in its entirety. This idea became vitally important in her discussions of management. In this book she also asserted the dynamic nature of human relations. Each present problem, she suggested, can be solved most effectively by integration, but the action taken to meet a present problem will inevitably influence the next problem to be faced. Thinking, Follett maintained, could not be seen in terms of any one situation or one problem, but must be viewed as a continuing process.

The examples quoted in *Creative Experience*[3] illustrate the shift to industrial relations. In the same year as this book was published she began to lecture publicly on business management. She gave a series of lectures at the recently formed Bureau of Personnel Administration in New York, which was under the direction of Henry Metcalf. The remaining nine years of her life were taken up with the study of industrial relations in the United States and Britain. These studies did not modify her social philosophy, nor her view of the individual and the explanation of behaviour. She had encountered entrepreneurial and organizational problems in setting up her social centres in Boston; she used her experience in this field to illuminate the problems of business, particularly in ordering and controlling activities, and of human involvement within the firm. Her philosophy of human behaviour in organizations was positively orientated; she believed that the truth about human relations was universal and applicable in all organizations. This feeling undoubtedly gave her the confidence to lecture to businessmen on their own problems. The application of her thought to business and management is found in a series of lectures she gave between 1923 and 1933, and republished under the title of *Dynamic Administration*.[4]

CONSTRUCTIVE CONFLICT

To Follett conflict was neither good nor bad. It was the expression of divergent interests, different opinions which can manifest themselves anywhere in life where one human being deals with another. She compared conflict to friction; an engineering problem which once understood seldom remained insuperable, and was, in fact, often a help. Management in its turn must know when to eliminate human friction and when to use it. When the conflict is an expression of diversity of approach, of varying environments rich in experience, there should always be an attempt to find a new synthesis. Looking at conflicts in such a constructive way often takes management a good deal of the way towards solving them. It constitutes a positive approach, a search for a totally new way of viewing a situation, which compromise, of course, does not.

Two methods of dealing with conflict were rejected by Follett: domination and compromise. Settlements based on domination were unsatisfactory, and based on only one view of the situation. Compromise was equally unsatisfactory although it was the most frequently used manner of ending the conflict. Follett's criticism of compromise was summed up in the obvious that 'nobody really wants to compromise because that means the giving up of something'.

If we can believe that integration is more profitable than domination or compromise, the bases of integration must be clearly analysed. First the differences must be brought out in the open. Evasion or suppression of the issues involved makes nonsense of any attempt to approach a problem constructively. Facing the real issues may well bring about revaluation of the whole position, and comparison of these issues may enable the opposing sides to see their own particular view as part of a panorama, incorporating their rivals as well. It might of itself bring about a realignment of groups and/or individuals involved; at its best it gives a new integration.

Once the content of conflict has been laid bare, Follett held that it must be broken into its constituent parts. This involved the analysing of the psychological implications of the demands put forward by each side to see which must be specifically met, and which were merely symbolic of a desire and could be satisfied in another way, to the mutual agreement of both parties.

Finally the very act of solving a conflict was not static, but part of the continuous pattern of circular response which typifies all human relations. To succeed, the responses and reactions of the two parties to each other and the way that those responses and reactions affect the evolving situation must be fully realized. To Follett, 'the conception of circular behaviour throws much light on conflict, for now I realize that I can never fight you alone, I must always fight you plus me. I respond not only to you, but to the relation of you plus me.'

This concept of power to influence the evolving situation has vital relevance to business administration.

The obstacles to achieving integration are substantial, and make great demands on the perceptive powers and sheer inventiveness of the individual. Language, leadership and theory can all be misused and blur the path to integration. Perhaps the most important of all the obstacles is the environment in which the individual has grown up. Often the environment of management is one of debate not cooperation; the manager approaches problems with preconceived ideas, and is unwilling to search for other methods of thought.

GIVING ORDERS

The issuing of orders from one person to another will often give rise to a conflict of some description which an analysis of the experience can help us to understand. The conflict may be a direct conflict between the two parties or it may be a Freudian conflict within the self of one or both parties, both of which will find expression in a partial or reluctant execution of an order. The precise form the conflict will take will depend on the habit patterns and attitudes of the two parties.

To solve such a conflict, the necessary integration must follow what Follett termed the 'law of the situation'. This law holds that when both parties see the logic of a situation, and try to gain a total understanding of all factors bearing on that situation, the conflict must dissolve in the face of the facts. The law of the situation will obviously work imperfectly so long as the facts are not available. In finding the law of the situation Follett felt a contribution would be made to the psychology of cooperation, and ultimately scientific management. Situations can be changed by orders, the implementation of orders, and the dynamics of any situation itself. Fresh orders bring into being a new situation, so that the next situation will be shaped by reactions to the first.

To sum up, Follett says of the giving of orders (i) that they come from the situation, (ii) that the situation is always evolving, and (iii) that the orders involve circular behaviour.

LEADERSHIP AND CONTROL

To be effective Follett felt that leadership must not be autocratic. The manager must not think solely of what effect he will have on the group, but also what influence the group will have on him. There is a two-way traffic. The leader must integrate, and not merely give orders.

Follett applied this constructive approach to leadership to the theory of checks and balances, the foundation of the American constitution. She concluded that the system was a compromise, and not one conducive to creative leadership. In its place she wished to see multiple leadership based on integrative thinking, adapting to the evolving situation.

She criticized the concept of a leader as a man taking quick decisions; to Follett the secret of leadership was the art of thinking ahead. One aspect of planning and thinking ahead is the ability to integrate the conflicting demands of the specialist and the general manager. The manager must provide creative leadership in the interrelating of the experience of the specialist and the line manager. The chief executive has the greatest responsibility in linking the activities of the various parts, looking at the proposed solutions in the light of the defined purpose of the group.

Leadership is not the product of position, but of knowledge. Effective leadership is therefore functional, based on knowledge of the situation. The degree of control which leadership can provide depends on the manager's ability to combine the ideas of others with his own. As ideas continually change, so the process of control must change. Furthermore, if social progress is to be made ideas must be continually integrated and co-ordinated. A failure of integration will have an effect on the running of the organization; one example is overselling.

Control is not differentiated but part of dealing with the whole organization. Having mastered the unifying aspect of control, the second step in attaining control is an understanding of the passage from one field to the next. Control is not a discrete event but a continuous process. It is more than forecasting and prediction; it is creating the next situation. The aim, for example, is not to meet a strike situation, but to create a strikeless situation.

FUNDAMENTALS OF PROGRESSIVE ORGANIZATION

Shortly before her death Mary Parker Follett answered some of her critics who saw the law of the situation and her view of control as a threat to individualism. Control to her meant fact-control, rather than human control, and central control meant synthesis rather than domination from the centre. Her ideas were deployed to defeat superimposed control and to move to the law of the situation. She summed up her idea of organizational control as a self-adjusting process under four headings.

(i) Co-ordination by direct contact with the responsible people concerned.

(ii) Co-ordination in the early stages.

(iii) Co-ordination as a reciprocal factor in all the relating stages.

(iv) Co-ordination as a continuing process.

Mary Parker Follett saw the work going on in business as trying to solve the kinds of questions about human relationships she had analysed in *Creative Experience*.[3] Management was at its best a service, but many other motives were present in the acts of managers. A single action stemmed from many motives and she accepted that profit, personal motives and desire for innovation were also present with the desire for service. She hoped that service would become the dominant motive in management. Science could show the benefit of service, for the experiences of managers and systematic observation would show the ultimate benefits of this approach. Science organized experience so that it could be used. Having experience and profiting by experience are two different matters. Experience may leave us with mistaken notions, prejudices and suspicion. Knowledge about human cooperation, situations and organizations should be analysed and spread. Techniques were not enough. The understanding of the organization was a craft, which had to be learned.

Much of what Follett said in her writings has become accepted and may now seem commonplace. But she interested managers in problems which writers such as Taylor were not dealing with, and indeed, considered unimportant. She took large questions and tried by examples and suggestions to make the problems susceptible to science. Her writings are a rich reward for anyone who takes them up. The simplicity of the analysis must not be allowed to conceal their true value and relevance.

NOTES

1. Mary Parker Follett, *The Speaker of the House of Representatives*, Longmans Green, 1909.

2. Mary Parker Follett, *The New State*, Longmans Green, 1920.

3. Mary Parker Follett, *Creative Experience*, Longmans Green, 1924.

4. Mary Parker Follett, *Dynamic Administration*, Pitman, 1941.

READINGS FROM MARY PARKER FOLLETT,
Dynamic Administration

Giving orders[1]

To some men the matter of giving orders seems a very simple affair; they expect to issue their orders and have them obeyed without question. Yet, on the other hand, the shrewd common sense of many a business executive has shown him that the issuing of orders is surrounded by many difficulties; that to demand an unquestioning obedience to orders not approved, not perhaps even understood, is bad business policy. Moreover, psychology, as well as our own observation, shows us not only that you cannot get people to do things most satisfactorily by ordering them or exhorting them; but also that even reasoning with them, even convincing them intellectually, may not be enough. Even the 'consent of the governed' will not do all the work it is supposed to do, an important consideration for those who are advocating employee representation. For all our past life, our early training, our later experience, all our emotions, beliefs, prejudices, every desire that we have, have formed certain habits of mind, what the psychologists call habit-patterns, action-patterns, motor-sets.

Therefore it will do little good merely to get intellectual agreement; unless you change the habit-patterns of people, you have not really changed your people. Business administration, industrial organization, should build up certain habit-patterns, that is, certain mental attitudes. . . .

If we analyse this matter a little further we shall see that we have to do three things; I am now going to use psychological language: (1) build up certain attitudes; (2) provide for the release of these attitudes; (3) augment the released response as it is being carried out. What does this mean in the language of business? A psychologist has given us the example of the salesman. The salesman first creates in you the attitude that you want his article; then, at just the 'psychological' moment, he produces his contract blank which you may sign and thus release that attitude; then if, as you are preparing to sign, some one comes in and tells you how pleased he has been with his purchase of this article, that augments the response which is being released.

If we apply this to the subject of orders and obedience, we see that people can obey an order only if previous habit-patterns are appealed to or new ones created. When the employer is considering an order, he should also be thinking of the way to form the habits which will ensure its being carried out. We should first lead the salesmen selling shoes or the bank clerk cashing cheques to see the desirability of a different method. Then the rules of the store or bank should be so changed as to make it possible for salesman or cashier to adopt the new method. In the third place they could be made more ready to follow the new method by convincing in advance some one individual who will set an example to the others. You can usually convince one or two or three ahead of the rank and file. This last step you all know from your experience to be good tactics; it is what the psychologists call intensifying the attitude to be released. But we find that the released attitude is not by one release fixed as a habit; it takes a good many responses to do that.

This is an important consideration for us, for from one point of view business success depends largely on this – namely, whether our business is so organized and administered that it tends to form certain habits, certain mental attitudes. It has been hard for many old-fashioned employers to understand that *orders will not take the place of training*. I want to italicize that. Many a time an employer has been angry because, as he expressed it, a workman 'wouldn't' do so and so, when the truth of the matter was that the workman couldn't, actually couldn't, do as ordered because he could not go contrary to life-long habits. This whole subject might be taken up under the heading of education, for there we could give many instances of the attempt to make arbitrary authority take the place of training. In history, the aftermath of all revolutions shows us the results of the lack of training.

In this matter of prepared-in-advance behaviour patterns – that is, in preparing the way for the reception of orders, psychology makes a contribution when it points out that the same words often rouse in us a quite different response when heard in certain places and on certain occasions. A boy may respond differently to the same suggestion when made by his teacher and when made by his schoolmate. Moreover, he may respond differently to the same suggestion made by the teacher in the schoolroom and made by the teacher when they are taking a walk together. Applying this to the giving of orders, we see that the place in which orders are given, the circumstances under which they are given, may make all the difference in the world as to the response which we get. Hand them down a long way from president or works manager and the effect is weakened. One might say that the strength of favourable response to an order is in inverse ratio to the distance the order travels. Production efficiency is always in danger of being affected whenever the long-distance order is substituted for the face-to-face suggestion.

Depersonalizing orders: The law of the situation[2]

Now what is our problem here? How can we avoid the two extremes: too great bossism in giving orders, and practically no orders given? I am going to ask how *you* are avoiding these extremes. My solution is to depersonalize the giving of orders, to unite all concerned in a study of the situation, to discover the law of the situation and obey that. Until we do this I do not think we shall have the most successful business administration. This is what does take place, what has to take place, when there is a question between two men in positions of equal authority. The head of the sales departments does not give orders to the head of the production department, or vice versa. Each studies the market and the final decision is made as the market demands. This is, ideally, what should take place between foremen and rank and file, between any head and his subordinates. One *person* should not give orders to another *person*, but both should agree to take their orders from the situation. If orders are simply part of the situation, the question of someone giving and someone receiving does not come up. Both accept the orders given by the situation. Employers accept the orders given by the situation; employees accept the orders given by the situation. This gives, does it not, a slightly different aspect to the whole of business administration through the entire plant?

We have here, I think, one of the largest contributions of scientific management: it tends to depersonalize orders. From one point of view, one might call the essence of scientific management the attempt to find the law of the situation. With scientific management the managers are as much under orders as the workers, for both obey the law of the situation. Our job is not how to get people to obey orders, but how to devise methods by which we can best *discover* the order integral to a particular situation. When that is found, the employee can issue it to the employer, as well as employer to employee. This often happens easily and naturally. My cook or my stenographer points out the law of the situation, and I, if I recognize it as such, accept it, even although it may reverse some 'order' I have given.

If those in supervisory positions should depersonalize orders then there would be no overbearing authority on the one hand, nor on the other that dangerous *laissez-aller* which comes from the fear of exercising authority. Of course we should exercise authority, but always the authority of the situation. I do not say that we have found the way to a frictionless existence, far from it, but we now understand the place which we mean to give to friction. We intend to set it to work for us as the engineer does when he puts the belt over the pulley. There will be just as much, probably more, room for disagreement in the method I am advocating. The situation will often be seen differently, often be interpreted differently. But we shall know what to do with it, we shall have found a method of dealing with it.

I call it depersonalizing because there is not time to go any further into the matter. I think it really is a matter of *repersonalizing*. We, persons, have relations with each other, but we should find them in and through the whole situation. We cannot have any sound relations with each other as long as we take them out of that setting which gives them their meaning and value. This divorcing of persons and the situation does a great deal of harm. I have just said that scientific management depersonalizes; the deeper philosophy of scientific management shows us personal relations within the whole setting of that thing of which they are a part.

Group responsibility[3]

I am often misunderstood on this point of collective responsibility. People sometimes think when I emphasize collective responsibility, that I do not believe in decentralization. I know no one who believes more strongly in decentralization than I do, but I believe that collective responsibility and decentralized responsibility must go hand in hand; more than that, I think they are parts of the same thing. Books on business administration often discuss concentrated authority versus distributed authority, but I do not think this discussible. I recently read in an article on business administration that we must find a happy mean between centralization and decentralization. I do not think that, for I believe we should have both. When the National Joint Council of Electrical Contractors and Electrical Workers was formed, it was found that joint local councils and joint district councils were necessary through which the national body could function and work out a national policy. That centralization and decentralization are not opposed is, I believe, the central lesson for business administration to learn. To understand this principle and to devise methods for its operation is what we must all work at daily if industry and the government of nations are not to fail. I do not minimize the difficulties we shall meet. This is one of our gravest problems: how to foster local initiative and at the same time get the advantages of centralization. The problem is grave, but we must face it; we want no compromise in this matter.

Let us note here a very marked difference between being responsible for a functional whole, what we are here considering, and being responsible for our function in the whole, which has been given far more consideration in the past. We have been so delighted with what has sometimes been called the functional theory, that is, the division of work so that each can do what he is best fitted for, that we have tended to forget that our responsibility does not end with doing conscientiously and well our particular piece of the whole, but that we are also responsible for the whole. A business should be so organized that all will feel this responsibility. We see it in the case of the home. The wife has her duties and the husband his, but in addition to these, or rather by means of these, each has to do his and her part to make the home bear its significance in the life of the community, serve its maximum degree of service to the community. We do try to make our children feel this; I wish we could extend it to the rest of our household, to our servants. What greater dignifying of labour could there be than that which comes from a sense of joint responsibility in community service?

This is the problem in business administration: how can a business be so organized that workers, managers, owners, feel a collective responsibility? The advantages of creating a sense of individual responsibility have long been noted as one of the cardinal principles of business administration, and many have leaned toward employee representation because they thought it was developing this. Some say in the language of the old maxim: Responsibility sobers. Or as one young manager said to me of his workmen, 'They don't have so many darn fool ideas now.' The idea of a collective responsibility, however, has been neither fully accepted nor the methods of obtaining it worked out.

I think myself that collective responsibility should begin with group responsibility, that a form of departmental organization which includes the workers is the most effective method for unifying a business. In one business, where there is a strong feeling on the part of the managers that the worker should be given responsibility to his full capacity, group responsibility is encouraged wherever possible. For instance, the chauffeurs asked for shorter hours. They were given a fifty-four hour week with overtime, and the chairman and secretary of the chauffeur group, acting for the group, assumed the responsibility for each man giving an honest week's work.

We see the next step in collective responsibility, *inter*departmental relations, in a store where, for instance, the elevator force has meetings at which are considered how the elevator force can help the store superintendent, how it can help the charge office, the advertising office, the information bureau, the mail order department, etc. Such steps are, of course, mere beginnings in the solving of what seems to me the crux of business administration, the relation of departments, of functions, however you wish to put it. Any study of business as an integrative unity should, I think, make this problem its chief concern.

An understanding of this principle of integrative unity which we are considering will keep us not only from a false individualism, but also from a false altruism. For instance, if we dislike many of the old ways of hiring and firing which often left too much to the mere whim of the foreman, we sometimes say that we dislike these methods because they are not fair to the workman, but the truth is that we do not change these methods in order to benefit the workman only, but because the change will benefit the business as a whole. Or take the necessity of regularizing employment so that seasonal or so-called 'cyclical' fluctuations will be reduced. This need should not be taken up solely as a grievance of labour, for there is loss in overhead as well as loss to the employees. Again, the arbitrator should arbitrate for the institution. This should go without saying, but a union girl asked, 'Is he pro-labour?' You can be *for* labour without being *against* capital; you can be for the institution.

When you have made your employees feel that they are in some sense partners in the business, they do not improve the quality of their work, save waste in time and material, because of the Golden Rule, but because their interests are the same as yours. Over and over again in the past we have heard it said to workmen, 'If this were your material, you wouldn't waste it,' and over and over again that admonition fails. We find, however, that when there is some feeling in a plant, more or less developed, that that business is a working unit, we find then that the workman is more careful of material, that he saves time in lost motions, in talking over annoyances, that he helps the new hand by explaining things to him, that he helps the fellow working at his side by calling attention to the end of a roll on the machine, etc. This is the Golden Rule taken behaviouristically. It is, by the way, the Golden Rule taken idealistically, too, for a functional whole is a much higher conception than our old notion of the Golden Rule.

In concluding my necessarily meagre treatment of what I have called integrative unity, I should say that the efficiency of many plants is lowered by an imperfectly worked out system of co-ordination of parts. In some instances what co-ordination there is depends chiefly on the ability of certain heads to get on together; their willingness to consult each other depends too often on mere chance qualities or conditions—perhaps whether certain men commute by the same train! An adequate system of co-ordination has not yet, so far as I know, been worked out for business administration.

It is impossible, however, to work most effectively at co-ordination until you have made up your mind where you stand philosophically in regard to the relation of parts to the whole. We have spoken of the relation of departments – sales and production, advertising and financial – to each other, but the most profound truth that philosophy has ever given us concerns not only the relation of parts, but the relation of parts to the whole, not to a stationary whole, but to a whole a-making. What does this mean in business? It means that the sales department, for instance, should have some principle by which to test the relation of a sales policy to general policy. Books on management sometimes tell us that the production manager should subordinate departmental policy to business policy. I do not agree with this. In the *Bulletin of the Taylor Society* for February, 1924, it is stated that 'any department head should recognize organization policies as more vital than his own.' I wonder why more 'vital'? Or I have seen it stated that department heads should realize that general policy is more 'important' than departmental policy. He should not, because it is not, any more than the United States is more important than New York, and I am no states-righter either. Co-ordinate manufacture and sales? Certainly, also work out the relation between manufacturing and general policy and between sales and general policy, always remembering that general policy is, or should be, no air plant, but that all the time manufacturing and sales policies are contributing to general policy. The production manager should not subordinate departmental policy to business policy; he should contribute it, and he should see that it is a contributable policy. That is the chief test of the production manager, whether his policy is a contributable policy.

The business environment [4]

And beyond all this, beyond the matter of the unifying of single plants, beyond even the unifying of all the plants in the same industry, there is still another way of looking at business unity which should be one of the chief concerns of the business administrator. He sees the three classes: (1) workers, including industrial and managerial workers, (2) consumers, and (3) investors. The chief job of business is to find a method for integrating the interests of these three classes. I have said nothing of the consumer, because there has not been time, but when we find employers and employees uniting against the consumer to secure higher prices, tariff regulations or other preferential advantages, when we are told that the cotton industry in England will always, in case of anticipated government interference, respond to the call of 'Lancashire against London', then we see how important is this branch of our subject.

Just as the *relation* of jobs is a part of job analysis, just as the *relation* of departments is a part of scientific management, so a study of all these relations just mentioned should be a part of the study of business administration. I wish it were not so often assumed that the subject of personnel relations in industry applies only to employers and employees. The manager has to get credit from the bankers, make dividends for the stockholders, and he has to deal with his competitors. To be more exact, the manager has relations with (1) bankers, (2) stockholders, (3) co-managers and directors, (4) wage-earners, (5) competitors, (6) the people from whom he buys, (7) customers.

The interweaving of authority and responsibility[5]

We are now ready to take a second step in the consideration of this subject. Authority and responsibility go with function, but as the essence of organization is the interweaving of functions, authority and responsibility we now see as a matter of interweaving. An order, a command, is a step in a process, a moment in the movement of interweaving experience. We should guard against thinking this step a larger part of the whole process than it really is. There is all that leads to the order, all that comes afterwards – methods of administration, the watching and recording of results, what flows out of it to make further orders. If we trace all that leads to a command, what persons are connected with it and in what way, we find that more than one man's experience has gone to the making of that moment. Unless it is a matter of purely arbitrary authority. Arbitrary authority, or the 'power over' which we considered in the paper on 'Power', is authority not related to all the experience concerned, but to that of one man alone, or of one group of men.

The particular person, then, identified with the moment of command – foreman, upper executive or expert – is not the most important matter for our consideration, although, of course, a very important part of the process. All that I want to emphasize is that there is a process. A political scientist writes, 'Authority co-ordinates the experiences of men'. But I think this is a wrong view of authority. The form of organization should be such as to allow or induce the continuous co-ordination of the experiences of men. A practical business man, the member of a firm of manufacturers in one of our Western States, said to me, while speaking of the necessity of business management's becoming a profession: 'And the essence of any profession is finding the law. That is what makes business management a science. The business manager has to find the law of every managerial activity in question.' This means that this man recognizes authority as inherent in the situation, not as attached to an official position. He would not agree with the political scientist that authority co-ordinates the experiences of men, because he sees that legitimate authority flows from co-ordination, not co-ordination from authority.

It would seem to go without saying that you cannot hold people responsible for anything unconnected with their experience. Yet this was what the Allies tried to do when they sought power over Germany through the Treaty of Versailles. The Treaty of Versailles failed because, not being related to the experience of the Germans, the Allies found it impossible to hold Germany responsible for the results. I am not responsible for anything which has not its roots in my experience or my potential experience, that is, the experience I am in a position to acquire by reason of my function.

It is because responsibility is the outcome of an interweaving experience that we often find it so difficult to 'fix' responsibility, as it is called. Is it the head of a manufacturing department who is responsible for the quality of a food product, or is it the consulting chemist? If a certain method you are using in your business proves a failure, who is responsible? The expert who suggested it? Or the head of the department who accepted it? Or those who engaged expert and head of department? Or the man who carried it out and knew it wouldn't work but obeyed orders? Again, if the quality of a piece of work is poor, it may be the fault of the last worker on it, or it may have been handed to him in poor condition from a previous operation, or the workers may have been given poor material, or all of these causes may have led to the final result. We might multiply these instances indefinitely; every one agrees, for instance, that managers and operators are both responsible for waste. This pluralistic responsibility, this interlocking responsibility, makes it difficult to 'fix' responsibility, yet business success depends partly on doing just this. We have a problem here to think out. We have to discover how far each one concerned has contributed to the failure or partial failure, not in order to blame, but in order to learn all we can from this experience.

Another corollary from this conception of authority and responsibility as a moment in interweaving experience is that you have no authority as a mere left-over. You cannot take the authority which you won yesterday and apply it today. That is, you could not if we were able to embody the conception we are now considering in a plan of organization. In the ideal organization authority is always fresh, always being distilled anew. The importance of this in business management has not yet been estimated.

*Summary – the leader's relation to the
fundamental principles of organization*[6]

I want to summarize this talk by taking the principles which I gave you in our discussion of 'Controls', and which I consider the fundamental principles of organization: namely, evoking, interacting, integrating, and emerging, and ask what part the leader has in all these.

Under evoking, we shall all agree, that it is one of the leader's chief duties to draw out from each his fullest possibilities. The foreman should feel responsible for the education and training of those under him, the heads of departments should feel the same, and so all along up the line to the chief executive. In fact several men at a meeting of the American Management Association voiced their conviction that 'leader' and 'teacher' are synonymous terms. If we are coming to think that the leader is not the boss, but the educator, that seems to me an indication that business thinking is taking a long step forward. Our old idea of leadership was that of being able to impress oneself upon others. But to persuade men to *follow* you and to train men to work *with* you are conceptions of leadership as far apart as the poles. The best type of leader today does not want men who are subservient to him, those who render him a passive obedience. He is trying to develop men exactly the opposite of this, men themselves with mastery, and such men will give his own leadership worth and power.

I say that it is the part of the leader to educate and train. He must know how to do this. He must himself understand, or get others who understand, the scientific methods which have lately been applied to production, to marketing, to office management, to finance, and, perhaps more important than all, the scientific methods which psychology is giving us for the understanding and controlling of human relationships.

Our second and third principles were interacting and integrating. The leader is more responsible than anyone else for that integrative unity which is the aim of organization. As our business undertakings are not only becoming vast in size but also more complex in character, the success of these undertakings depends on their parts being so skilfully related one to another that they function effectively as a whole. The leader should be leader of a coherent group, of men who are finding their material welfare their most effective expression, their spiritual satisfaction, through their relations to one another, through the functioning of the group to which they belong. If the old idea of leader was the man with compelling personality, the idea today is the man who is the expression of a harmonious and effective unity which he has helped to form and which he is able to make a going affair. We no longer think that the best leader is the greatest hustler or the most persuasive orator or even the best trader. The great leader is he who is able to integrate the experience of all and use it for a common purpose. All the ramifications of organization are the ways he does this; they are not set up to provide a machinery of following.

The fourth fundamental principle of organization which I gave you was what I called the emerging, because that is the expression so much used today to denote the evolving, the creating of new values, the forward movement. It is the word with most significance in modern literature. Scientists are using it to describe evolution – emergent evolution – and the business man is as interested as the scientist in the emerging. As a certain psychologist speaks of those moments in creating when evolution turns a corner, as Huxley spoke of the mystery moments in evolution, so the leader in business is one who understands the creative moment in the progress of business, who sees one situation melting into another and has learned the mastery of *that* moment.

To sum up my summary: the leader releases energy, unites energies, and all with the object not only of carrying out a purpose, but of creating further and larger purposes. And I do not mean here by larger purposes mergers or more branches; I speak of larger in the qualitative rather than the quantitative sense. I mean purposes which will include more of those fundamental values for which most of us agree we are really living.

These extracts are all taken from Mary Parker Follett, *Dynamic Administration*, Pitman, 1941.

1. pp. 52–4.
2. pp. 58–60.
3. pp. 79–82, 88–9.
4. p. 93.
5. pp. 149–51.
6. pp. 267–8.

4.3 Psychology in Industry;
New Techniques and Approaches

MICHAEL TRAVIS

ALTHOUGH many readers may take it for granted that modern psychology is universally applied to the human problems of industry, the evidence is often to the contrary. A current survey of personnel recruitment procedures in a group of northern industrial concerns[1] suggests that a good many doubtful and unscientific assessment techniques are in current use. Indeed, only in a minority of firms could the investigators find evidence of psychologically planned selection techniques which included effective job analysis, reliable assessment procedures and follow-up of work progress. Few of the individual selectors had had any formal training in selection work and yet a majority expressed a dissatisfaction with their current procedures and a willingness to consider improved methods. It seems hard to reconcile these research findings of the late 1960s with the fact that, even by the early twenties, a number of techniques of job analysis and methods of measuring individual traits were known. In the same way, a number of years was to elapse before Elton Mayo's Hawthorne work[2] had much impact upon management practices. Indeed, the questions unanswered in the various relay and wiring room experiments have since provoked a multitude of studies of supervisory and leadership behaviour, but with the exception of investigations which tend to support current management values, few of these found mention in management textbooks. A scrutiny of appointments advertisements with their references to 'integrity' and character traits will suggest to the reader that another monumental study of the late twenties – the Character Education Enquiry conducted by Hartshorne and May[3] – has failed to break through to practitioners in selection. Of course few selectors have the time to peruse psychological journals and there is the traditional resistance towards the intrusion of the scientist, especially where he is likely, as in the case of Hartshorne and May, to challenge the generality of the character traits personnel selectors have been seeking and perhaps quietly admiring.

Just as industry has been slow to utilize general psychology in certain of its practices, so it has shown a striking willingness to make use of psychology in other areas. Originally mental testing had appeared as a simple solution to a multitude of selection problems and brought unconditional enthusiasm from a section of industry and education. Indeed, Florence Goodenough[4] writing about the hey-day of testing in the U.S.A. refers wryly to the days when an I.Q. was an I.Q. and no one challenged its validity. The limitations of mental testing were not appreciated, nor was the need for training in the use and interpretation of test material. Otherwise effective tools were discarded because they did not live up to false expectations, or their interpretation was beyond the skills of their users. William McGehee[5] points to the tendency for industry readily to adopt training methods which have high 'face validity'. These techniques which look good but have only a limited usefulness and may require highly trained staff, may not facilitate and may even retard learning. The case study method, he points out, may increase the elegance with which executive training is approached but have absolutely no effect upon the quality of the solution. For example, psychologists in industry occasionally have to spend time restraining the over-enthusiastic administrator from adopting the relatively unproven techniques which have high face validity or some other special appeal. Group selection methods, selection techniques which involve the observation of expressive gesture, constitutional psychologies, motivational research and group dynamics techniques have occasionally met with specific acceptance that their usefulness would fail to justify.

THE SHORTCOMINGS OF EARLY
INDUSTRIAL PSYCHOLOGY

Occasionally outright naivety has been attributed to behavioural scientists in their attempts to cope with industrial problems. One example of this may be seen in the tendency of some management writers to over-generalize from the findings of the Hawthorne Experiments and of investigators of the same tradition, such as Likert, McGregor and Argyris. All these researchers, by way of an impressive programme of investigation, had investigated the consequences of participative management – that is, extensive participation at all levels in decision taking; their findings were immensely instructive and provided a valuable commentary about traditional scientific management and its attempts at consultative methods. But managers and researchers have queried whether all industrial workers actually seek a high degree of participation and have pointed to the fact that the cultural, economic and technical circumstances in which industrial production is carried out have an effect on attitudes towards participation and power equalization. 'There can be no general prescription for every patient,' writes Tom Lupton[6], and it may be that entrepreneurs of industrial psychology have done the behavioural sciences a disservice by their over-generalization of findings.

In fact, some of the blame for the selective use of psychology in industry must rest with psychologists themselves. A number of factors may be considered. First, for many early psychologists there was much stigma attached to the idea of experimentation or observation which might lead to some practical end. Thus, in 1898 when Cattell was writing about the tests he administered to Columbia University freshmen he was careful to note that he wished to study the effects of environment and heredity on growth and the interrelation of traits. The practical aspects of student selection find less emphasis. Secondly, there has been in my opinion an emphasis upon a speculative outlook in the teaching of psychological techniques on management courses. In interview instruction one may occasionally see this tendency. Rather than an understanding of the personality dynamics of the individual candidate it may be more valuable to assist selectors in the choice of appropriate personality and ability traits and to advise on techniques of assessment. Many have made persuasive cases for an actuarial rather than a clinical approach to personnel assessment. Thirdly, it must be admitted that the experimental tradition begun by Wundt in his first psychological laboratory in 1879 and which has been central to psychology to the present day is sometimes difficult to maintain in industry. In the laboratory it is relatively easy to carry out experiments and repeat them, while in industry repetition under exactly similar conditions is sometimes impossible. Furthermore, the experiment itself may interfere with the particular variable under scrutiny, for if employees know that they are part of an experiment or involved in a survey of attitudes and opinions they may respond in a way which is very untypical of their normal behaviour. Control of the variables under observation is another problem, since while experimenting with one variable the psychologist may find difficulty in resisting other changes which management may wish to make. Only by effective planning, experimental design and sophisticated statistical treatment can these problems be minimized, and it must be admitted that by no means all of the current experimental and survey work can be considered adequate. Indeed in the face of industrial problems psychologists are sometimes tempted to rely a little too heavily on imprecise survey and clinical evidence. For example, much of the discussion of accident proneness as a continuing human trait has had a very inadequate survey basis. Similarly studies which have correlated the extent of a manager's concern with his subordinates' personal well-being with the subordinates' general effectiveness are frequently quoted to support the view that employee-centred management is the best. Here the causal direction is difficult to identify and the evidence does not justify generalized pronouncements on the best way to manage.

Finally it can be argued that industrial psychologists have sometimes failed to grasp the essential features of an industrial setting. An example may be drawn from what is often called the criterion problem. In assessing the effectiveness of a new training scheme, changed selection methods, or redesigned work layout, the investigator has to have some criterion or standard of performance of workers. Before new procedures are started or redesign begun, it is necessary to state what performance is desired. Frequently experimenters have been prepared to put in psychological tests, training methods and new works methods, and then begin a search for a criterion which would justify them. Indeed it is only within recent years that the criterion problem has gained the attention it deserved.[7] Job satisfaction has often emerged as the criterion, although it has little appeal to industrialists and it does not always tie up with work performance, particularly in manual occupations. Needless to say, criteria which are suitable at one point in time may not be appropriate at another, since with changing technology we may need different types of organization and personnel practices. Some psychologists have been slow to recognize these problems. In the application of mental testing and personality assessment techniques to the process of vocational guidance we may see a lack of attention to such long-term goals.

THE SCOPE OF INDUSTRIAL PSYCHOLOGY

Ideally industrial psychology has attempted to combine the methods of the experimenter, survey psychologist and the clinician to investigate the behaviour of people at work. Frequently it is compartmentalized into a number of problem areas. Selection, training, physical environment, optimum incentive conditions and human engineering problems have been traditional research areas in industrial psychology. Roughly speaking they may be seen as applications of knowledge about individual differences, learning phenomena, physiological psychology, motivation and general experimental psychology. These classifications may reflect the chapter headings of industrial psychology textbooks, but in reality the problems faced by a practising personnel officer or industrial consultant are rarely so easily categorized.

An appraisal of existing selection schemes may frequently provide a number of insights into training, organization and incentive questions within the firm. Consultants frequently report that what begins as a selection problem ends with recommendations for action in several of these areas. For example, a call to a psychologist for a number of selection tests which would measure the emotional stability required to cope with a mentally tiring job might end with a redesign of the job in question and a reorganization of the incentive conditions of the work. In the same way a call for the use of intelligence tests for the selection of personnel for training might result in a redesign of current training methods.

INDIVIDUAL DIFFERENCES

Initially the pioneer area of industrial psychology, personnel selection remained for a long time the scapegoat of many administrators. It was assumed that if people had ability and well-developed skills they would show them in a way which was supportive to the organization. Evidence of under-performance from educational psychology and later from occupational studies has shown otherwise. Indeed, the early investigators in industrial psychology had tended to see the worker as an individual with a collection of abilities and skills working within a physical environment. They were less concerned with the working group as a social unit and with its effects upon the attitudes and affiliations of its members. Nevertheless, with this interest in individual capacities came a number of important developments. As has often been the case in industrial psychology, some of the inspiration for research came from non-industrial sources. By the turn of the century the severe problem of retardation of large numbers of school children and the increasing demand for advanced education created a need for appropriate selection techniques. Similarly the changing of attitudes towards the mentally handicapped during the eighteen hundreds and the consequent founding of special schools in the western world drew the attention of many psychologists to the problems of selection and the measurement of individual differences. In Britain, Sir Francis Galton had published his *Inquiries into Human Faculty and its Development*[8] in 1883 and was concerning himself with individual differences in intellect and mental imagery, while in the United States J. Mc K. Cattell was measuring certain physical and mental characteristics of his students. Keenness of vision, hearing, colour vision, sensitivity to pain, reaction-time and memory were measured but when scores were correlated with college grades several years later, no significant relationships were established. Similar work by J. A. Gilbert utilizing tests of auditory acuity, speed of tapping and anthropometric measures on child subjects revealed scores which showed no relationship with teachers' ratings of the children concerned. In fact it was Alfred Binet working under the education authorities in Paris who was first able to produce an effective device for the selection of children for the authorities' special schools. His method was a simple one of sampling the reasoning and problem-solving abilities he wanted to measure. His first intelligence scale contained material for the classification of low-grade defectives and material appropriate for children in higher grades. In 1910, seeing the usefulness of his tests for allocation and grading in the army, Binet recommended the psychological testing of French soldiers. His advice was rejected by the French War Ministry and it was left to the German and American military authorities during World War I to first undertake systematic selection by standardized test. Indeed, at the time of Binet's recommendation several psychologists had outspokenly defended pure psychology and attacked all attempts to develop applied fields. E. B. Titchener, a distinguished psychologist of the time, called on psychologists to renounce applied studies and W. Wundt, distinguished for his contribution to experimental psychology, deplored specifically the applications of general psychology to education, psychiatry and law. In fact, those psychologists in the United States who had become interested in making practical applications of their work frequently avoided publicity and made only limited reports on their work. Seashore writing in *Psychology and Daily Life*[9] in 1913 points to a lack of progress except in the applied psychology of music. In the same conspicuously modest way Münsterberg in discussing the progress of applied psychology writes, 'the only fields in which psychological experiment has been somewhat translated into practical use are those of education and medicine.' A general unwillingness to communicate findings could explain these incomplete accounts by Seashore and Münsterberg.

In spite of this resistance of academic psychologists, progress in applied psychology was becoming apparent in time study, motion study and job analysis. Frederick W. Taylor's book *The Principles of Scientific Management*[10] and Frank B. Gilbreth's *Motion Study*[11] appeared in 1911. Münsterberg, who finally became director of the Psychological Laboratory at Harvard, published several texts on the application of general psychology to such varied topics as crime detection, teaching practice and management techniques. Viewed by many as the father of industrial psychology as a result of his paper *Psychology and Industrial Efficiency*,[12] Münsterberg not only indicated how psychology might help in the process of selection but also cited examples of his own personal successful selection work with motor men, telephone operators, and other occupations.

INDUSTRIAL PSYCHOLOGY IN BRITAIN

In this country it is due to Bernard Muscio that the possibilities of industrial psychology were made known. A one-time demonstrator in experimental psychology at Cambridge and later investigator of the Industrial Fatigue Research Board, Muscio gave in 1916 a series of lectures on Industrial Psychology, in which he defined the subject area which, he felt, could incorporate the scientific management movement. However, the emphasis in scientific management upon the increased output which would result from more efficient working methods aroused some antagonism from workers and the trade unions. The suspicions engendered in this country were to continue, according to P. E. Vernon, until the World War II period and were responsible, he points out, for the lack of cooperation between service psychologists and the Ministry of Labour. Nevertheless, an important number of researches were begun in British factories during the World War I period. At first the work was done under the Health of Munition Workers Committee and continued by the Industrial Fatigue Research Board (later the Industrial Health Research Board), a branch of the Medical Research Council. The Industrial Fatigue Research Board was established to 'consider and investigate the relation of hours of labour and other conditions of employment, including methods of work, to the production of fatigue, having regard both to industrial efficiency and the preservation of health among the workers'.[13] Rest pauses, hours of work, work rhythm, noise, temperature, training and accidents were typical areas to be investigated – most of which had the consideration of industrial fatigue well to the fore. From the start, investigators found difficulty in establishing a clear-cut definition of fatigue and in obtaining adequate measurement of this condition. Most researchers were compelled to find indirect measures, although most discontent was recorded regarding the adequacy of output as a measure. As P. M. Elton observed in 1922, 'fatigue is not to be measured in terms of work performed and is not distributed between workers in the ratio of the work they do, whether necessary or unnecessary'. In their study of inspection processes in industry, Wyatt and Langdon note[14] 'there is reason to believe that boredom is responsible for a greater loss in output than fatigue'. Difficulty was experienced in attributing observed effects to the influence of fatigue, and investigators were further handicapped by their limited knowledge of worker motivation and social psychology. McDougall's instinct theory held weight with many psychologists and Elton Mayo's *Human Problems of an Industrial Civilisation*[2] (1933) had not yet revealed the shortcomings of a non-social industrial psychology. Regarding the practical issues of hours of work, rest pauses, etc., the British investigators produced a number of instructive findings. It was demonstrated that the extension of working hours beyond a given point brought little or no increase in production, and where suitable rest pauses were introduced the result was generally an improvement of quality and quantity of output. Interesting findings emerged suggesting that output often fell in the middle of a work period and that when this trough was given over to a rest period production rose, not only after the rest, but also before it.[15] The evidence sometimes pointed less to fatigue than to changes of incentive and motivation.

By 1938, after twenty years of existence, the Board had produced eighty-three reports on special industrial problems. Several of these reports were to become much quoted standard texts with their statistics reworked from time to time. Greenwood and Woods in I.F.R.B. Report No. 4 provided subsequent authors with survey data which has caused long controversy regarding accident proneness as a permanent and consistent trait. Their investigation was to lead to the development of a number of theories of 'accident proneness'. In the tradition of early industrial psychology, initial attempts to account for this condition emphasized individual differences such as nervous instability and poor motor co-ordination, though more careful statistical treatment has drawn attention to chance factors in the distribution of accidents, to differences of exposure to hazard and to the existence of a number of social determinants.

C. S. MYERS AND THE N.I.I.P.

It is difficult to know just what impact these findings were having on British industry in the early days. Perhaps some insight might be gained from the fact that in 1919 a Summer School of Industrial Administration was held at Cambridge under the auspices of the University Psychological Laboratory and organized by Dr C. S. Myers. The subject was a 'study of certain industrial management problems, chiefly from a psychological point of view'. That it was well attended and that many of the participants were responsible industrial executives sounds promising, but apparently 'the teachings fell largely on barren soil'.[16] In fact, one of the contributors is alleged to have remarked, 'We are bound to deduce that, on the whole, British industry is either undermanaged or mismanaged.' Undaunted, C. S. Myers founded the National Institute of Industrial Psychology in 1921. The Institute was founded as a non-profit making scientific association to promote and encourage the practical application of psychology to commerce and industry. Its activities have since included research, advisory services to individuals and firms, training in different branches of industrial psychology and dissemination of information on the subject through lectures, discussions, publications and the maintenance of a reference library.

Myers was soon able to gather several eminent psychologists to the Institute's staff, and support was enlisted from a number of industrial concerns. In fact at a time when university departments were small, and there existed few posts in educational and clinical psychology, N.I.I.P. represented a major avenue for the employment of applied psychologists. Myers himself brought a sound experimental background to his work with N.I.I.P. He had held the post of director of the Cambridge Laboratory and had investigated auditory problems and individual differences. In 1909 he had published his *Textbook of Experimental Psychology*[17] and during his Cambridge period gained a reputation for sound middle-of-the-road empiricism at a time when psychology was tending to divide into various schools. He sought advances in experimental and applied psychology – aims which saw fruition in his reorganization of the Cambridge Laboratory and his establishment of the N.I.I.P. During the war period Myers had been consultant on psychological matters to the British armies in France and was involved in the training of medical officers in neurological centres. Influenced strongly by Muscio's lectures on Industrial Psychology, Myers became interested in the idea of applying the findings of psychology to industrial problems, and in his lectures at the Royal Institution, London, in 1918 he proposed the establishment of a number of institutes of applied psychology in each of our largest cities. Although this hope was never to be completely fulfilled, N.I.I.P. had opened a Scottish branch in 1930 and by the mid-thirties possessed a staff of about forty. In view of its need to earn fees in order to survive the Institute was compelled to undertake extensive private consultancy work for firms, government departments and other public organizations. Much of the data produced in these investigations into staff selection, training, environmental conditions, work methods, production planning and marketing were private and remained unpublished. L. S. Hearnshaw, in his book *A Short History of British Psychology, 1840–1940*,[18] has suggested that pioneer work was carried out at this time in what later became known as human engineering, ergonomics and human relations. It may be that several of the post-war findings in these areas were anticipated at this time.

Industrial relations, however, remained a less important area of investigation even though as early as 1920 Myers in *Mind and Work*[19] had briefly dealt with industrial unrest and discussed its relation to mental worry, conflict and individual adjustment. Although the social aspects of work were not yet fully appreciated some British psychologists had been prepared to absorb into their conception of industrial psychology the principles of scientific management and time and motion study propounded by Taylor and Gilbreth and to undertake projects in these areas. In fact during the early days of industrial psychology in Britain, psychologists may have sometimes overstepped their competence. L. S. Hearnshaw writes,[18] 'Not all the investigations in this area were founded firmly in psychological research; they often involved operational rather than psychological analysis and psychologists were not specially, by virtue of their training, competent to carry them out.'

PERSONNEL TESTING

During the inter-war years, the I.H.R.B. and the N.I.I.P. were primarily concerned with the application of underlying sciences such as physiology, individual and early group psychology to problems of work and the formulation of personnel techniques. Through its journal, *Occupational Psychology*, the Institute has continued to make known research within a broad area of industrial problems. By dint of its own research activities it has remained an authority in the area of ability measurement, personnel selection, training techniques and vocational guidance procedures. The experience it has gained in survey investigations in industry has similarly rendered it an authority on interest and attitude measurement methodology. However, it was in the United States that the first widespread use of standardized selection procedures occurred, as a result of the need in 1917 to allocate two million recruits into appropriate military categories. The problem was to select the rather dull recruits who would require specialized training, eliminate the really backward, select possible officer candidates and arrange for a reasonable degree of homogeneity of ability in training groups. The individual tests of Binet and his successors were too lengthy and unsuited to this population, which had to be tested in batches of several hundred. The answer was found in the famous Army Alpha tests and the non-verbal Army Beta Tests for illiterates. Military selection provided certain conditions which were ideal for validating the effectiveness of these procedures. Unlike the industrial setting, it is often possible to follow not only the careers of the selected individuals, but also to evaluate the later performance of the unselected group where suitable common criteria of job performance can be found. The military testing schemes were found to be effective and the new group tests formed the basis of many later tests which were used in industrial selection work. The immediate post-war availability of these measures and the increasing interest shown towards mental testing techniques made possible several investigations into the importance of intellectual characteristics in occupational behaviour. In fact a start was made by using the vast collection of data accumulated during the massive military testing programmes. One of the first projects was concerned with the relationship between intelligence and attainment on the occupational scale. Obviously this was a matter of the utmost concern to vocational advisers, training departments and selectors. If attainment on the occupational scale was closely dependent upon intelligence then the usual form of encouragement to young people to aspire to high-level occupations was mistaken. The data were first published in the *Memoirs of the National Academy of Sciences* in 1921, and provided a first look at this question, showing a tendency for mean intelligence scores to rise with attainment on the occupational scale. Most revealing of course was the immense element of overlap between the various necessary occupational intelligence levels (a finding which was brought out again by the World War II data). Soon occupational psychologists were dealing in detail with individual careers, and the search for the fundamental qualities of successful managers was on. Writing in the *Journal of Applied Psychology* in 1924, Bingham and David reported a study of 102 business executives who underwent army-type intelligence tests and a complete analysis of their business performance. Their conclusion was that superiority in intelligence, beyond a certain minimum, contributes less to business success than does superiority in several non-intellectual traits of personality.[20] This finding was echoed by similar studies of selling and teaching occupations and suggested that much more investigation was required in the area of personality and interests.

As early as World War I personality tests had been in existence. R. S. Woodworth had produced his Personal Data Sheet and various devices had been used to screen off recruits with disturbed personalities. As selection tools they and their successors have proved to be one of the most disappointing ventures in industrial psychology. It soon became known that anxious candidates become wary about tests of this sort and tend to modify their responses accordingly. Highly intelligent subjects are able to identify items as measures of emotional stability, dominance and social acceptability, etc., and where a job is at stake, they do not hesitate to impress their selectors on these counts. For selectors themselves these tests provided further problems. First, personality inventories needed to be long if they were to possess any degree of reliability. The consequent problems of administration and scoring were sufficient to dissuade many organizations from using them, but second, there was the really serious question of what personality characteristics to look for in candidates for a given job. The real danger lay in the use of personality tests to select a 'neutral' breed of men whose scores all fell close to the mean, for the task of carrying out detailed surveys of existing staff to identify the personality test profiles of successful employees was more than most firms could undertake. The introduction of projective testing techniques in the form of the Rorschach Ink Blot Test in 1932 and the Thematic Apperception Test published by H. H. Murray in 1935 provided measures of greater penetration than conventional inventory tests, but introduced new problems of administration, scoring and interpretation. More recent endeavour in the field of personality testing has attempted to overcome the problems of faking, sets of response and interpretation. The introduction of forced-choice type tests where items are balanced regarding favourability has been a promising innovation but it is unlikely that much improvement in the efficiency of personality testing can be expected until test users are able to identify the critical personality requirements for a given job and to devise effective criteria to assess employee behaviour. It is the author's contention that many selectors fail to realize that in some occupations a broad range of personalities may be able to cope adequately with the task involved. In fact, it has been demonstrated in social psychology that the presence of a wide range of personality types with the consequent conflict of individuals may provide a creative and productive work group, especially where the exchange and refinement of ideas is involved. The occupational profiles which become available from the use of a personality test upon a cross-section of people employed often provide a good deal more interest to the sociologist than to the personnel selector. For example, typical cross-sectional studies of an occupation may reveal high mean scores on traits such as tendermindedness, emotional insecurity, introversion and group dependence, but are these the traits which the selector should encourage within the occupation through selection according to degree of fit with existing norms – a practice not uncommon at one time in selection work?

INTEREST AND ATTITUDE MEASUREMENT

The measurement of interests and attitudes has been a more successful activity. The World War I psychologists had already attempted to devise standardized tests which would measure a candidate's information about certain interests and activities. Tests of mechanical information still remain to this day, and often form part of batteries for the selection of craft apprentices. However, information testing is cumbersome and general information tests need frequent revision. Without doubt the most interesting and valuable contributions to the study of interests and their occupational relevance have been stimulated by the inventory studies of E. K. Strong. First published in 1927 and followed by several revisions, Strong's interest inventory provided a comparison of the vocational interests of an individual with those of successful men in over forty occupational groups. The natural desire to fake a questionnaire of this sort, dealing as it does with interests, leisure activities and job preferences, has given the Strong Vocational Interest Blank only limited value as a direct selection tool. However, the main value of Strong's inventory and more recent tests has been in their use in studies of the relationship of interests to intelligence, aptitudes and personality. He was able to test many of the widely held views on these subjects – in particular the relationship between occupational interests and levels of intelligence. Further work concerned the stability and predictive value of leisure and interest patterns, for, whereas he was able to show that single interests or leisure activities are continually changing and are poor predictors of job performance, interest patterns frequently do have predictive value in respect of the type of work in which the individual is likely to find the greatest satisfaction – presumably where he will tend to show involvement in his work and long tenure of post.

THE INTERVIEW AS A METHOD OF APPRAISAL

The interview was well established as assessment technique and needed no pioneer, but even as early as 1916 investigators were questioning its value. In that year W. D. Scott, writing in an article called *Selection of Employees by Means of Quantitative Determination*, described an experiment in which he had sales managers judge the ability of applicants for sales positions. The results were a serious challenge to the reliability and validity of the traditional interview. The unreliability of the technique was underlined by the considerable disagreements amongst the judges and the low validity by the low correlations between ratings and the actual production records of the applicants. These were no chance judgements, for similar results were reported by H. L. Hollingworth and the search had begun to identify and eliminate the sources of error in the interview technique. An interesting study in this direction was carried out in Britain by E. H. Magson, who attempted to discover how estimates of general ability are normally made in everyday life.[21] Magson, besides reporting that his untrained interviewers drawn from a wide variety of careers were unable to assess general intelligence with any degree of accuracy, showed that the estimates that were made were at least in part based upon the manner, facial expression and personal appearance of the subject. W. Spielman and C. Burt, writing in 1926 in Industrial Fatigue Research Board Report No. 33,[22] went on to show that a further source of the varied assessments amongst judges or assessors was that of fundamental disagreement about the meaning of the trait or quality which was being assessed. Further analysis showed that certain simple qualities could be estimated much more easily than complex moral and character descriptions about which assessors may disagree, and in which assessment is likely to be affected by the moral standpoint of the judge himself. Further evidence on this matter of the effects of the attitudes and values of assessors upon their judgement of a person or situation was brought to light in startling fashion by Stuart A. Rice's report 'Contagious Bias in the Interview'.[23] His study of the interviews of 2,000 homeless men showed clearly how a belief or opinion such as socialism or prohibitionism may affect diagnosis of a welfare problem.

At about the same time a number of studies were conducted to compare the effectiveness of psychological techniques of assessment and traditional methods. In Britain the Borstal studies carried out by Alec Rodger demonstrated the clear superiority of psychologically planned assessment procedures over traditional unplanned interviews.[24]

The need for the selection of interviewers, specialized training in the conduct of the technique and for detailed attention to the choice and description of traits or qualities to be assessed was known by the early thirties, but a lengthy time lag was to go by before much attention was given to this problem. Little systematic selection of personnel selectors took place and there appeared for many years to be a trickle of people into selection work, whose suitability was distinctly suspect. For many years the only comprehensive courses in interview technique were available from N.I.I.P., but interviewing is something that many people feel they do rather well, and the small demand for training is not surprising. However, an early outcome of the experiments into interview unreliability was the appearance of a series of plans or guides which could be used both as an aid to the specification of qualities for the job in question and as a guide to the interview assessment of the candidate. On the British scene the Seven Point Plan devised by Alec Rodger for use in vocational guidance and selection work probably found the greatest favour, and had the merits of providing a short list of reasonably simple qualities and characteristics under which job and candidate could be assessed. Other systems have been proposed by J. Munro Fraser and more recently by Elizabeth Sidney and Margaret Brown in *The Skills of Interviewing*.[25] Further attempts to eliminate the drawbacks to the interview included efforts to standardize the whole procedure. It was known that questioning technique can influence candidate response and several standardized interviews have been produced. That they did not answer the problem became known from Rice's studies where bias in assessment remained even though the same questions were put to all subjects. These findings were later strengthened by the experience of the social and market surveys conducted between the wars, but these did not prevent the publishing of several standardized interviews intended for use in personnel selection. One of the best known of these, *The Diagnostic Interviewer Guide*, published in America by E. F. Wonderlic, structured the interview by giving sets of questions related to certain major areas – work, family and personal history. Limited successes were reported with these devices but most interviewers feel that standardized interviews make for awkward breaks in conversation and do not facilitate the maintenance of rapport throughout the procedure. Even within the area of market and social surveys there is not complete agreement about the value of the standardized interview and the 'free' interview still finds a place for itself in studies of attitudes and values.

OTHER ASSESSMENT TECHNIQUES

In face of the difficulties of interviewing, some investigators attempted to develop the application form in such a way that it would contribute directly towards the assessment. The idea of devising application forms so that they are concerned mainly with matter that is known to be critical to the successful carrying out of a job or group of jobs seems obvious, but few organizations have developed them to this extent. Practices differ, of course, on either side of the Atlantic; for the American population seems to expect to give more detailed personal information on an application blank, but the traditional British application form, with its requirement for name, address, age, schooling and work history, frequently adds nothing to what is known from the letter of application. By 1925, as a result of all the interest in the selection of salesmen in the United States, investigators had been able to conclude that a good deal could be gained from the use of a blank in which items were known to have significance for success in a job. Other devices including interview summary forms and rating scales were soon produced, but these did not answer the serious problem, first raised by Spielman and Burt in their 1926 paper; namely that the most difficult qualities to assess in interview are those which are never shown during the procedure – cooperation with equals, attitudes to seniors, etc. From this problem were born the situational tests in which the candidate could be observed exhibiting the behaviour which would not normally appear in the comfort and quiet of the interview room. The 'command group situations' and the 'leaderless group situations' used as part of the British War Office Selection Boards are well known. For once, industry has not been slow to utilize these new techniques, for executives have seen in them ways of assessing those elusive qualities of 'leadership', 'toughness' and 'competitiveness' for which they are continually searching. A good deal of the fundamental work of evaluating these techniques has come from this country. P. E. Vernon has pointed out that the correlations between W.O.S.B. assessments and those of officer success were small, but suggested the unreliability of the criterion of success as an explanation. The experience of the Civil Service Selection Boards suggested that by setting group exercises of very high face-validity it was possible to create great interest amongst the candidates. But it was P. E. Vernon's article, 'The Validation of Civil Service Selection Board Procedures', in *Occupational Psychology* in 1950, which constituted the classic evaluation of these selection devices. Here he was able to show evidence of the value of psychologically planned procedures but again, probably due to criterion problems, the correlations were not high. The gradings given by observers in one part of the procedure may have been affected by their previous impressions, and this contamination renders separate evaluation of group discussions difficult. Other studies by J. Munro Fraser, John Handyside and David Duncan, utilizing group exercises for the selection of management trainees and supervisors, showed promising results, but P. E. Vernon's cautious observations remain the most authoritative view on the subject. Although group exercises may have some superiority over the conventional interview, Vernon illustrates how successful use of these techniques is dependent upon the skill and experience of the observers. The face validity, the appeal to the candidates and the reality for the users may be rather deceptive. Once again one must wonder how many of these observations have permeated through to the many executives who regularly utilize techniques of this kind without the training and experience of the War Office and Civil Service Selection Boards. Without specially prepared projects, detailed job specifications and rating scales, the task of evaluating the suitability of a candidate for a supervisory post is likely to be a hopeless one.[26]

In fact in selection, vocational guidance and training, the emphasis has often been upon the lower level job. This does not imply that the psychologist is always more efficient in the lower levels. Referring to military experience in selection and allocation work, N. A. B. Wilson[27] has drawn attention to the likelihood that many low-level jobs are organized in such a way that each job requires a variety of specialized aptitudes. Thus, assessments of individuals by aptitude test may be of little value as aptitude indicators. Since the pool of high general ability must be limited in some occupational groups, Wilson suggests that if tasks could be reorganized so that most jobs consisted of psychologically homogeneous elements, 'it might be possible to make the limited pool of general ability go further, while utilizing some hitherto under-used special aptitudes'. This is an interesting thought and certainly one to be borne in mind when new jobs are to be created and old ones reorganized. Could it be, though, that job simplification of the work of the less able employee produces effects which are not entirely desirable? Current research into the effects of job enlargement upon individuals of different capacities highlights the possible dangers of over-simplification.[28] These investigations are concerned with attitudinal, production and adjustment correlates of job redesign. Regarding higher level allocation in the military field, N. A. B. Wilson has asserted that with so much organizing and technical content the assumption of dependence on general as opposed to special ability seems to be justified. However, there remains a good deal of research to be undertaken in the senior levels of management, and executive development research looks like being an interesting field.

WORLD WAR II AND NEW DEVELOPMENTS

It will be seen that during the early period of the application of psychology to the problems of business and personnel management probably the principal contribution was made through tests and other devices for appraising personnel. Since the start of World War II a number of major developments have taken place. The mobilization of personnel required improved allocation techniques, adequate training schemes and attention to problems of motivation and adjustment. Equipment, too, posed special problems since the radar and aviation equipment of the day frequently outstripped the capacities of its operator. At first there existed a gap between the designer and the psychologist with his knowledge of individual capacities and skills. Later the employment of psychologists with a background and interest in experimental psychology did much to overcome these difficulties. The war period also saw the introduction of widespread research into training problems. Improved techniques in the U.S. services resulted in 90 per cent of illiterates acquiring a speaking, reading and writing vocabulary of 1400 words in eight weeks. Furthermore the growth of studies of small groups and social behaviour provided a stimulus for the study of combat groups, effective military leadership and the nature of military morale, and studies in these areas of military psychology have continued to develop since the war. In *Occupational Psychology* (October, 1966), N. A. B. Wilson[29] notes developments in the use of programmed instruction, in engineering psychology and in studies of work environment within the military field. Naturally the findings of military psychologists have had a considerable impact upon thinking in industrial psychology, and many present occupational psychologists have a background in military personnel research. Since the war a number of new applications of psychology to industry have developed and the contribution of research has increased. For example, regarding the use of group selection methods, research has appeared which tackles questions regarding the optimum size of groups, the qualities to be assessed during the session, the type of project to be tackled and the number of observers required. Disturbing questions relate to the effects of a group's quality upon an observer's assessment of individual members, and to the effect of the introduction of an extremely dominant or destructive individual into the group. Experience may help to answer some of these questions, but frequently it is only the researcher working in a college, university or private institution who has the opportunity to set up experimental groups in an attempt to answer these problems. In 1945 the Research Center for Group Dynamics was formed by Kurt Lewin at the Massachusetts Institute of Technology. The researches of this centre awakened a good deal of interest in problems of motivation and productivity as they are related to group structure. Group dynamics brought a new look at the way people work together and provided a number of insights into managerial problems. Furthermore the development of an empirical social psychology brought with it a greater understanding of attitude change and effective communications. Findings in these areas had considerable relevance to consumer behaviour and advertising techniques, and there has developed since 1945 a branch of knowledge called consumer psychology. Experts in this field have found it possible from their knowledge of perceptual and cognitive processes to give advice regarding optimum advertising format, and the experience gained in survey techniques and psychometrics has enabled them to test the effectiveness of different advertising media. Less sound have been the attempts by a number of psychologists to develop the technique of motivational research as an aid to solving marketing problems. Speculative and heavily dependent on psychoanalytic theory, this approach has held some attractiveness for people in marketing. Recently there has grown an interest among psychologists concerning problems of organization and communication within companies. With engineers and mathematicians, psychologists have become involved with discovering what kinds of communication networks are best likely to suit the organization and its technology.

COOPERATION BETWEEN SPECIALISTS AND A MORE INTEGRATED INDUSTRIAL PSYCHOLOGY

Although one can look back to 1916 as the year when the first psychiatrist was appointed within industry, it is only recently that there has been extensive investigation of mental health at work. Just as differential psychology has developed from simple selection work into personnel planning, forecasting, executive development and the establishing of data concerning occupational failure, so clinical psychology has been given greater recognition in the industrial setting. Absenteeism, turnover and accidents are serious industrial problems which demand psychological enquiry, and social and clinical psychology have contributions to make in this area. In a society strongly influenced by moral views regarding the adaptive value of work and labour, psychology has attempted to discover the relationship of work satisfactions to general mental health and to anticipate the problems which an increased leisure existence could provide. In engineering psychology, as well, the period since the war has seen the development of an entirely new conception of the machine operator. No longer is he taken to be an independent attachment or machine minder, but he is seen as an integral part of a man-machine system. With the increasing complexity of equipment, the high costs of error and the shortage of individuals with adequate skills, it is often unrealistic for the equipment designer to match the demands of his machine to his own assumed capacities. Within the man-machine system there lies the problem of arriving at the best combination of the decision-making skills of the operative and the capacities of machines.[30] Current problems in aviation involve deciding which functions of flying shall be allotted to the human operator and which ones to the machine. Information regarding human capacities, the availability of adequate selection devices, the training problems involved, the availability of job aids and future machine technology, have to be taken into account when decisions of this sort are made. Frequently the costs of operator failure have to be weighed against the costs of delaying the introduction of a man-machine system which would put too strong an onus upon operator capacities. Systems development illustrates the concern of industrial psychologists with both the human and the hardware aspects of industry and highlights the need for cooperation between psychologists, engineers, economists and other scientists. Further, it illustrates the more integrated nature of contemporary industrial psychology.

NOTES

1. *An Enquiry into Recruitment and Selection Practices in the West Riding*, Management Centre, University of Bradford, 1967.

2. E. Mayo, *Human Problems of an Industrial Civilisation*, Routledge & Kegan Paul, 1933.

3. H. Hartshorne and M. A. May, *Studies in Deceit*, vol. I, Columbia University, 1928.

4. F. L. Goodenough, *Mental Testing*, Staples, 1950.

5. William McGehee, 'Are We Using What We Know about Training? Learning Theory and Training.' *Personnel Psychology*, vol. 2, 1958, pp. 1–12.

6. T. Lupton, *Management and the Social Sciences*, Hutchinson, 1966.

7. M. H. Brolly, 'The Criterion Problem in Selection and Guidance', *Occupational Psychology*, vol. 39, No. 2, April, 1965, pp. 77–113.

8. Sir F. Galton, *Inquiries into Human Faculty and its Development*, Macmillan, 1883.

9. C. E. Seashore, *Psychology and Daily Life*, Appleton, 1913.

10. F. W. Taylor, *The Principles of Scientific Management*, Harper, 1911.

11. F. W. Gilbreth, *Motion Study*, Constable, 1911.

12. H. Münsterberg, *Psychology and Industrial Efficiency*, Cambridge, Mass., 1913.

13. For a review of the early work on fatigue, see E. G. Chambers,

'Industrial Fatigue', *Occupational Psychology*, January and April, 1961.

14. S. Wyatt and J. N. Langdon, *Inspection Processes in Industry – a Preliminary Report*, London, 1932. (Industrial Health Research Board Report, No. 63.)

15. H. M. Vernon and T. Bedford, *Two Studies on Rest Pauses in Industry*, London, 1924. (Industrial Fatigue Research Board Report, No. 25.)

16. L. Urwick and E. F. L. Brech, *The Making of Scientific Management*, vol. 2, Pitman, 1949.

17. C. S. Myers, *Textbook of Experimental Psychology*, Arnold, 1909.

18. L. S. Hearnshaw, *A Short History of British Psychology, 1840–1940*, Methuen, 1964.

19. C. S. Myers, *Mind and Work*, University of London Press, 1920.

20. Bingham and David, 'Intelligence Test Scores and Business Success', *Journal of Applied Psychology*, vol. 8, 1924.

21. E. H. Mason, 'How We Judge Intelligence', *British Journal of Psychology*, Mono. Suppl. No. 9, 1926.

22. W. Spielman and C. Burt, *A Study in Vocational Guidance*, London, 1926. (Industrial Research Board Report, No. 33.)

23. S. A. Rice, 'Contagious Bias in the Interview', *American Journal of Sociology*, 1929.

24. A. Rodger, *A Borstal Experiment in Vocational Guidance*, London, 1937. (Industrial Health Research Board Report, No. 78.)

25. E. Sidney, and M. Brown, *The Skills of Interviewing*, Tavistock, 1961.

26. For a review of personnel selection procedures, see C. H. Stone and W. E. Kendall, *Effective Personnel Selection Procedures*, Staples, 1957.

27. N. A. B. Wilson, 'Psychology and Military Proficiency', *Occupational Psychology*, vol. 40, No. 4, October, 1966.

28. A. B. Hill and J. M. B. Thickett, 'Whither Work Study – A Suggestion', *Journal of Work Study and Management*, October, 1966.

29. N. A. B. Wilson, op. cit.

30. R. Conrad, 'Beyond Industrial Psychology', third C. S. Myers lecture, 1967, *Bulletin of British Psychological Society*, vol. 20, No. 67.

4.4 Elton Mayo and the Empirical
Study of Social Groups

DAVID ASHTON

THE importance of Elton Mayo as a pioneer of scientific management lies in his approach to employee cooperation. He was the
first person to reveal the inadequacy of studying the individual in
isolation and of only taking into account the purely physical
aspects of an industrial environment. His work indicated the
importance of the primary, informal groups in every industrial
context; he studied the worker as part of a group, saw how the
group affected each of its members, and how it was related to the
formal structure of its particular industrial organization.

George Elton Mayo was born in Australia in 1880 and was
trained in psychology at Adelaide University before he went to
the United States. In 1926, he became Professor of Industrial
Research at the Harvard Graduate School of Business, remaining
in that position until he retired in 1947. He died in September
1949.

Though Mayo is now considered responsible for the general
approach to much of modern sociological and psychological
industrial research, up to the present day, his own first researches
were developed along orthodox, 'work study' lines. In 1923, for
example, his treatment of the problem of high labour turnover in
one section of a Philadelphia textile mill reflected the techniques
of F. W. Taylor. Mayo introduced rest pauses to a labouring task,
and explained the eventual success of these pauses as due to the
relief of postural fatigue and impaired circulation. Further he
assumed, at that time, that the monotony of the task had led to
'pessimistic reveries', which the rest periods had managed to
eliminate.

A complete reversal of these conclusions is to be found in his
last book, *The Social Problems of an Industrial Civilization*,
written over twenty years later. It is now appropriate to trace the

gradual evolution of his new approach to industrial problems which was to invalidate his original, orthodox conclusions on the textile mill developments.

THE HAWTHORNE EXPERIMENTS

Mayo's major research was associated with the Hawthorne plant of the Western Electric Company. It was during his years of work at the plant that doubt grew about the adequacy of the 'technical', 'mechanical' approach of Taylor and other pioneers to all human industrial problems, and eventually he consolidated an entirely revolutionary attitude to the difficulties of men at work.

In 1924, an orthodox experiment at the Hawthorne plant began, related to the physical environment of work; it attempted to examine the influence of illumination upon the level and maintenance of output. Parallel observations were made of two groups of operatives. For one group, the intensity of the lighting was varied periodically; for the second group, it remained constant throughout the experiment.

This test resulted in very appreciable production increases in both groups and of almost identical magnitude. The difference in efficiency of the two groups was so small as to be less than the probable error of the values. Consequently, we were again unable to determine what definite part of the improvement in performance should be ascribed to improved illuminations.[1]

The output of the first group, however, rose steadily throughout the experiment, even when the operatives considered the light to be worse. More significantly, the output of the second group also rose steadily – since there had been no changes in the physical environment, the key to improved production must, apparently, have been elsewhere.

At this point it was decided to develop a further experiment to clarify the anomalies of the previous problem. Departing from tradition, Mayo set up the Relay Assembly Test Room to enquire into the 'total human situation'. Initially, there was no closely defined sequence established – only the overall desire to resolve the earlier inconsistencies.

The Relay Assembly Test Room was a small section of the main department partitioned off from the rest, and six girls occupied the room, seated at a long bench. Their actual work was the assembly of telephone relays, which involved the intricate task of fitting together the forty separate pieces which made up the small part. Production levels were recorded throughout the experiment, which lasted five years. During this entire period, an observer sat with the girls, giving them information and noting everything that went on. The Test Room was frequently visited by senior company officials and others interested in the progress of the experiment.

During the experiment a series of changes was introduced, such as piece-work, rest pauses, shorter working hours. With most changes the output increased. One of the final changes reverted to the original conditions – i.e. long hours, no rest pauses; only the group piece-work scheme was retained. However, during the period of twelve weeks when this change was in operation, the output rose to a record level.

The significance of the experiment was made clear in 1933 in Mayo's book on the Hawthorne experiments, *The Human Problems of an Industrial Civilization*:

The records of the test room showed a continual improvement in the performance of the operators regardless of the experimental changes made during the study. It was also noticed that there was a marked improvement in their attitude toward their work and working environment. This simultaneous improvement in attitude and effectiveness indicated that . . . we could more logically attribute the increase in efficiency to a betterment of morale than to any of the alterations made in the course of the experiments.

It became evident that production had risen because of a change in the girls' attitudes to their situation. Their attitude to authority changed.

By Period XIII, however, their apprehension of authority was almost entirely dissipated. In this period the girls expressed full confidence toward those in charge of the experiment. They were no longer afraid that they would be the losers from the experimental changes. This increased confidence was expressed not merely by the absence of obsessive doubts and qualms, but also by verbal expressions of satisfaction with the test room situation. . . . Over and over again the girls expressed their contentment with the test room and its pleasanter, freer, and happier working conditions. . . . In their eyes their first-line supervisor ceased to be one who 'bawled them out' in case things went wrong: instead he came to be regarded as a friendly representative of management. This was what Operator 2 meant when she said, referring to the observer, 'Say, he's no boss. We don't have any boss.'[2]

They were responding to the interest shown in their work and the apparent importance of it. The discipline necessary to achieve the higher production came from *within* the group:

A change in morale had also been observed. No longer were the girls isolated individuals, working together only in the sense of an actual physical proximity. They had become participating members of a working group with all the psychological and social implications peculiar to such a group. In Period X a growing amount of social activity developed among the test room girls outside of working hours and outside of the plant. The conversation in the test room became more socialized. In Period XIII the girls began to help one another out for the common good of the group. They had become bound together by common sentiments and feelings of loyalty.[3]

The conclusions drawn from the Relay Assembly Test Room results were to guide the approach for all further research at the Hawthorne plant. Emphasis now switched from study of the individual worker in isolation and the straightforward adjustment of his physical environment, to concentration on the informal groups of workers, their social norms and attitudes.

STRONG INFORMAL GROUP

The enquiry known as the Bank Wiring Observation Group constituted a further major piece of research, this time specifically designed to investigate the social pattern of a group of workers:

'The investigators' attention had been drawn to the fact that social groups in shop departments were capable of exercising very strong control over the work behaviour of their individual members.' The chief feature which the investigation revealed was the restriction of output throughout the group, which was effectively maintained by various forms of social pressure applied to all members of the group. The studies were carried out between November 1931 and July 1932.

In contrast to the Relay Assembly Group, there was no increase in production by the members of the Bank Wiring Observation Group. The group consisted of fourteen men, engaged in three different jobs – nine were wiremen, three soldermen, and two were inspectors. The men were paid on a group basis. Production remained steady from week to week, and it became obvious that the workers were operating well within their capabilities. The researchers' conclusions included the following points:

1. Each individual in the group was restricting his output.
2. Restriction of output manifested itself in two ways: (a) The group had a standard of a day's work which was considerably lower than the 'bogey' and which fixed an upper limit to each person's output. This standard was not imposed upon them, but apparently had been formulated by the workmen themselves. Furthermore, it was in direct opposition to the ideas underlying their system of financial incentive, which countenanced no upper limit to performance other than physical capacity. (b) In each individual case it manifested itself in an output rate which remained fairly constant from week to week. The departmental output curves were devoid of individuality and approximated a horizontal line in shape.
3. Differences in weekly average hourly output rates for different wiremen did not reflect differences in capacity to perform. This conclusion was based on the following observations: (a) Most of the wiremen stated definitely that they could easily turn out more work than they did. (b) The observer said that all the men stopped work before quitting time. Frequently, a wireman finished his work quite early and stalled until quitting time. In general the men who ranked highest in output were the first to be finished. This point was verified by a comparison of individual morning and afternoon output rates, which showed the greatest differences in the cases of

the faster wiremen. (c) Tests of dexterity and intelligence showed no relation between capacity to perform and actual performance.[4]

Such was the strength of their informal group standards that no single member attempted to reach official production targets or to vary from the informal norm. Many methods were used by members of the group to ensure that everyone conformed to the limitations on output. These methods included 'binging' – punching on the upper arm –

In addition to its use as a penalty and as a means of settling disputes, binging was used to regulate the output of some of the faster workers. This was one of its most significant applications and is well illustrated in the following entry:

w[orker]8 [*to* w6]: Why don't you quit work? Let's see, this is your thirty-fifth row today. What are you going to do with them all?

w6: What do you care? It's to your advantage if I work, isn't it?

w8: Yeah, but the way you're working you'll get stuck with them.

w6: Don't worry about that. I'll take care of it. You're getting paid by the sets I turn out. That's all you should worry about.

w8: If you don't quit work I'll bing you. [w8 *struck* w6 *and finally chased him around the room.*]

OBS[erver] [*a few minutes later*]: What's the matter, w6, won't he let you work?

w6: No. I'm all through though. I've got enough done. [*He then went over and helped another wireman.*][5]

Here was a coherent, informal, social group, with its natural leaders, complete in attitudes to work, management, and level of production – i.e. with its own full group culture. The clash between the aims of the company and the aims of this group became obvious, as did the ineffectiveness of purely financial incentive to maximize production. For one reason or another, the group had established its rates of work. The chief function of the informal organization was to resist all changes to its standards; it was, therefore, necessarily at variance with the company's aims.

Differences in status and prestige within the group were complex, and, though based on subjective, often erroneous, views, the personal interrelations were of major importance to all members of the group. 'The men had elaborated spontaneously and quite unconsciously an intricate social organization, around their collective beliefs and sentiments.' The Bank Wiring Observation Group enquiry consolidated Mayo's discovery of the importance of the informal group in employee behaviour.

Mayo's research upon work situations at the Hawthorne plant was backed by an interview programme. This ran for more than two years and covered over 20,000 employees. It provided important additional information in three main ways. Firstly it corroborated the findings of the other research projects; secondly, it helped the management of the company by revealing some of the actual kinds of problems which they faced; and, thirdly, it enabled the management to revise their schemes for supervisory training.

The first references to the Hawthorne experiments are in Mayo's book, *The Human Problems of an Industrial Civilisation*, published in 1933. In one section of the book he deals with the Relay Assembly Room and the Interview Programme. The rest of it reproduces a number of his lectures on fatigue, monotony, morale and social relations. Other writings based on the Hawthorne experiments are by associates, Roethlisberger, Dickson and Whitehead. Mayo's last book, *The Social Problems of an Industrial Civilisation*, published in 1945, has a further chapter on three experiments. (Comments on this book are made later in this chapter.)

SUMMARY OF IDEAS

The conclusions to be drawn from Mayo's researches can best be summarized in three main points:

1. The importance of the work group

The studies at the Hawthorne plant show that work is a group activity, and the informal primary group has important effects upon work performance. A group will tend to develop its own norms, values and attitudes, and exert strong social control upon the individual members of the group and their behaviour at work. Group collaboration with management's objectives is important and must be planned for rather than expected.

2. The importance of recognition and security

Physical conditions were shown to have little influence upon workers' performance and attitudes to work in comparison with their need for security, recognition and belonging.

3. Complaints as symptoms of disturbance

The interview programme showed that comments and criticisms made by workers were often best regarded as manifestations of other deeper or more basic dissatisfactions about their changing status or lack of recognition.

MAYO'S LIMITATIONS

Mayo's contributions to the understanding of people at work is impressive, and one cannot really doubt his importance in the development of scientific management. The main ideas of his research, as set out above, continue to be valid and relevant today, and have provided a basis for many further developments. There are, however, a number of criticisms which may be made of Mayo's work and ideas, and these are discussed below.

One of Mayo's limitations derives from his approach to his industrial research, which was that of a social psychologist rather than a sociologist. He omitted detailed study both of the wider social context and its relation to work behaviour, and the total social situation within the workplace. He was at least partially aware of the first inadequacy in his writings, but by ignoring the total social situation within an organization he reduced the value of his work. An industrial organization may be seen as a plural society, in which the organization chart does not mirror the true pattern of social relationships. Because of the variety of group cultures and aims within any organization there will always be lateral pulls against any attempt to give the vertical (i.e. formal) organization a social meaning. Since he studied only single groups as a social psychologist, Mayo underestimated the value and importance of the broader, inclusive approach of the sociologist.

It was not until he came to write his last book, in 1945, *The Social Problems of an Industrial Civilisation*, that Mayo attempted to relate his work to a wider social context. Unfortunately his final book, which might have given a satisfying completeness to his work, serves only to clarify his limitations. Parts of the book are effective, such as his destruction of the 'rabble hypothesis'. He demonstrates the falsity of that part of economic theory, derived from Ricardo, which considers natural society as a horde of unorganized individuals, who think and act logically in their own self-interest. In reference to his first researches in a Philadelphia textile mill, Mayo commented:

The 'expert' assumptions of rabble hypothesis and individual self-interest as a basis for diagnosis led nowhere. On the other hand, careful and pedestrian consideration of the workers' situation taken as part of a clinical diagnosis led us to results so surprising that we could at the time only partly explain them.[6]

In this book, Mayo reveals an attitude of extreme empiricism to social science research. He assumes the superiority of the physical over social sciences, and sees this as a limiting factor upon the effective use of theory in the social sciences. His conclusion is that the much greater use of theory in politics, economics and sociology has restricted their development and limited their effectiveness. He emphasizes the primary importance of observations and collection of facts and gravely underestimates the importance of theory as a framework and guidance for research. His recurrent theme – 'If our social skills had advanced step by step with our technical skills, there would not have been another European war' – is unfortunately coupled with a naivety regarding the nature and relationships of different areas of knowledge.

Another of Mayo's limitations is his management bias: he puts forward a business case for treating workers better, but ignores the ethical grounds. This does not, of course, affect the value of his research discoveries – but means, simply, that he was an industrial psychologist who saw his role as primarily providing assistance to management. His emphasis upon social skill as a means for aligning all groups to the aims of the organization, though relevant to a large extent, led him to ignore the necessity of conflict of interests within an organization. He postulated a static industrial society, where management, by use of social skills, fully co-ordinated the aims of every group.

Mayo's static, co-ordinated, industrial society would seem to have only limited relevance to the majority of industrial communities, including Great Britain. His solutions might have had more relevance if resolved within the industrial framework of a dynamic society with continuing conflicts of interest. Thus his conclusions have a doubtful validity for Britain, where attitudes have been more deeply entrenched and class and political struggles deeply involved. The reactions of a group of American women can hardly be taken as sufficiently representative to provide a valid solution in such a different context as British industry.

All these limitations, however, must be put into perspective, in order not to diminish the tremendous contribution Mayo has actually made to the development of modern scientific management. His faults mainly occur in generalization and summary. As an empiricist, his strength lay much more in the actual research he carried out, and it is the importance of this by which he should be judged.

CONCLUSION

The Hawthorne researches must be regarded as a milestone and a major turning point in the study of men at work. The specific conclusions, summarized earlier, which Mayo drew from his work remain valid, and form an impressive testimony to his enduring importance. His work has formed the basis for a large part of research since the Hawthorne experiments. Equally important, the achievements of Mayo and his associates have led to a revised approach to personnel problems in many organizations. By demonstrating that industrial man is a social animal, Mayo has revealed the advantages of treating him as a human being, and this new approach is perhaps the greatest single development in the study of men at work.

NOTES

1. C. E. Snow, 'A Discussion of the Relation of Illumination Intensity to Productive Efficiency', *Tech Engineering News*, November, 1927.

2. F. J. Roethlisberger, William J. Dickson and Harold A. Wright, *Management and the Worker*, Harvard University Press, 1956, pp. 85–6.

3. ibid., p. 86.

4. ibid., pp. 445–6.

5. ibid., pp. 422–3.

6. Elton Mayo, *The Social Problems of an Industrial Civilisation*, Routledge & Kegan Paul, 1952, p. 59.

READINGS FROM ELTON MAYO,
The Human Problems of an Industrial Civilization

Fatigue [1]

THE physiological conception of work pays small tribute, therefore, to the business-economic theory. Work can be done only in a steady state; interruption comes, in any ordinary industrial situation, not from any partial exhaustion of fuel reserves but from some 'interference'. This interference is of the nature of an external condition which carries as a consequence for certain individuals an actual organic disequilibrium which makes continuation of effort for such individuals impossible.

We can say that fatigue is not an entity but merely a convenient word to describe a variety of phenomena. The common fallacy of supposing that the word 'fatigue' corresponds to a definite thing has been the source of much confusion. Fatigue from short bursts of activity, whether by the whole body or by isolated muscle groups, is characterized by increase in lactic acid and temporary inability to continue. Fatigue from depletion of fuel reserves does not occur commonly in man but when it does, chemical analysis of the blood reveals a low level of blood sugar. Fatigue from working in a hot environment has several manifestations, the most simple to measure being an increase in heart rate. Finally, of two individuals doing the same task one may be more fatigued than the other because the poor nervous coordination of the unskilful man makes it necessary for him to expend more energy than the other. In general, fatigue from any of these causes is greater the more nearly the individual approaches his capacity for work.

We cannot be surprised, then, that the English Research Board has dropped the word 'fatigue' from its title. It is too fatally easy to conclude that because we have a word 'fatigue' there must be a simple thing or fact that corresponds with it – a common fallacy discussed by Henderson in his studies of Pareto. The industrial investigator is constantly forced in his enquiries to take account of many factors in a complex situation; wherever the general effect is unsatisfactory to the worker and to industry, he sets himself to discover the nature of the disequilibrium and the nature of the interference. The monographs published by the scientific workers under the Fatigue Board do not discuss fatigue directly; they inquire into hours of work and rest pauses, atmospheric conditions, vision and lighting, vocational selection (i.e. individual differences with respect to a particular task), posture and physique, and so on.

Monotony [2]

Monotony, like fatigue, is a word which is used to denote any sort of induced unbalance in the worker such that he cannot continue work, or can continue only at a lower level of activity. There are many possibilities of such unbalance – different individuals and different situations. Inquiry into such situations looks for some contributing factor or factors in external conditions, something also in the individual himself. The unbalance is, in Cannon's words, both interofective and exterofective; there is disequilibrium within the individual and between him and his work. In the case cited, the complicating problem was that of the mental preoccupations – pessimism and rage – induced in the workers by the conditions of their work. But neither they nor their immediate supervisors had been able to define or specify the contributory external conditions.

Equilibrium [3]

The Fatigue Laboratory researches show us a number of mutually dependent factors in equilibrium, a change in external conditioning, and a change throughout the whole organization which is the organism. In the presence of such a change the individual may be able, by virtue of a shift of inner equilibrium, to keep going without effort or damage; the diagram which showed the difference between the athlete and untrained persons illustrated this. Or the inner equilibrium may be temporarily overthrown, in which case the untrained man stops running. The athlete can achieve a 'steady state' in a greater variety of external changes and under conditions demanding much greater effort – having achieved this adjustment of inner equilibrium he 'keeps going indefinitely'. The Western Electric experiment was primarily directed not to the external condition but to the inner organization. By strengthening the 'temperamental' inner equilibrium of the workers, the company enabled them to achieve a mental 'steady state' which offered a high resistance to a variety of external conditions.

Interview programs [4]

The improvement in production, they believe, is not very directly related to the rest pauses and other innovations. It reflects rather a freer and more pleasant working environment, a supervisor who is not regarded as a 'boss', a 'higher morale'. In this situation the production of the group insensibly lifts, even though the girls are not aware that they are working faster. Many times over, the history sheets and other records show that in the opinion of the group all supervision has been removed. On occasion indeed they artlessly tell the observer, who is in fact of supervisory rank, very revealing tales of their experiences with previous 'bosses'. Their opinion is, of course, mistaken: in a sense they are getting closer supervision than ever before; the change is in the quality of the supervision. This – the change in quality of supervision – is by no means the whole change, but it is an important part of it. Two questions, therefore, propose themselves to the directors of the inquiry. The first is a question as to the actual quality of the supervision outside the experimental room and in the plant. The second is a question as to the nature of an ordinary working environment from a worker's point of view. Is it so little free and happy as the development of the test room seems to suggest? Almost simultaneously, therefore, the industrial research division embarks upon two inquiries designed to develop further these questions. These two inquiries are the 'mica room' experiment, begun in August, 1928, and the interviewing program, which was instituted in September of the same year.

Output, morale, personality [5]

After some time, the economic situation compelled this girl to return to living with her family. Subsequently to this her output curve once again descended and developed something of its former irregularity. This, in spite of the fact that for some time after this the conditions in the experimental room were maintained.

This was not the only instance discovered by the research division of the relation between output, morale, and heavy personal preoccupation. It is, however, the instance which best lends itself to comparatively objective demonstration before an audience. It had become clear to the interviewing department that, in those many instances where personal situations of this or some similar type were divulged in the intimate anonymity of an interview, it was fair to assume the existence of a condition of affairs essentially similar to that which had revealed itself in the mica room. It was evident that such persons would be less well able to support pressure of any kind than those more fortunately placed. 'Pressure' in this use must be interpreted to mean much more than, for example, merely working overtime; indifferent supervisory methods, unfriendliness in fellow workers, monotonous or repetitive work, all these would possibly serve to provoke a distorted interpretation, an irrational response. In something of this fashion did the interviewing group begin its effort to understand the questionable reliability of personal comments in the interviews. A comment in one interview reads 'Between the hard luck at home and the unfair treatment round here [i.e. in the Works], why, I certainly feel "dumpy" many a day.' With respect to comments of this type, and they were not infrequent, the division began to believe:

1. Such an individual – hard luck at home and feeling 'dumpy' – is not a reliable judge of departmental conditions.

2. He is probably caught in a vicious circle; he feels 'dumpy' in any event and consequently every event is interpreted to increase his conviction of hard luck and unfair treatment.

3. One cannot 'handle' such an individual adequately without understanding his history, his present circumstances, and so his method of thinking and consequent attitude.

Communication [6]

In a particular instance it was found that neither the supervisors nor any of the working group really knew the 'bogey' that had been set nor the facts considered in its determination. They did not clearly understand the method of payment on the job. The whole department echoed with protective devices, some of which were known to the supervisor and others not so known. On a first observation there was a tendency to ascribe this to an alleged habit of 'restricting output'; it was speedily found that this phrase expresses a gross simplification which is essentially untrue. Apparently it is not enough to have an enlightened company policy, a carefully devised (and blue-printed) plan of manufacture. To stop at this point, and merely administer such a plan, however logical, to workers with a take-it-or-leave-it attitude has much the same effect as administering medicine to a recalcitrant patient. It may be good for him, but he is not persuaded. If an individual cannot work with sufficient understanding of his work situation, then, unlike the machine, he can only work against opposition from himself. This is the essential nature of the human, with all the will in the world to cooperate he finds it difficult to persist in action for an end he cannot dimly see. From this it follows that the more intelligent an industrial method, the more difficulty does it encounter in performance and action. This is because if intelligent it changes as a method in response to externally dictated need or with the progress of invention – and fails to carry its workers intelligently with it. Many varieties of situation were discovered at Hawthorne, but wherever the symptoms described as 'restriction' clearly showed themselves, something of exasperation or a sense of personal futility was also revealed. There was a conflict of loyalties – to the company, to the supervisor, to the working group – and no possibility of solution, except by improved understanding. Whether they admitted 'stalling' or no, workers expressed their dislike for a situation which imposed upon them a constraint and a disloyalty. Evidently the more intelligent a company policy, the more necessary is it that there shall be a method of communicating understanding 'down the line'. And this method of communication must include the interview – that is, it must know and effectively meet the real difficulties which workers themselves experience and express, and must take account also of personal disability.

At this point in the inquiry a relation had established itself between the 'interview program' and the results obtained in the experimental rooms. The source of those constraints, relief from which the relay assemblers had so freely expressed, had, at least in part, revealed itself. Human collaboration in work, in primitive and developed societies, has always depended for its perpetuation upon the evolution of a non-logical social code which regulates the relations between persons and their attitudes to one another. Insistence upon a merely economic logic of production – especially if the logic is frequently changed – interferes with the development of such a code and consequently gives rise in the group to a sense of human defeat. This human defeat results in the formation of a social code at a lower level and in opposition to the economic logic. One of its symptoms is 'restriction'. In its devious road to this enlightenment, the research division had learned something of the personal exasperation caused by a continual experience of incomprehension and futility. It had also learned how serious a consequence such experience carries for industry and for the individual.

Categories of adult response [7]

Generally speaking, therefore, the responses of any adult individual to his surrounding are of three types:

(a) *Logical.* In this area he has developed skill and capacity for discrimination and independent judgement.

(b) *Non-logical.* This type of response is described above as 'signal response'. The individual's actions may be adequate to the situation, but any intelligence they exhibit is socially and not personally derived. This form of response is the effect of training in a social code of behaviour.

(c) *Irrational.* Non-logical response is typical of social adjustment. Irrational response, on the other hand, is symptomatic of social maladjustment and shows all the signs of obsession. Both types of response are rooted in individual unreason, but it is only the latter which technically interests the psychopathologist.

The non-logical response, that, namely, which is in strict conformity with a social code, makes for social order and discipline, *for effective collaboration in a restricted range of activity,* and for happiness and a sense of security in the individual.

Collaboration [8]

There is one important aspect of the employer-employee problem which has persisted through a century of change in industrial organization, in wages and in working conditions. This is the problem which was tentatively stated in the final phase of the interview study at Hawthorne. It may be briefly expressed in a claim that at no time since the Industrial Revolution has there been, except sporadically here and there, anything of the nature of effective and wholehearted collaboration between the administrative and the working groups in industry. To 'take sides' immediately on an issue such as this and to assign heavy blame to one side or other is useless. The failure is due to our incapacity to define the actual problem with sufficient precision. And until such definition is attempted, public discussion of the issues will do little except to load upon an already complicated situation an added burden of mutual suspicion and distrust.

These extracts are taken from Elton Mayo, *The Human Problems of an Industrial Civilisation*, Macmillan, New York, 1933, numbers as indicated:

(1.) *Fatigue*, pp. 25–6.
(2.) *Monotony*, p. 52.
(3.) *Equilibrium*, p. 72.
(4.) *Interview programs*, pp. 75–6.
(5.) *Output, morale, personality*, pp. 101–102, 102–103.
(6.) *Communication*, pp. 114–16.
(7.) *Categories of adult response*, pp. 157–8.
(8.) *Collaboration*, pp. 171–2.

4.5 C. I. Barnard and the Theory of Organizations

ANTHONY TILLETT

THE work of C. I. Barnard is very much that of a practical man of business. His work is not the product of formal empirical investigations, but of experience tempered by speculation. The speculation is disciplined by his concrete objectives and his own beliefs about organization. The development of his ideas about human action and organization were strongly influenced by a group of men at Harvard, particularly L. J. Henderson. Like Barnard, Henderson was not a social investigator by profession. He came to the study of social phenomena through physiology and the work of Vilfredo Pareto. Henderson's work stressed the nature of society as a working system, and the equilibrium of that system. These same concepts were to be extremely important for the development of American sociology.

Barnard's work is not difficult to read, but it is subtle; no discussion of his writings can do justice to the careful refinements of concepts found in his work. The major part of his work consists of lectures and talks. His most important book, *The Functions of the Executive*[1], was delivered at the Lowell Institute as lectures, and the majority of his views were given in the form of talks and lectures.[2]

Barnard's interests as an executive shaped his intellectual interest. He was for a time the President of the New Jersey Bell Telephone Company, and later served in government agencies and charitable positions. His main interest lay in the role of the executive in organizations, and his main concern was to show how behaviour and action within an organization differed from other kinds of behaviour, particularly by the degree of reciprocity that exists between the person and the organization.

Barnard saw all organizations as having certain essential properties in common. His examples came not only from business but from the army and the Roman Catholic Church, from large

312

organizations as well as small, for 'the same principles that govern simple organizations may be conceived as governing the structure of complex organizations which are composite systems'. To understand the small organization was to understand the large organization. However, his interest lay more in discovering the component elements of the organization than in finding the 'principles' of such organizations. Unlike Fayol (see 2.4) he was more interested in understanding the way an organization functions as a 'living body', rather than discovering the right way to administer a firm. A reader may feel that such an approach is too abstract and simple. But Barnard's aim was to develop a common language for organizational analysis, so that the problems of the executive would not be seen solely in terms of industry, but as problems relevant to all cooperative activity.

The present account will deal with his work on the general theory of organizations, which has had a major influence on later developments in the social sciences and management studies. Many of the points will be made by direct quotation from his works.

THE ORGANIZATIONAL FIELD

The most distinctive feature of Barnard's work is the idea that the organization is a field, distinct both from the persons participating in the organization, and the environment in which the organization functions. Thus actions of persons in an organization differ from their activities outside, not only because of the different activities, but because the activities inside the organization are motivated by no clear indication of self-interest. Persons contribute services, not themselves. The organization is not, however, a 'leviathan' able to act without personal or social support; the pejorative sense of bureaucracy, and the figure of the 'organization man', are not found in Barnard's organizational elements. Barnard avoids the idea of the organization as able to make its own decisions, independent of influence, an autonomous power centre. His central concept is of the organization as a 'system of consciously co-ordinated activities', resulting in a collective synthesis of individuals, whose very cooperation brings into focus a new form of activity.

The individual has a personal and an organizational role. The organization must recognize this and create an equilibrium of rewards and satisfactions for the participants. The idea of an organizational equilibrium is to be understood in a general way, not as being something specific or measurable. 'Thus the efficiency of the cooperative system is the capacity to maintain itself by the individual satisfaction that it affords. This may be called its capacity of equilibrium, the balancing of burdens by satisfactions that result from its continuance', and he continues in a footnote to this passage, that efficiency is not the product of one type of organizational structure, but can be achieved with many different types.

The equilibrium for Barnard is not static, for as individual demands change these are channelled into the organization and have to be satisfied. The higher up in the organization one goes, the more satisfaction one derives from work in the company, and so the better the equilibrium for the company. Satisfaction is only partly psychological, and involves the concepts of work interest and role performance. The reasons for the identity of interest of the person and the organizational role come from an understanding of the goal and purpose of cooperation and from the awareness that organizations can achieve what persons cannot. Identity of interest is not to be understood as the dominance of the firm over the man, as in the ideal 'organization man', for Barnard recognizes that persons in organizations always have concerns and interests outside. One of the important tasks of the executive is to extend this satisfaction to individuals who work for money alone, and to whom the rationality of cooperative action is unimportant.

The equilibrium of the organization is not based on the individual alone but also on other organizations, and the larger society. Thus, any kind of social change, in the economy, the distribution of power in society, or the labour market, will alter the organization, even though the goals of the organization may not formally change. The relationship of the organization to the environment is not a static but a functional one:

This external equilibrium has two terms to it; first the effectiveness of the organization which comprises the interchange between the organization and individuals. Thus the elements stated will each vary with external factors, and they are at the same time interdependent; when one is varied, compensating factors must occur in the other if the system of which they are components is to remain in equilibrium, that is to persist and survive.

The perception of this equilibrium is not a logical appraisal, but subject to both analysis and intuition. The adjective that Barnard would apply is 'rational' which must be distinguished from 'logical'. In his earliest published work, *Mind in Everyday Affairs* (reprinted as an appendix to *The Functions of the Executive*), Barnard was anxious to show the equal validity but different use of the two processes of thought that are overtly rational, namely the logical and the non-logical. The former deals with reason and evidence, while the latter deals with action and decision. In our everyday lives it is the latter which predominates, for in making choices and taking decisions, we rely on 'fictions' (beliefs and intuitions) which should have a place in any discussion of rationality and organizations. The executive, like the spendthrift wife, must be able to present reasons, for

reasons must be given, but they must appeal to those attitudes, predilections, prejudices, emotions, and the mental background that cover actions. This implies a task of great difficulty. It requires discerning the mental state and the processes of the person to be convinced, adopting his mentality.

Both ways of thinking are important, and their interaction produces a dialectic which gives a larger view of the organization. Rationality takes on a different form under the stress of decision, and to treat reason as mere analysis has 'blinded us to an appreciation of structure and organization'. To this feeling must be added a comprehensive but unanalysed understanding of the whole organization.

THE INTERNAL ECONOMY OF THE ORGANIZATION

Three main elements are distinguished by Barnard as being needed to maintain an organization: (i) a willingness of persons to serve, (ii) a common purpose, and (iii) internal communication. These elements are linked together by the informal social organization which exists in all formal organizations; for both willingness and communications are characteristics of the small group in the organization, and the quality of these relations will influence the ability of the organization to have an identifiable goal.

The commitment of persons to the organization has been defined above, as part of the equilibrium between society and the organization. Persons are not organizational animals, for they have a variety of obligations and interests which have little to do with the workplace. The logic of motivation in Barnard is in direct opposition to those who see income as the only reason for work, with the implication that the organization bestows goods on its members. Barnard rejects the concept of membership, because persons only offer services and activities, not the whole of their life. There is a complex if unspoken bargain concerning the person and the time and work required by the organization, a bargain of satisfactions and limits, contributions and rewards, which originates with the willingness of the person to serve. The worker is not a tool, but a member of society first, and then a participant in the organization. To encourage service a large number of inducements can be developed by the organization but the relationship remains one of bargain based on choice. Choice may include persuasion, and the creation of a moral commitment becomes an important satisfaction, particularly where there is little else to offer. Barnard makes the point explicit:

If an organization is unable to afford the incentives adequate to the personal contributions that it requires, it will perish unless it can by persuasion so change the desires of enough men that the incentives that it can offer will be adequate. Persuasion, in the broad sense in which I am here using the word, includes (a) the creation of conditions, (b) the rationalization of opportunity, and (c) the inculcation of motives.

Examples of such persuasion would be found in the army where the task of the organization depends on discipline, in the creation of a career structure where the rewards come in later years, as in the law, and finally in inculcation of motives. Motives are found in all organizations, but they are strongest in voluntary organizations with political or religious aims.

Persuasion is an important task for the executive and requires a different formulation in each organization. In addition incentives differ according to the organizational position held, but whatever the position, material rewards are not sufficient. The executive faces the question of 'choice and degree of emphasis on different incentives'. Barnard felt that such a choice could not be replaced by the provision of welfare arrangements or 'smart tricks', which are unrelated to the services of the person to the organization, for

as a substitute for the proper conduct of employee relations they are futile and dangerous. They tend to create in the minds of management a presumption of fair and constructive relations with employees when in fact they may present merely a philanthropic attitude or an attempt to buy off hostile states of mind. It is clear to my mind that philanthropy as such has no legitimate place in industrial relations, and that the idea of buying good relations is abortive. The very notion creates a state of mind on the part of management that will blind it to the essential problems.

An understanding of the goals of the organization must also take account of the fact that every participant will have different ideas of these goals which are based on his task and position in the organization as well as his background. This is not to be deplored but to be understood and accepted, for

a purpose may serve as an element in the cooperative system only so long as the participants do not recognize that there are some serious divergencies of their understanding of that purpose as the object of cooperation. If, in fact, there is an important difference between the aspects of the purpose objectively viewed, then divergencies become quickly evident when the purpose is concrete, tangible, physical; but when the purpose is general, intangible, and of sentimental character the divergencies can be very wide and not recognized.

So the normative element becomes crucial to the functioning of the organization. Belief papers over the cracks. 'Non-logical' thought, discussed above, has a positive function for the organization, and is related to organizational position. Goals are distinguished not only by belief but by authority and so the organization

requires a pyramiding of the formulation of purpose, that becomes more and more remote in the future time. Responsibility for abstract generalizing, prospective long run decisions is delegated up the line; responsibility for definite action remains always at the base where the authority of effort resides.

Goals hold the organization together, and are the responsibility of the executive. An understanding of these distinctions, and the creation of myths to avoid a conflict or division of purpose is one of his major tasks.

Finally the element which co-ordinates these different views, incentives and aspects of the organization is the communications system of the organization. This concept is used to explain the working of the organization at all levels. The main characteristics of communication in organizations are carefully stated and include formal channels, efficiency, rules and personal competence. Hopkins has pointed out that these characteristics are very similar to those that are used by Weber in his discussion of bureaucracy.[3] Barnard interestingly places little emphasis here on office, although he was to do so in a later essay. But there are differences between his concept of communications in administration, and Weber's concept of hierarchical authority. Communication involves much more than the giving of orders and technical directions, although these are part of the process. Communication is far more a property of the organization than a property of the individual, and executive positions are seen as 'communication centres', transferring messages within the system. Forms of communication are not discussed, for flexibility not hierarchy is the key to the system. The style of communication differs with the number of people concerned; as the number of communications increase an organization must differentiate its functions. Hierarchic leadership is limited by the number of communications which it can undertake, for the 'capacity of people to maintain relationships is obviously limited'. Authority is not only limited by the number of communications, but by the way that the communication is transferred in organizations. Communications cannot only use formal channels. Much communication goes through informal channels which are based on the informal groupings of participants. Communication, unlike bureaucracy, has to take account of informal groups, and the information they possess. Such informal passing of information is 'dysfunction' in the Weberian scheme of organization.

The informal group is the most important link between the formal organization and the contributing individual. It provides not merely a means of communication and cohesion but also a means by which the integrity of the individual is protected. Unlike the formal group which always tries to put forward general objectives the informal group is largely 'unconscious' in its effect on the organization. Even where, as in specialized tasks, the objective purpose would seem to be paramount, the influence of the informal group is important. The process of specialization, for example, is changed by the nature of the informal group and must take this into account. 'Each unit of the organization has a specific objective, specific locational characteristics, specific time schedule and involves a specific selection of individual contributors.' So the 'associational situation' (informal group) affects the capacity and character of specialization.

It is here that the function of the executive properly begins, with a feeling for the organization, the informal group, and the needs of the individual participant. Barnard succinctly stated the interrelationship between elements in the organization, and implicitly states the responsibility of the executive within the organization.

The end of cooperation cannot be accomplished without special organization. The co-ordination implied is a functional aspect of the organization. The function is to correlate the efforts of the individual in such a way with the conditions of the cooperative situation as a whole that the purpose [of the organization] may be accomplished.

The purpose is the particular responsibility of the executive, and the authority and use of decisions intimately depends on the characteristics of formal organization already discussed.

EXECUTIVE AUTHORITY

The executive has the task of guiding the organization, setting goals and understanding the long-range character of decisions. Such general goals can neither be the grounds for commitment by persons, nor the basis for the day-to-day running of the organization. Authority does not come from enthusiasm for a grand design, nor from domination, but from accepting a compromise between the complexity of contributions, and the limited absolute power of the organization. Authority does not depend on commands, but on a reciprocal relationship; a communication becomes authoritative by 'virtue of its acceptance by a contributor'. Thus there is a degree of consent needed from the worker, or the group, if the purpose of the communication is to be achieved.

The form and nature of the acceptance of the communication differ, and if this were not so, the organization would not be taking into account the difference between contributors. The acceptance depends on what Barnard calls the 'zone of indifference' which he defines in the following passage:

If all the orders for actions, reasonably practicable, be arranged in order of their acceptability to the person affected, it may be conceivable that there are a number which are clearly unacceptable, that is will certainly not be obeyed; there is another group somewhere more or less in the neutral line, that is barely unacceptable; and a third group unquestionably acceptable. This last group lies within the 'zone of indifference'. The person will accept an order lying within this zone and is relatively indifferent as to what the order is so far as the question of authority is concerned.

Effective orders must be limited to this area. The 'zone of indifference' may apply to both a person or a group. There are difficulties in discovering the boundaries between the 'zones', but empirical work like the Hawthorne investigations has shown this to be more than a fanciful idea.

The 'zone of indifference' becomes a useful interpretative concept by which to explain the behaviour of persons in organizations. The origin of such zones is not the concern of Barnard, but it is clearly related to general ideas current in society about work, equity and social standards.

Executive authority depends on communication. Authority and communications, rather than authority and position, must go together. Authority without communication is a fiction of the superior, a fiction which may have influence as a myth, but does not add to the objective functioning of the organization. But the myth does have a function which is important for the organization. Barnard, in his important essay 'The Functions and Pathology of Status Systems in Formal Organizations' (in *Organization and Management*, 1948), considered the question of status in more detail:

... a system of status in formal organizations is necessary as a matter of need in individuals, and as imposed characteristics of the cooperative system, especially with respect to techniques of communication essential to co-ordination. But it also appears that systems of status generate uncontrolled and uncontrollable tendencies of rigidity, hypertrophy, and unbalance that often lead to the destruction of the organization.

Status can become pathological and interfere with the system of communication. This essay deals in a far more specific way with the individual behaviour of the executive, whereas in *The Functions of the Executive* the focus is on the contributions of the individual to the organizational system. He distinguishes two kinds of status: the functional, where there is no command structure and which depends on the division of labour; and scalar status which is determined by 'the relationship of superiority or subordination in the chain of command'. The latter kind can become institutionalized and limit the potential capacity of the organization to change. Executive authority at its most effective must be based on function.

Status and other satisfactions are part of the way that contributions are secured. The acceptability of the organization to the person who possesses skills and services must be created by the executive. The executive needs to understand both the limits of his power, and the forces which make the organization effective. The path to that understanding charted by Barnard is not clear-cut, but it does present a more realistic and complex picture of the nature of authority in the organization than hitherto. Authority depends on the relations of the organization to the individual, or of the organization to society, not on the mastery of the executive alone. The organization limits the authority of the executive, for it is compliant only under specific conditions: conditions like communications, acceptance, and informal relations, which must be recognized for the organization to be effective.

EXECUTIVE RESPONSIBILITY

The executive must recognize the importance of the preceding elements and be prepared to work with them. Although his main task lies in the maintenance of the organization through the communications system, there is a special and interesting element emphasized by Barnard which he calls 'creative morality'. By now it must be clear that the executive does not have the power of the entrepreneur, dictating conditions of work and loyalty by personal fiat. The executive's task is more difficult because he does not have this power. By creative morality Barnard means the creation of a sense of purpose and commitment towards the organization in those who are most marginal to it, such as the mass production worker in a tedious and repetitive job. Barnard recognizes that this is '... the most inherent difficulty in the operation of the cooperative system – the necessity for indoctrinating those at the lower levels with general purposes, and the major decisions so that they remain cohesive and able to make the ultimate detailed decisions coherent'. Common values are important, for in this way the purposes of the organization can be shared, even if not shared equally. The need for such acceptance by the marginal workman is more important for the organization than the individual and yet, particularly in times of change, such common values in the organization must not counter those in the society. The balance of these interests – technological, organizational and personal – and the preservation of some kind of common code is one of the severest tests of the executive.

ORGANIZATIONAL DECISIONS

The organization is not just a communications system; in the process of communicating, decisions are taken. Both the conditions for the acceptance of the decisions and the creation of common values to facilitate the decisions have already been discussed. Decisions are not all of one type, but are personal and organizational, long-term and short-term, and are relevant to every person who contributes to the organization. If the number of decisions is taken as a criterion, then the most important contribution comes from the 'non-executive' participants. But 'it is precisely for this reason that many executive decisions are necessary – they act to facilitate correct action involving appropriate decisions of others', so the executive has the role of a self-corrective mechanism to bring the organization back to equilibrium where necessary, and pursue the goals that the organization has set itself.

The tool of the executive in making decisions is the capacity to analyse and perform 'technologically correct conduct'. But such a decision must account for the complexity of the organization, so that 'the analysis of present circumstances is in part the definition of purpose in immediate terms; but it is also the process of finding what present circumstances are significant with reference to that purpose.' But there are no blue-prints for making correct decisions, no principles of procedure on which the executive can rely. By recognizing the diversity of organizations, the conflicting interests that make up cooperation, Barnard has made the study of organizations more difficult but more realistic; simple principles – the maxims of good management behaviour – have little relevance to the executive.

The complexity of decision making and the circular effect of decisions are well illustrated in the following discussion:

The ideal process of decision is to discriminate the strategic factors and redefine or change the purpose on the basis of the estimate of future results of action in the existing situation, in the light of history, experience, knowledge of the past. The discrimination of the environment is inevitably unbalanced as respects its several elements because of differences in available techniques and because to some extent the past will be misread into the present instead of being used as part of estimating the future. The inherent limitation then imposed upon the process of decisions is itself a strategic factor in the making of major and general decisions.

The decisions of the executive can never be completely objective, for what seem 'objective' decisions are opportunistic, rather than long-term, and are limited to specific processes. By the creation of common values, the long-term interests of the organization can flourish. The executive must take both into account in making organizational decisions.

ORGANIZATIONAL ASSESSMENT

From Barnard's work there is no clear-cut test of an organization. Any assessment of an organization will have to take into account a large number of factors, not all of which can be measured. One of the tests of the organization is the capacity of the executive to integrate these disparate 'economies'. Simple judgements of organizations are more likely to mislead than illuminate. Thus, '... the only statement of the organization economy is one that is in terms of success or failure; and the only analysis of the decisions as to the actions of the organization. There is no unit of measurement for the economy of organizational utility.' Finding and judging success and failure involves an understanding of the complexity and elements of the organization, particularly the organization as one system, rather than a series of disparate departments. In looking at the total organization, the criterion of organizational equilibrium, the balance of contributions and satisfactions, is one of the most important for the health of the organization. Survival rather than efficiency becomes the test for the whole organization over time.

Two other judgements about the organization are important for its assessment. First, the importance of the 'lower participants', who have little power yet on whom the output of the organization depends. They are concerned with 'efficiency of detail' in translating the general goals into present decisions. They must have their satisfactions linked to the company in the form of a feeling of worth, and the acceptance of organizational values. Second, the organization must provide creative solutions, not only for itself, but for the economy as a whole. Organizations must be service-orientated in their policies.

Barnard did not study firms and companies *per se*, but organizations. He showed that simple economic criteria are not enough for an understanding of the organization, and that the executive has to understand social and personal phenomena. The role of the executive is not only to maximize production, but to maximize the effectiveness of the total organization in all its forms. Cooperation was not a choice between paternalism and authority, but a necessary condition for obtaining the services of participants. Individual influence was limited – personality, principles, these were secondary. No one solution for the effective executive was possible, so that the work which advocated the one best way was limited by this analysis. Many of these points are illustrated in the extracts from his book which follow.

Barnard founded a new type of analysis for organizations, and his ideas have continued to be the source of much work in the field of 'organizational analysis'. Decisions and the communication system,[4] leadership and creative morality,[5] and the type of contributions which individuals bring with them,* have all been refined and specified. Barnard's work resulted in a new theory of organizations, and by seeing the business as one type of organization he liberated the study of management from the narrow interests with which it had previously been concerned, and provided a framework for future empirical work.

NOTES

1. C. I. Barnard, *The Functions of the Executive*, Harvard University Press, 1938.

2. *Organization and Management*, Harvard University Press, 1948.

3. T. K. Hopkins, 'Bureaucratic Authority: Convergence of Weber and Barnard', in *Complex Organizations: a Sociological Reader*, ed. A. Etzioni, Holt, Rinehart & Winston, pp. 82–98.

4. The work of H. A. Simon, particularly *Administrative Behaviour*, Macmillan, 1947.

5. For example, P. Selznick, *Leadership in Administration*, Harper and Row, 1957.

READINGS FROM C. I. BARNARD,
The Functions of the Executive

The effectiveness and efficiency of cooperation[1]

WHAT we mean by 'effectiveness' of cooperation is the accomplishment of the recognized objective of cooperative action. The degree of accomplishment indicates the degree of effectiveness.

It is apparent that an objective of cooperation is non-personal, that it is an aim of the system of cooperation as a whole. It follows that the definition of effectiveness in any given case is also to be determined in some way by the cooperative system as a

---

*In his book *A Comparative Analysis of Complex Organizations*, Free Press, 1961 Etzioni takes Barnard's idea of contributions, and shows how organizations differ by the kind of compliance they can gain from their participants.

whole. The basis of this determination will be whether the action taken *and* the objective result secured prove sufficient to acquire for the system of cooperation the supplies of forces or materials necessary to satisfy personal motives. In either individual action or cooperative action the satisfactions may be secured even though the end is not attained, but the attainment of some end, and belief in the likelihood of attaining it, appears necessary to the continuance of co-ordinated action. Thus, even though the attainment of a given end is not necessary for itself, it is necessary to keep alive the cooperation. Effectiveness from this point of view is the minimum effectiveness that can be tolerated. Hence it can be seen that the attempt to do what cannot be done must result in the destruction or failure of cooperation.

It remains to note here that the effectiveness of cooperative action implies effectiveness, in a special sense, of constituent 'individual' actions within the cooperative system. If five men are pushing a stone, the effort of each individual is a constituent action; it has not independent non-cooperative existence; its effectiveness is a function of the total action. The effectiveness of one man can only be appraised on the assumption that the other actions remain equal, that is, effectiveness of constituent efforts has meaning only in a differential sense, its value varying inversely as the values of other efforts vary. For convenience in maintaining effectiveness, however, it is frequent to assign to the constituent effort an artificial or individual objective, such as that man A should exert x pounds of force for y minutes. If he does so he is effective, otherwise not.

Although effectiveness of cooperative effort relates to accomplishment of an objective of the system and is determined with a view to the system's requirements, efficiency relates to the satisfaction of individual motives. The efficiency of a cooperative system is the resultant of the efficiencies of the individuals furnishing the constituent efforts, that is, as viewed by them. If the individual finds his motives being satisfied by what he does, he continues his cooperative effort; otherwise he does not. If he does not, this subtraction from the cooperative system may be fatal to it. If five men are required and the fifth man finds no satisfaction in cooperating, his contribution would be inefficient. He would withhold or withdraw his services, so that the cooperation would be destroyed. If he considers it to be efficient, it is continued. Thus, the efficiency of a cooperative system is its capacity to maintain itself by the individual satisfactions it affords. This may be called its capacity of equilibrium, the balancing of burdens by satisfactions which results in continuance.

Efficiency or equilibrium can be secured either by changing motives in individuals (or securing substitute individuals of appropriate motives), which is operation on a social factor, or by its *productive* results which can be distributed to individuals. These productive results are either material or social, or both. As to some individuals, material is required for satisfaction; as to others, social benefits are required. As to most individuals, both material and social benefits are required in different proportions.

The limitations to which cooperative effort must conform imply that even in the case of efficient systems the supplies of material and social benefits are restricted, so that efficiency from the productive viewpoint depends not merely upon what or how much is produced but upon what or how much is given for each individual contribution. If more than sufficient material is given to some, it may be that there will not be enough to go around and only an insufficient amount will be available to others. To the latter the situation would then be unsatisfactory. Similarly, the social benefits are limited, and if they should be improperly distributed there would be a deficiency as to some. Hence, efficiency depends in part upon the distributive process in the cooperative system.

If the distribution were such that benefits just equalled burdens in each case, which would require ideal precision in distribution, each individual would have no margin of inducement as against other alternatives. The cooperative system must create a surplus of satisfaction to be efficient. If each man gets back only what he puts in, there is no incentive, that is, no net satisfaction for him in cooperation. What he gets back must give him advantage in terms of satisfaction; which almost always means return in a different form from that which he contributes. If he puts forth effort, he requires a changed condition for himself, just as he would if he put forth effort individually rather than cooperatively. Efficiency, for the individual, is satisfactory exchange. Thus the process of cooperation also includes that of satisfactory exchange.

From this point of view the process of cooperation could be merely one of exchange, that is, of distribution. Viewed in isolation we are accustomed to this process as a basis for efficient cooperation in the exchanges – stock, commodity, etc. – which are not productive in a direct sense. Much cooperation, especially that of the 'social' types, is of this character; in these cases, the formal objective of cooperation is merely a pole around which cooperation organizes. But many important systems of cooperation depend upon a production secured through the accomplishment of a tangible objective. Thus human energy is focused in cooperation upon a physical objective which produces a physical material which may be distributed to individuals in amounts required; as to some individuals these amounts may be more than they could secure by individual efforts; as to others, less. In the latter case, other satisfactions secured or produced through cooperation are the basis of efficiency. These other satisfactions are social.

The efficiency of cooperation therefore depends upon what it secures and produces on the one hand, and how it distributes its resources and how it changes motives on the other. Everything that it does involves physical, biological, and social forces, applied to particular factors – physical, biological, personal, and social – in the situation as a whole. From the change in this situation it furnishes inducements or satisfactions. The distribution of these satisfactions is itself an application of physical, biological, and social forces to changing the total situation. A cooperative system is incessantly dynamic, a process of continual readjustment to physical, biological, and social environments as a whole. Its purpose is the satisfaction of individuals, and its efficiency requires that its effect be to change the history of its environment as a whole; it does this by changes in the physical, biological, and social components of that environment.

The cooperative system [2]

It is the central hypothesis of this book that the most useful concept for the analysis of experience of cooperative systems is embodied in the definition of a formal organization as a *system of consciously co-ordinated activities or forces of two or more persons.* In any concrete situation in which there is cooperation, several different systems will be components. Some of these will be physical, some biological, some psychological, etc., but the element common to all which binds all these other systems into the total concrete cooperative situation is that of organization as defined. If this hypothesis proves satisfactory it will be because (1) an organization, as defined, is a concept valid through a wide range of concrete situations with relatively few variables, which can be effectively investigated; and (2) the relations between this conceptual scheme and other systems can be effectively and usefully formulated. The final test of this conceptual scheme is whether its use will make possible a more effective conscious promotion and manipulation of cooperation among men; that is, whether in practice it can increase the predictive capacity of competent men in this field. It is the assumption upon which this essay is developed that such a concept is implicit in the behaviour of leaders and administrators, explaining uniformities observed in their conduct in widely different cooperative enterprises, and that its explicit formulation and development will permit a useful translation of experience in different fields into common terms....

The system, then, to which we give the name 'organization' is a system composed of the activities of human beings. What makes these activities a system is that the efforts of different persons are here co-ordinated. For this reason their significant aspects are not personal. They are determined by the system either as to manner, or degree, or time. Most of the effective cooperative systems are easily seen to be impersonal. For example, a clerk writing on a report form for a corporation is obviously doing something at a place, on a form, and about a subject that clearly never could engage his strictly personal interest. Hence, when we say that we are concerned with a system of co-ordinated human efforts, we mean that although persons are agents of the action, the action is not personal in the aspect important for the study of cooperative systems. Its character is determined by the requirements of the system, or of whatever dominates the system.

Theory of formal organization [3]

EFFECTIVENESS OF COOPERATION

The continuance of an organization depends upon its ability to carry out its purpose. This clearly depends jointly upon the appropriateness of its action and upon the conditions of its environment. In other words, effectiveness is primarily a matter of technological processes. This is quite obvious in ordinary cases of purpose to accomplish a physical objective, such as building a bridge. When the objective is non-physical, as is the case with religious and social organizations, it is not so obvious.

It should be noted that a paradox is involved in this matter. An organization must disintegrate if it cannot accomplish its purpose. It also destroys itself by accomplishing its purpose. A very large number of successful organizations come into being and then disappear for this reason. Hence most continuous organizations require repeated adoption of new purposes. This is concealed from everyday recognition by the practice of generalizing a complex series of specific purposes under one term, stated to be 'the purpose' of this organization. This is strikingly true in the case of governmental and public utility organizations when the purpose is stated to be a particular kind of service through a period of years. It is apparent that their real purposes are not abstractions called 'service' but specific acts of service. A manufacturing organization is said to exist to make, say, shoes; this is its 'purpose'. But it is evident that not making shoes in general but making specific shoes from day to day is its series of purposes. This process of generalization, however, provides in advance for the approximate definition of new purposes automatically – so automatically that the generalization is normally substituted in our minds for the concrete performances that are the real purposes.

Failure to be effective is, then, a real cause of disintegration; but failure to provide for the decisions resulting in the adoption of new purposes would have the same result. Hence the generalization of purpose which can only be defined concretely by day-to-day events is a vital aspect of permanent organization.

ORGANIZATION EFFICIENCY

It has already been stated that 'efficiency' as conceived in this treatise is not used in the specialized and limited sense of ordinary industrial practice or in the restricted sense applicable to technological processes. So-called 'practical' efficiency has little meaning, for example, as applied to many organizations such as religious organizations.

Efficiency of effort in the fundamental sense with which we are here concerned is efficiency relative to the securing of necessary personal contributions to the cooperative system. The life of an organization depends upon its ability to secure and maintain the personal contributions of energy (including the transfer of control of materials or money equivalent) necessary to effect its purposes. This ability is a composite of perhaps many efficiencies and inefficiencies in the narrow senses of these words, and it is often the case that inefficiency in some respect can be treated as the cause of total failure, in the sense that if corrected success would then be possible. But certainly in most organizations – social, political, national, religious – nothing but the absolute test of survival is significant objectively; there is no basis for comparison of the efficiencies of separate aspects.

A more extensive consideration of the inducements that result in personal willingness to cooperate is given in Chapter XI. The emphasis now is on the view that efficiency of organization is its capacity to offer effective inducements in sufficient quantity to maintain the equilibrium of the system. It is efficiency in this sense and not the efficiency of material productiveness which maintains the vitality of organizations. There are many organizations of great power and permanency in which the idea of productive efficiency is utterly meaningless because there is no material production. Churches, patriotic societies, scientific societies, theatrical and musical organizations, are cases where the original flow of *material* inducements is toward the organization, not from it – a flow necessary to provide resources with which to supply material inducements to the small minority who require them in such organizations.

In those cases where the primary purpose of organization is the production of material things, insufficiency with respect to the non-material inducements leads to the attempt to substitute material inducements for the non-material. Under favorable circumstances, to a limited degree, and for a limited time, this substitution may be effective. But to me, at least, it appears utterly contrary to the nature of men to be sufficiently induced by material or monetary considerations to contribute enough effort to a cooperative system to enable it to be productively efficient to the degree necessary for persistence over an extended period.

If these things are true, then even in purely economic enterprises efficiency in the offering of non-economic inducements may be as vital as productive efficiency. Perhaps the word efficiency as applied to such non-economic inducements as I have given for illustration will seem strange and forced. This, I think, can only be because we are accustomed to use the word in a specialized sense.

The non-economic inducements are as difficult to offer as others under many circumstances. To establish conditions under which individual pride of craft and of accomplishment can be secured without destroying the material economy of standardized production in cooperative operation is a problem in real efficiency. To maintain a character of personnel that is an attractive condition of employment involves a delicate art and much insight in the selection (and rejection) of personal services offered, whether the standard of quality be high or low. To have an organization that lends prestige and secures the loyalty of desirable persons is a complex and difficult task in efficiency – in all-round efficiency, not one-sided efficiency. It is for these reasons that good organizations – commercial, governmental, military, academic, and others – will be observed to devote great attention and sometimes great expense of money to the non-economic inducements, they are indispensable to fundamental efficiency, as well as to effectiveness in many cases.

The role of incentives [4]

It will be evident, perhaps, without more elaborate illustration, that in every type of organization, for whatever purpose, several incentives are necessary, and some degree of persuasion likewise, in order to secure and maintain the contributions to organization that are required. It will also be clear that, excepting in rare instances, the difficulties of securing the means of offering incentives, of avoiding conflict of incentives, and of making effective persuasive efforts, are inherently great; and that the determination of the precise combination of incentives and of persuasion that will be both effective and feasible is a matter of great delicacy. Indeed, it is so delicate and complex that rarely, if ever, is the scheme of incentives determinable in advance of application. It can only evolve; and the questions relating to it become chiefly those of strategic factors from time to time in the course of the life of the organization. It is also true, of course, that the scheme of incentives is probably the most unstable of the elements of the cooperative system, since invariably external conditions affect the possibilities of material incentives; and human motives are likewise highly variable. Thus incentives represent the final residual of all the conflicting forces involved in organization, a very slight change in underlying forces often making a great change in the power of incentives; and yet it is only by the incentives that the effective balancing of these forces is to be secured, if it can be secured at all.

Two general consequences of this inherent instability are to be noted. One is the innate propensity of all organizations to expand. The maintenance of incentives, particularly those relating to prestige, pride of association, and community satisfaction, calls for growth, enlargement, extension. It is, I think, the basic and, in a sense, the legitimate reason for bureaucratic aggrandizement in corporate, governmental, labor, university, and church organizations everywhere observed. To grow seems to offer opportunity for the realization of all kinds of active incentives – as may be observed by the repeated emphasis in all organizations, upon size as an index of the existence of desirable incentives, or the alternative rationalization of other incentives when size is small or growth is discouraged. The overreaching which arises from this cause is the source of destruction of organizations otherwise successful, since growth often so upsets the economy of incentives, through its reactions upon the effectiveness and efficiency of organization, that it is no longer possible to make them adequate.

A second and more important result of the inherent difficulty of securing an adequate scheme of incentives is the highly selective character of the organizational recruiting practice. This has two aspects, the acceptance of desirable and the rejection of undesirable contributions or contributors; and its chief process is the maintenance of differential incentives. Since all incentives are costly to organization, and the costs tend to prevent its survival, and since the balancing of organization outgo and income is initially to be regarded as impossible without the utmost economy, the distribution of incentives must be proportioned to the value and effectiveness of the various contributions sought.

This is only too much accepted as respects material incentives, that is, material things or money payment. No enduring or complex formal organization of any kind seems to have existed without differential material payments, though material compensation may be indirect to a considerable extent. This seems true up to the present even though contrary to the expressed attitude of the organization or not in harmony with its major purpose, as often in the case of churches and socialistic states.

The same doctrine applies in principle and practice even more to non-material incentives. The hierarchy of positions, with gradation of honors and privileges, which is the universal accompaniment of all complex organization, is essential to the adjustment of non-material incentives to induce the services of the most able individuals or the most valuable potential contributors to organization, and it is likewise necessary to the maintenance of pride of organization, community sense, etc., which are important general incentives to all classes of contributors.

Authority [5]

A communication has the presumption of authority when it originates at sources of organization information – a communications center – better than individual sources. It loses this presumption, however, if not within the scope or field of this center. The presumption is also lost if the communication shows an absence of adjustment to the actual situation which confronts the recipient of it.

Thus men impute authority to communications from superior positions, provided they are reasonably consistent with advantages of scope and perspective that are credited to those positions. This authority is to a considerable extent independent of the personal ability of the incumbent of the position. It is often recognized that though the incumbent may be of limited personal ability his advice may be superior solely by reason of the advantage of position. This is the *authority of position.*

But it is obvious that some men have superior ability. Their knowledge and understanding regardless of position command respect. Men impute authority to what they say in an organization for this reason only. This is the *authority of leadership.* When the authority of leadership is combined with the authority of position, men who have an established connection with an organization generally will grant authority, accepting orders far outside the zone of indifference. The confidence engendered may even make compliance an inducement in itself.

Nevertheless, the determination of authority remains with the individual. Let these 'positions' of authority in fact show ineptness, ignorance of conditions, failure to communicate what ought to be said, or let leadership fail (chiefly by its concrete action) to recognize implicitly its dependence upon the essential character of the relationship of the individual to the organization, and the authority if tested disappears.

This objective authority is only maintained if the positions or leaders continue to be adequately informed. In very rare cases persons possessing great knowledge, insight, or skill have this adequate information without occupying executive position. What they say ought to be done or ought not to be done will be accepted. But this is usually personal advice at the risk of the taker. Such persons have influence rather than authority. In most cases genuine leaders who give advice concerning organized efforts are required to accept positions of responsibility; for knowledge of the applicability of their special knowledge or judgment to concrete *organization* action, not to abstract problems, is essential to the worth of what they say as a basis of organization authority. In other words, they have an organization personality, as distinguished from their individual personality, commensurate with the influence of their leadership. The common way to state this is that there cannot be authority without corresponding responsibility. A more exact expression would be that objective authority cannot be imputed to persons in organization positions unless subjectively they are dominated by the organization as respects their decisions.

It may be said, then, that the maintenance of objective authority adequate to support the fiction of superior authority and able to make the zone of indifference an actuality depends upon the operation of the system of communication in the organization. The function of this system is to supply adequate information to the positions of authority and adequate facilities for the issuance of orders. To do so it requires commensurate capacities in those able to be leaders. High positions that are not so supported have weak authority, as do strong men in minor positions.

Thus authority depends upon a cooperative personal attitude of individuals on the one hand; and the system of communication in the organization on the other. Without the latter, the former cannot be maintained. The most devoted adherents of an organization will quit it, if its system results in inadequate, contradictory, inept orders, so that they cannot know who is who, what is what, or have the sense of effective co-ordination.

337

Executive decisions [6]

The fine art of executive decision consists in not deciding questions that are not now pertinent, in not deciding prematurely, in not making decisions that cannot be made effective, and in not making decisions that others should make. Not to decide questions that are not pertinent at the time is uncommon good sense, though to raise them may be uncommon perspicacity. Not to decide questions prematurely is to refuse commitment of attitude or the development of prejudice. Not to make decisions that cannot be made effective is to refrain from destroying authority. Not to make decisions that others should make is to preserve morale, to develop competence, to fix responsibility, and to preserve authority.

From this it may be seen that decisions fall into two major classes, positive decisions – to do something, to direct action, to cease action, to prevent action; and negative decisions, which are decisions not to decide. Both are inescapable; but the negative decisions are often largely unconscious, relatively non-logical, 'instinctive', 'good sense'. It is because of the rejections that the selection is good. The best of moves may be offset by a false move. This is why time is usually necessary to appraise the executive. There is no current evidence of the all-important negative decisions. The absence of effective moves indicates failure of initiative in decision, but error of action probably often means absence of good negative decisions. The success of action through a period of time denotes excellence of selection and of rejection of possible actions.

Where decisions are personal, the *fact* of decision is specialized to the individual, but the *processes* of decision within the individual are perhaps not specialized, except that decisions are made in some order of time and at particular places. Organization decisions as *accepted facts*, that is, having authority, on the contrary are not specialized to individuals but are *functions* of the organization as a whole; but the *processes* of decision are necessarily specialized. The purposes and action of organization are non-personal. They are co-ordinated. The efforts of the individual in organization result from decisions which in part are *necessarily* made by others acting non-personally. The concept of organization implies a system of human efforts in which the processes of decision are distributed and specialized. But since decision is a matter of definition of purpose and discrimination of strategic factors, the specialization of the process of decision involves distinctions in the distribution of emphasis upon either purpose or the other environmental aspect of decision. Neither is ever completely absent at any position in organization, but at some points the emphasis is upon definition of purpose, at others upon the discrimination of the environment and the determination of the strategic factors. The emphasis in the executive functions is upon definition of purposes; among other functions the emphasis is upon discrimination of the environment. Thus, in an industrial organization, workmen, clerks, testers, laboratory assistants, salesmen, technicians, engineers, are characteristically occupied with the strategic factors of the environment external to the organization as a whole. The direct environment of executive decision is primarily the internal environment of the organization itself. The strategic factors of executive decision are chiefly and primarily strategic factors of organization operation. It is the organization, not the executive, which does the work on the external environment. The executive is primarily concerned with decisions which facilitate or hinder other decisions in the effective or efficient operation of the organization.

Purpose [7]

Thus the organization for the definition of purpose is the organization for the specification of work to do; and the specifications are made in their final stage when and where the work is being done. I suspect that at least nine-tenths of all organization activity is on the responsibility, the authority, and the specifications of those who make the last contributions, who apply personal energies to the final concrete objectives. There is no meaning to personal specialization, personal experience, personal training, personal location, personal ability, eyes and ears, arms and legs, brains and emotions, if this is not so. What must be added to the indispensable authority, responsibility, and capability of each contributor is the indispensable coordination. This requires a pyramiding of the formulation of purpose that becomes more and more general as the number of units of basic organization becomes larger, and more and more remote in future time. Responsibility for abstract, generalizing, prospective, long-run decision is delegated *up* the line, responsibility for definition, action, remains always at the base where the authority for effort resides.

The formulation and definition of purpose is then a widely distributed function, only the more general part of which is executive. In this fact lies the most important inherent difficulty in the operation of cooperative systems – the necessity for indoctrinating those at the lower levels with general purposes, the major decisions, so that they remain cohesive and able to make the ultimate detailed decisions coherent; and the necessity, for those at the higher levels, of constantly understanding the concrete conditions and the specific decisions of the 'ultimate' contributors from which and from whom executives are often insulated. Without that up-and-down-the-line coordination of purposeful decisions, general decisions and general purposes are mere intellectual processes in an organization vacuum, insulated from realities by layers of misunderstanding. The function of formulating grand purposes and providing for their redefinition is one which needs sensitive systems of communication, experience in interpretation, imagination, and delegation of responsibility.

Morality [8]

The creative aspect of executive responsibility is the highest exemplification of responsibility. As to the great proportion of organization decisions required of the executive, the conflict of morals is within organization codes, and personal codes are not directly involved. The 'organization personality' alone is concerned. The conflict may be treated with relative objectivity, as a 'problem.' In fact, probably most executive decisions appear in the guise of technical decisions, and their moral aspects are not consciously appreciated. An executive may make many important decisions without reference to any sense of personal interest or of morality. But where creative morality is concerned, the sense of personal responsibility – of sincerity and honesty, in other words – is acutely emphasized. Probably few persons are able to do such work objectively. Indeed, few can do it long except on the basis of personal conviction – not conviction that they are obligated as officials to do it, but conviction that what they do for the good of organization they *personally* believe to be right.

The creative function as a whole is the essence of leadership. It is the highest test of executive responsibility because it requires for successful accomplishment that element of 'conviction' that means identification of personal codes and organization codes in the view of the leader. This is the coalescence that carries 'conviction' to the personnel of organization, to that informal organization underlying all formal organization that senses nothing more quickly than insincerity. Without it, all organization is dying, because it is the indispensable element in creating that desire for adherence – for which no incentive is a substitute – on the part of those whose efforts willingly contributed constitute organization.

These extracts are taken from C. I. Barnard, *The Functions of the Executive*, Harvard University Press, 1938, page numbers as indicated:

(1.) pp. 55–9.
(2.) pp. 73–4, 77.
(3.) pp. 91–4.
(4.) pp. 158–60.
(5.) pp. 173–5.
(6.) pp. 194, 210–211.
(7.) pp. 232–3.
(8.) pp. 281–2.

The Authors and Editors

DAVID ASHTON is Assistant Director of Post-Experience Programmes at the Management Centre in the University of Bradford. He is a graduate of Nottingham University and holds the Postgraduate Diploma in Management Studies. Before entering the academic world he worked in the Metal Box Company.

DENNIS CHAPMAN is Senior Lecturer in Social Sciences and Administration in the University of Liverpool. He worked with B. Seebohm Rowntree at York on *Poverty and Progress*, and has been in contact with the Cocoa Works for thirty years.

NORMAN CUTHBERT is Senior Lecturer in Industrial Relations at the Management Centre in the University of Bradford. He was educated at Nottingham University and worked in accounting before developing his interest in personnel management and labour relations. He has written extensively on manpower planning and payment systems.

THOMAS KEMPNER is Director and Professor of Management Studies at the Management Centre in the University of Bradford. He graduated from University College, London, and taught at Henley Administrative Staff College and Sheffield University before going to Bradford to establish its Business School in 1963.

IAN MCGIVERING is Reader in Industrial Sociology at the Management Centre in the University of Bradford. He has taught and written widely and was a member during the 1950s of the Social Sciences Department in the University of Liverpool.

MICHAEL MARTIN is Senior Lecturer in Management Science at the Management Centre in the University of Bradford. Originally a physicist, he worked in Operational Research with the National Coal Board and studied and taught at Sheffield University before he took up his present post.

MICHAEL THICKETT is Director of Personnel with Hepworth and Grandage Limited. He is a graduate of Leeds and California Universities and joined the academic staff at the Management Centre in the University of Bradford from the National Coal Board. He left the University in 1967 for his present industrial post.

ANTHONY TILLETT is a social historian, who graduated from the

Universities of Reading and Essex. He has also taught and studied at the Universities of Wisconsin and Mexico. He is currently engaged in sociological research in Mexico.

MICHAEL TRAVIS is Personnel Manager of Thor Tools Limited. He lectured in Industrial Psychology at the Management Centre in the University of Bradford until 1967, and before joining the Centre worked with the National Institute of Industrial Psychology.

GORDON WILLS is Professor of Marketing at the Management Centre in the University of Bradford. He graduated from Reading University in Politics and Economics and holds the Postgraduate Diploma in Management Studies with distinction. He has worked in marketing intelligence with I.C.I. and Foote Cone & Belding, and it was from the latter firm that he took up his present post. He is Editor of *Management Decision* and the *British Journal of Marketing*, and a director of Roles and Parker Ltd.

Index

A.S.M.E., *see* American Society of Mechanical Engineers

Accident proneness, 271, 277

Accountancy *and* Accountants (professional), 41, 42, 44, 47, 49, 51

Adams, Henry, 229

Administration and factory organization, 41–5

Administration, business, integration of (*see also* Follett, Mary Parker), **247–67**: constructive conflict, 249–51; giving orders, 251–2, 254–6; leadership and control, 252–3; progressive organization, fundamentals of, 253–4; *Readings from Follett*, 254–67: on giving orders, 254–6; on depersonalizing orders ('law of the situation'), 257–8; on group responsibility, 258–62; on business environment, 262–3; on interweaving authority and responsibility, 263–5; on the leader's relation to the fundamental principles of organization, 265–7

Administration, Dynamic (Follett), 249; *readings from*, **254–67**

Administration, Fayol's views on, 108, 110–11

'Administration, General Principles of, Discourse on the' (Fayol, 1908), 108

Administration, Industrial, Summer School of (Cambridge, 1919), 277

'Administration' *or* 'Management'? 109–10

Administrative personnel, *see* Bureaucracies

Adult response, categories of (Mayo) 310

Advertising, 229–30, 237, 239, 290; media, 239, 290; TV and Press, 239

Air Ministry: Committee for the Scientific Survey of Air Defence, 141

Aitken H. J., *quoted*, 40

Alexander Magnus, 181

Allocation problems, 155–8

Amalgamated Society of Engineers (1851), 173

America *and* Americans, *see* United States

American Institute of Social Service, 175 n.

American Machinist, The, 49

American Management Association, 266

American Railroad Gazette, 50 *bis*

American Society of Mechanical Engineers (A.S.M.E.), 54, 55, 57 *bis*, 64, 86, 102

Analytical apparatus, Gilbreth's, 99

Apperception Test, Thematic (1935) 282

Application forms (blanks), 286

Applied Psychology, Journal of, 281

Applied science, 45

Appraisal of (personnel), methods of, 284–6, 286–9

Arkwright, Richard, 172

Army Alpha and Beta Tests (U.S.A.). 280

Army: analogies for industrial organization and management vocabulary in, 49–50, 60; psychology in selection tests for, 61

Assessment of organizations, 324–6

'Athletic contests' (work efficiency competitions), Gilbreth's, 105–6

Atlantic, Battle of the, 143

MORE ABOUT PENGUINS
AND PELICANS

Penguinews, which appears every month, contains details of all the new books issued by Penguins as they are published. From time to time it is supplemented by *Penguins in Print*, which is a complete list of all books published by Penguins which are in print. (There are well over three thousand of these.)

A specimen copy of *Penguinews* will be sent to you free on request, and you can become a subscriber for the price of the postage. For a year's issues (including the complete lists) please send 4s. if you live in the United Kingdom, or 8s. if you live elsewhere. Just write to Dept EP, Penguin Books Ltd, Harmondsworth, Middlesex, enclosing a cheque or postal order, and your name will be added to the mailing list.

Some other books in the Pelican Library of Business and Management are described on the following pages.

Note: *Penguinews* and *Penguins in Print* are not available in the U.S.A. or Canada

Pelican Library of Business and Management

COMPUTERS, MANAGERS AND SOCIETY

Michael Rose

Computers, Managers and Society is an account, part technical, part sociological and part philosophical, of the computer revolution.

After a general survey of the development of computer-controlled data processing. Michael Rose examines the complex effects of the computer upon the clerical worker – the new opportunities, the dangers of alienation, the threat of technological unemployment. He then focuses upon the fast-developing problems of managers. Many of the standard managerial functions can already be programmed. But should executives delegate qualitative decisions to a machine? And if so, how far can and should these changes go?

'Computerization' presents managers with new opportunities on a structural scale unmatched since the Industrial Revolution. Do they really understand the new situation? Can they, when it is transforming itself so rapidly? And are we aware enough of the effects of the computer upon an even larger social group – society itself – now faced with the need to clarify its whole attitude to technological change?

AN INSIGHT INTO MANAGEMENT ACCOUNTING

John Sizer

Management accountancy is the key to modern business strategy and technique. No department specialist – and certainly no general executive – can cope without an insight into its principles and practices. This book is designed to give just such an insight: to enable every businessman to understand the finances and internal costing of his company – and to keep its accountants on their toes.

John Sizer, who has practical experience of several industries, is now Senior Tutor in Accounting at the London Graduate School of Business Studies. In this book he discusses such subjects as stewardship, cost accounting, the measurement and control of profitability, long-range planning, capital investment appraisal, budgetary control and marginal costing. Other chapters cover the accountant's contribution to the pricing decision, and company taxation. But whilst he provides an admirably succinct description of modern accounting techniques, John Sizer's main achievement has been to relate them all to essentially functional and practical situations within the firm. This is a no-nonsense manual which firmly removes from accounting all the mystique which overawes managers and often merely masks muddle.